First published in 2015 by Voyageur Press, an imprint of Quarto Publishing Group USA Inc., 400 First Avenue North, Suite 400, Minneapolis, MN 55401 USA

The information in this book is true and complete to the best of our knowledge. All recommendations are made without any guarantee on the part of the author or Publisher, who also disclaims any liability incurred in connection with the use of this data or specific details.

We recognize, further, that some words, model names, and designations mentioned herein are the property of the trademark holder. We use them for identification purposes only. This is not an official publication.

Voyageur Press titles are also available at discounts in bulk quantity for industrial or sales-promotional use. For details write to Special Sales Manager at Quarto Publishing Group USA Inc., 400 First Avenue North, Suite 400, Minneapolis, MN 55401 USA.

To find out more about our books, visit us online at www.VoyageurPress.com.

ISBN: 978-0-7603-4730-0

Library of Congress Cataloging-in-Publication Data
Routson, Ashley V.
The beer wench's guide to beer : an unpretentious guide to craft beer /
by Ashley V. Routson.
        pages cm
ISBN 978-0-7603-4730-0 (paperback)
1. Beer. 2. Brewing. 3. Brewing--Amateurs' manuals. I. Title.
TP577.R68 2015
663'.42--dc23
                    2014045117

Acquisitions Editor: Thom O'Hearn

Project Manager: Jordan Wiklund

Design Manager: James Kegley

Layout: Diana Boger

On the title page: An explosion of flavor—and Belgian lace!

Printed in China
10 9 8 7 6 5 4 3 2 1

THE BEER WENCH'S GUIDE TO BEER

AN UNPRETENTIOUS GUIDE TO CRAFT BEER

ASHLEY ROUTSON

Voyageur Press

INTRODUCTION 7

SECTION ONE

WHAT DID I JUST DRINK?
A GUIDE TO BEER STYLES (AND HISTORY!)

chapter one

BREAKING DOWN BEER STYLES 11

chapter two

THE LIGHTEST OF LIGHT 17

pale lagers – Bohemian (Czech) pilsener – Munich helles – German pilsner – dortmunder export – hefeweizen/weissbier – class (premium) American pilsner – kölsch

chapter three

THE DARKER SIDE OF LIGHT 31

amber and dark lagers – schwarzbier (black lager) – Munich dunkel – Vienna lager – Oktoberfest (marzen) – steam beer/California common

chapter four

THE IPA AND ITS EMERGING SUBCATEGORIES 39

English IPA – American india pale ale – imperial (double) india pale ale – black IPA/American black ale – Belgian-style IPA– white IPA – india session ale/session IPA – brettanomyces/wild IPA – red IPA – rye IPA – spiced/herbed tea

chapter five

THE OTHER HOPPY BEERS 49

ordinary bitter (session ale) – extra special bitter (ESB) – American pale ale – American amber ale – American brown ale

chapter six

THE DARKER SIDE OF ALE   59

English mild – porter – (Irish) dry stout – sweet/milk stout – oatmeal stout – foreign export stout – American stout – Russian imperial stout – chocolate stout – coffee stout – oyster stout – Scottish ales – Irish red ale

chapter seven

MEANWHILE, IN BELGIUM . . .   67

Belgian blonde ale – Belgian tripel – Belgian dubbel – witbier – saison (farmhouse) – Biere de Garde

chapter eight

BIG, BOLD, AND BRAZEN   77

English barleywine – American barleywine – Baltic porter – Russian imperial stout – bock – maibock (helles bock) – doppelbock (double bock) – eisbock – weizenbock

chapter nine

SOUR AND BARREL-AGED BEERS   87

gueuze – Flanders red ale – Flanders oud bruin (brown ale) – Leipzig-style gose – Berliner weisse

SECTION TWO

BECOMING AN EXPERT

THE BREWING PROCESS, BREWING INGREDIENTS, EVALUATING BEER, AND RESPECTING BEER

chapter ten

BREWING AND BEER INGREDIENTS   101

malt – hops – yeast – brettanomyces – water

chapter eleven

EVALUATING BEER 129

tasting conditions – appearance – aroma – flavor – mouthfeel – overall impression

chapter twelve

RESPECTING BEER 139

storing beer – freshness – cellaring beer – pouring beer – temperature (bottles) – temperature (draft) – glassware

SECTION THREE

HAVING FUN WITH BEER
PAIRING BEER WITH FOOD, COOKING WITH BEER, BEER MIXOLOGY

chapter thirteen

PAIRING BEER WITH FOOD 155

getting started, 157 – pairing beer with cheese, 174 – pairing beer with tacos, 179 – pairing beer with pizza, 180

chapter fourteen

COOKING WITH BEER 183

the basics, 184 – soups, stews, and chili, 186 – breads and batters, 191 – condiments, sauces, and dressings, 197 – meat and seafood, 204 – vegetarian recipes, 211 – desserts, 216

chapter fifteen

BEER MIXOLOGY 225

getting started, 226 – beer blends (the spiritless cocktails), 227 – beer cocktails (with spirits), 232 – bourbon cocktails, 235 – gin cocktails, 237 – rum cocktails, 240 – beer flips, 242 – tequila and mezcal cocktails, 245 – vodka cocktails, 248

BEER RESOURCES 250

INDEX 252

ABOUT THE AUTHOR & ACKNOWLEDGMENTS 256

INTRODUCTION

When you think about it, learning about beer is similar to dating, or even just getting to know a new person. The first thing you notice are all the physical traits. For beer, that starts with the color, the vessel in which it's served, and the amount of foam and head retention. But then you move in—oh, the aroma! You just have to take a sip. Then, the all-important attribute: the flavor.

When you're infatuated with beer, you start to dig a little deeper. There are fun details to unearth as you figure out what you like—the alcohol level, the bitterness, and maybe even a little bit about the history of the style. Who knew history could be so fun? Once you spend enough time hanging out with beer, understanding her little nuances, you fall in love.

So she takes you home, to the brewery, where she shows you where she came from and how she was made. She lets you meet her parents (water, yeast, malt, and hops) and tells you how to take care of her (she is a fickle little thing). Now you can't imagine your life without her. You're cooking together and drinking together every week.

OK, maybe that was a little bit of a stretch, but it does explain my particular approach to writing this book. First, we're going to walk through many of the beer styles you'll find today. We'll learn the defining factors of each style, some science-y numbers to impress your friends, a little bit about the history of how these styles came to be, and tasting notes that will help you know what to expect from each style. You'll learn what beers you like, what beers you don't like, and just as important, why you feel the way you do.

The second section, "Becoming an Expert," contains a description of the brewing process, the ingredients used in brewing, and how to properly store and serve beer. While that might sound dry, it's anything but. Playing with glassware and learning how to taste beer is all sorts of nerdy fun. And if you've ever wondered what goes into making beer—or if you just want to be better at pub trivia—this section is not to be skipped.

Last, but certainly not least, we'll have some fun with beer. (In fact, feel free to skip straight to this section if it's where you want to start.) We'll learn all about beer pairings—with plenty of cheese, of course. We'll cook with beer, making everything from breakfast to dinner and dessert. We'll even make blends and cocktails with beer, from the classic Black and Tan to my signature Beermosa. Oh, and if you just rolled your eyes or made a face at the thought of using beer in cocktails, just wait. I will convert you.

What are we waiting for? Let's get started.

SECTION
ONE

WHAT DID I JUST DRINK?

A Guide to Beer Styles
(and History!)

chapter one

BREAKING DOWN BEER STYLES

In the past, beer books and other so-called official sources have traditionally organized beer styles by country or region. I've taken a different approach and created a guide that relates to the way most people actually drink. For example, if you already know you like hoppy beers, you can jump straight to the IPA or Other Hoppy Beers chapters. If you love malty and dark beers, it's clear which chapters are for you as well. I hope that means you can easily flip through and figure out exactly where you want to start reading (and sampling, of course!).

The exception to this is the Belgian beer chapter. Since those styles are so unique, and their signature flavors are largely determined by particular Belgian yeasts, they really belong together rather than mixed among the other chapters. Also, I've found that even though the beers have a wide range of flavors, many beer drinkers either fall in love with almost all of them or none at all.

It's important to note that some beer styles might have been not-so-accidentally left out and some not-exactly-recognized-yet beer styles might have been thrown into the mix. Some styles also get a ton of attention, while others barely get a mention. What can I say? The beer world is ever expanding and our collective attention span is ever diminishing. And this is my book so I get to play favorites, right?

So here's what will happen: I'll start each section with some general notes to provide some context and some backstory behind the styles that follow, then dive into a handful of specific beers. Once you get into the beers, the entries will contain the same parts to make an apples-to-apples, or should I say beer-to-beer, comparison as easy as could be:

Style name: This is pretty self-explanatory.

The gist: You'll find this in italics right under the style name. It's a 140-character or less description of the style, so it's perfect for skimming and tweeting while reading (hint hint).

My two cents: This is where things get fun. How does it look, smell, and taste? Pour one for yourself and compare notes with me. Since some styles are more dynamic than others, some descriptions may be a little wackier than others. Keep in mind that this section is somewhat based on the style standards, but it is more than a bit subjective. It's the beer style as seen through the eyes of the wench. If a particular description gets you excited, and you want a full-on download of straight style knowledge, the websites for both the Brewers Association (www.brewersassociation.org) and the Beer Judge Certification Program (BJCP, www.bjcp. org) have links to the most up-to-date style guidelines that both organizations use for judging beer competitions.

Key stats:

Standard Reference Method (SRM): SRM is one of the most common ways that beer pros determine the color of a beer. I'm not going to tell you how it's scientifically determined; it's complicated and way above my head. However, whether you're a brewer, beer judge, or beer drinker, you can easily reference a set of swatches to figure out where the beer in your hand falls on the scale. If you don't have a set of swatches handy, remember the lower the SRM number, the lighter the color of the beer. The higher the number, the darker the beer. The highest number is about 40, which is typically reserved for an imperial stout. I've included the chart at 113.

International Bittering Units (IBU): The IBU scale measures a beer's bitterness, most of which comes from the hops, specifically the alpha acids in hops (see page 111). The scale takes into consideration two key factors: the level of alpha acids in the hop varietal and the length of extraction during the boil. It is important to note that while IBU measures the bitterness in beer, it does not necessarily measure a beer's hoppiness. A beer may be high in hop aroma and flavor, yet low in bitterness. There is no official scale for hop aroma or flavor, only subjective observations.

The IBU Scale: This technically ranges from 0 to 100, but most beer styles fall between 20 and 45 IBUs. Some styles, like lighter lagers, gruits (hopless beers), and sour beers, can fall below 20 IBUs. Other styles, such as big imperial IPAs or aggressive imperial stouts, could hit the 80–100 mark.

A few brewers and beer geeks argue that they can detect even higher levels of bitterness, but the threshold for most people is 100 IBUs. This essentially means that most people can't tell the difference between a beer with 100 IBUs and a beer with more than 120 IBUs. The bitterness is just saturated on the palate at that point.

Alcohol by Volume (ABV): ABV tells you how much alcohol is in the beer. It is determined by taking the starting (original) gravity of the beer, subtracting the final gravity, and then dividing that number by the final gravity and multiplying *that* number by 100. Once again, it's not a big deal to know how to determine this number. You should just understand that the lower the ABV, the less alcohol there is in a beer, and the higher the ABV, the more alcohol there is in a beer.

Original Gravity (OG): OG is a number that a lot of breweries and bars like to put on sales and marketing materials, menus, and tap lists, but few people know what it actually means. Essentially, it tells a brewer the level of fermentable sugars in the wort (sugar water made from barley, discussed on page 104). If you are a total science nerd, you might be into calculating the OG vs. the ABV. Or eventually you may be able to see a high OG with a lower than usual ABV and figure out that the beer will taste sweeter than usual. I look at OG numbers and I'm all like, whatever. To each their own. Since it may be of interest or useful to some readers, I'm including them.

In one word: If I had to sum up this beer style into one word, this is what I would say. There may be a time or two where I repeat the same word. After all, if a beer style is sexy, I'm going to call it like it is.

Ales vs. Lagers

Almost all beer styles fall under one of two parent categories: ales or lagers. The difference between these two is not color, a common misconception. It's not region of origin or the types of malts and hops used either, though all those factors can lead to subcategories. What it really comes down to is the type of yeast.

We will discuss the yeast at greater length starting on page 18, but for now it's only important to know that ales are fermented at warmer temperatures, typically for shorter periods of time, with top-fermenting yeast, the most common being *Saccharomyces cerevisiae*. Conversely, lagers are fermented at colder temperatures over longer periods of time (typically one to two weeks longer than ales) with bottom-fermenting yeast, the most common being *Saccharomyces pastorianus*.

A few beer styles, namely sour beers, are spontaneously fermented with wild yeast strains and bacteria, but for the most part, all beers fall into one of these two categories.

Pour it into this: Beer is tasty in just about any clean glass, but have some fun. Pour that British bitter in a nonic pint glass and pull out your favorite tulip for that Belgian tripel. What better way is there to give yourself the full armchair-travel experience? If a particular style should be imbibed at cooler or warmer temperatures than the recommended average, I'll also mention proper serving temperature here.

Drink instead of: Hey you! Put down the wine and step away from the cocktails. Grab a beer instead. For example: Instead of water, drink domestic lagers brewed with adjuncts such as corn and rice. Okay, okay. Bad joke, but you get where I'm going.

Pair with: This will be a brief list of a few cuisines, foods, and cheeses that I recommend pairing with this style. This is just a cheat sheet. We'll discuss beer and food pairings at greater length starting on page 155.

Brief history lesson: I assume your attention spans are as short as mine, so think of this section as the abridged version of beer history—the cliff notes, if you will. There are a lot of beer history books out there, many of which focus on one particular style or region, if you want to dive deeper.

Try it: You are drinking along with the book, right? I'll do my best to recommend commercially produced beers in this style category, and I hope you can find at least one of them. However, bear in mind that availability of beer can be seasonal and regional, so my apologies if you strike out trying to find an Oktoberfest in April. Also, if you're after a particular style that a nationwide brewery doesn't make, check out your local breweries. (And if you haven't already, check them out regardless.)

That should do it. Grab yourself a beer, and let's begin.

chapter two

THE LIGHTEST OF LIGHT

Pale Lagers

It might come as a surprise to learn that pale-colored lagers are a relatively recent invention, considering their popularity and abundance. If you were to draw out the entire timeline of beer styles, pale-colored beer would fall toward the modern-day end of the spectrum. Light lagers brewed with adjuncts, like rice and corn, are even more contemporary.

Many factors came together for the creation of the pale lager family, but three scientific advances were absolutely crucial: the discovery of yeast, innovations in kilning, and the invention of refrigeration.

Discovery of Yeast

When humans accidentally discovered the awesomeness of fermentation thousands of years ago, no one knew exactly how or why it happened. They just knew that eating and drinking fermented things made them feel good, and they wanted more.

It wasn't until the 1800s that brewers would learn that single-celled organisms were actually the ones responsible for turning the sugary, grain-based liquid called *wort* into beer. French chemist Louis Pasteur was responsible for identifying these beautiful little booze-excreting creatures we now know to be yeast.

At first, scientists only knew about the yeast strain called *Saccharomyces cerevisiae*, the same yeast used in bread making and the primary strain for the fermentation of ales (but not lagers). Eventually, scientists discovered that all sorts of yeasts and bacteria could be used in fermentation.

The first person to isolate a cell of lager yeast was Danish mycologist (aka fungi expert) and fermentation physiologist Emil Christian Hansen. Ultimately, this yeast would be called *Saccharomyces pastorianus*, a tribute to the yeast legend himself, Louis Pasteur.

The isolation of the lager yeast strain was a pinnacle moment for lager brewers. They could finally learn how to control the unknown factor and perfect lager fermentation down to a T.

Innovations in Kilning

Did you know that until the late 1600s most beer was brownish or black in color? That's because most styles of beer are brewed with malted barley, which must be kilned after drying and germinating (the malting process will be discussed more in depth on page 106). Before the 1600s, most beer was kilned over wood fires. This produced smoky malts that were fairly dark in color, not ideal for brewing pale beers.

Eventually, the Brits discovered that kilning over coke could successfully produce pale malts. (Coke is coal heated in the absence of oxygen that gives off heat with little to no smoke.) The lager brewers ultimately picked up on the pale malt trend in the 1800s, hence the birth of the pale lager.

Invention of Refrigeration

It is important to note that lager yeast in particular requires cooler temperatures for fermentation. The invention of refrigeration allowed the Germans to brew a more consistent product year round and made it possible to keep beer cold prior to serving. Refrigeration also played a role in keeping beer stabilized, helping it better survive exportation.

The first large-scale refrigerated lagering tanks were developed for the Spaten Brewery in 1870. This allowed lagers to be produced on a larger scale, completely revolutionizing the lager beer industry. The invention of refrigeration is often referenced as a major turning point in the history of beer. It is a key mark of modern-era brewing.

Reinheitsgebot and Prohibition

The *Reinheitsgebot* ("rye-n-heights-ge-bot") is the ever-famous German Purity Law. It states that beer must only be brewed with water, hops, and barley (yeast was grandfathered into this list once it was discovered). Although this law is no longer enforced, most German brewers still uphold its rigorous standards. Increased enforcement of the *Reinheitsgebot* in 1871 forced the extinction of many "impure" beer styles and brewing traditions in Germany. As a result, pilsners and pale lagers became king, dominating the German marketplace from there on out.

Then things were mostly quiet—until that fateful year, 1920. Although advances in science have been extremely important for the evolution of beer, no single discovery or invention has had as huge of an impact on the history of beer as Prohibition in the United States.

I'm assuming that everyone reading this book has heard of Prohibition. (If not, then I seriously question the credentials of your American history teachers.) Prohibition essentially started with the ratification of the Eighteenth Amendment in 1920 and lasted until 1933. For thirteen years, ten months, nineteen days, seventeen hours, thirty-two minutes, and thirty seconds the manufacturing and sale of alcoholic beverages was illegal in the United States of America.

Prohibition single-handedly destroyed the craft and artisanal booze industry in the United States. Before Prohibition, there was something like three thousand breweries in the country, but only a couple dozen survived Prohibition, and most of those breweries consolidated to form larger breweries. This set the stage for mass production of domestic beers (in this case, lagers) and the market dominance of said beers.

It is important to note that before Prohibition even started, imported lagers, especially pilsners, were all the rage. The largest flow of German immigration occurred between 1820 and World War I. The immigrants brought a taste for German-style beers with them, as well as the knowledge and skills for brewing lagers. By the time Prohibition hit, lager sales were outpacing those of ales. And then there was World War II.

World War II also sucked.

Before the American beer industry had a chance to recover from Prohibition, World War II hit the nation. War has been known to breed innovation out of necessity. Important supplies and raw materials are often rationed, forcing industries dependent on those resources to seek out comparable alternatives. In times of war, food is often the resource that is rationed the most.

During World War II, barley was rationed for beef farmers and most brewers were forced to brew with other "cereal" grains. Although brewers had already been experimenting with supplemental starches like corn before Prohibition, it wasn't until World War II that it became a common practice. And thus began the mass production of light adjunct-based domestic lagers, yet another reason to hate Hitler.

The Craft Lager Revolution

Despite the fact that the overwhelming majority of beer consumed in the world today is mass-produced, adjunct-riddled pale lagers that bear little to no semblance to the traditional pilsners that inspired them, there has been a recent resurgence of craft lagers and pilsners. Some writers have referred to this phenomenon as the "third wave of lagers," but I prefer to think of it as a part of the overall craft beer revolution.

As with most traditional styles, American brewers like to tweak and manipulate pale lagers by, what I refer to as, "Americanizing" them. Some brew with American hops instead of the traditional Saaz or noble hops, some like to push the alcohol boundaries by brewing imperial versions of pale lagers, some push the bitterness boundaries by using more hops, and some even add weird, nontraditional ingredients into the mix. Examples of Americanized pale lagers include Firestone Walker Pivo Pils (an extra-hoppy pilsner), Dogfish Head Piercing Pils (pilsner brewed with white pear tea and pear juice), and Ballast Point Fathom (an imperial pale lager, aka a super-hoppy imperial lager).

Keep in mind, not all modern-day brewers step outside the box on styles. Some brewers are purists who choose not to adulterate or change traditional recipes. They prefer to brew to style and uphold certain brewing traditions. These brewers should be commended for their work. In an ever-growing world of extreme and weird beers, simple is refreshing.

BOHEMIAN (CZECH) PILSENER

The original pale lager: light yellow, lots of bubbles, notes of sweet hay and tree bark spice. Refreshing.

BJCP Stats

SRM: 3.5–6   IBU: 35–45   ABV: 4.2–5.4 percent   OG: 1.044–1.056

My two cents: The pilsner is quite possibly the most successful and popular beer style in the world. The majority of beer brewed and consumed in the world is either a pilsner or a derivative of it (aka adjunct lager).

Brilliant pale gold with a large white head and medium body, it's easy to see why the style quickly took over once brewers could make it. The classic Bohemian pilsener is fizzy and refreshing but also filled with subtle complexity.

In fact, it's one of the best styles for observing water's impact on the overall flavor of beer. It's technically the hoppiest of the pale lagers, but the perceived bitterness varies notably with water.

Soft water, in this particular case, tends to take the edge off the bitterness in hops. As a result, the Bohemian pilsener has a slightly lower level of perceived hoppiness than its hard water–brewed German counterpart (discussed next).

The other important ingredient in this style is Saaz hops, a varietal commonly described as earthy and spicy. I equate Saaz hops to being something like cocktail bitters. It adds a subtle bitter and wood-like herbal quality that you would notice more in its absence than in its presence.

In the glass: Light yellow with lots of bubbles

In the nose: Unsalted crackers, fresh hay and grass

In the mouth: Sweet hay, biscuits with a drop of honey, dash of Angostura bitters

In one word: Refreshing

Pour it into this: Pilsner glass (tall, thin, and tapered)

Drink instead of: Vodka soda and white zinfandel (BTW, if you drink white zin, put down this book and reevaluate your life. And don't get me started on vodka.)

Pair with: Pilseners of all types are a great match for fried foods but can also work nicely with grilled foods, salads, and even sushi. When it comes to cheese, think American varieties—mild cheddar, havarti, colby jack, and cream cheese all work well with pale lagers. Or go super traditional with Czech foods such as potato dumplings filled with smoked meat, bramboráky (fried potato pancakes spiced with marjoram, salt, pepper, and garlic), beer cheese (soft cheese mixed with raw onions and mustard), and goulash.

Brief history lesson: The Bohemian pilsener was the first pale-colored lager. Josef Groll developed the original recipe at Pilsner Urquell, a collective brewery at the time, using Bavarian yeast that had been smuggled into Bohemia by a local monk (those robes can hide just about everything).

In lieu of using the heavily kilned malts his stubborn colleagues in Germany were using, Groll found inspiration in relatively new, but not really that new, pale malt coming from England. As legend has it, Pilsner Urquell was the first brilliant beer to ever see the light of day. (In the beer world, brilliant refers to pristine clarity.)

Try it: Pilsner Urquell, Gordon Biersch Czech Style Pilsner, Lagunitas Pils, Samuel Adams Noble Pils, Oskar Blues Mama's Little Yella Pils

Beer Hates Ultraviolet Light

Hops hate UV light. When hops come into contact with UV light, a chemical reaction occurs that causes the beer to smell as if a skunk had sprayed it. Hence, light-struck beers are commonly referred to as "skunked." Beers packaged in green bottles are extremely susceptible to light. A lot of imported lagers come in green glass bottles and, more often than not, are skunked by the time they reach your glass. That's because green glass bottles, unlike brown bottles, offer little to no protection from UV light.

Heineken now purposefully exposes its wort to light during the brewing process, forcing it to become skunked prior to bottling. Yep, you read that right. Because most of its beer was already skunked during exportation, US-based Heineken consumers became accustomed to its "unique" skunk flavor—so much so that light-struck flavor became an attribute of the beer, rather than a flaw. If you really want to know what light-struck tastes like, grab a Heineken.

Munich Helles

MUNICH HELLES

Pronounced hell-us, it's the first German knock-off of Bohemian pilsener. Brilliant yellow, super grassy, hints of honey and lemon peel. Crisp.

BJCP Stats

SRM: 3–5   IBU: 16–22   ABV: 4.7–5.4 percent   OG: 1.045–1.051

My two cents: Have you ever heard the saying, "not your Dad's beer?" Well, the helles is "your Dad's beer"—at least it was my dad's beer. I didn't really understand his preoccupation with the style, especially the one produced by Spaten. To me, it seemed flavorless, lackluster, and dull, barely a step up from the domestic lagers everyone else drank. It took me a really long time to embrace its simplicity and, ultimately, enjoy its flavor. When I finally did, I fell in love with the helles.

Of all the pale lager styles, the helles is typically the sweetest. But it's not sugary sweet; it's chewing-on-fresh-grass sweet. It is also the least bitter of the pale lagers, hence seeming sweeter than the others; but it's not overly sweet. The ability to brew a perfect helles, or a pilsner for that matter, is a true testament of the talent and skill of the brewer. Its ingredients might seem simple, but it requires a delicate touch that most extreme brewers have a hard time mastering. Because the style is so soft and clean, any and all flaws extracted during the brewing process are extremely evident in the final product. A helles should never taste fruity or have any hint of dank or citrusy American hops.

In the glass: Bright straw yellow, lots of little bubbles, fluffy head

In the nose: Fresh cut grass, sweet hay, honey, and slightly stale bread

In the mouth: Sweet hay, sweet grass, lemon peel

In one word: Flawless

Pour it into this: Pilsner glass

Drink instead of: A cosmopolitan or pinot grigio

Pair with: Weisswurst (traditional Bavarian sausage made from finely minced veal and fresh back bacon), pretzels (soft and hard), vinaigrette-based salad dressings, Chinese food, grilled chicken, lighter seafood, and soft mild cheeses like mozzarella, goat, and muenster

Brief history lesson: In German, the term *hell* is an adjective meaning light or bright. The Munich helles was the first pale lager brewed in Munich. It was created by Spaten Brewery to compete with the Bohemian pilsener, which was becoming so popular it was scary.

What most differentiates the helles from the pilsners is its significantly lower level of hop bitterness. Germans historically have had lower tolerance levels for hop bitterness, and the beers they brew are a reflection of this.

Outside of Germany, the style is often labeled "Munich Original Lager," probably because most consumers know the word *lager*, but not the term *helles*.

Try it: Spaten Premium Lager (the classic), Paulaner Premium Lager, Stoudt's Gold Lager, Maui Brewing Co. Bikini Blonde Lager, Ballast Point Longfin Lager

GERMAN PILSNER

Straw-colored, highly carbonated, clean and crisp with notes of fresh grass, dried flowers, and bitter herbs.

BJCP Stats

SRM: 2–5   IBU: 25–45   ABV: 4.4–5.2 percent   OG: 1.044–1.050

My two cents: This is by far my favorite of the pale lagers. It's interesting how two seemingly similar beer styles—the Bohemian pilsener and the German pilsner—can have such subtle, yet defining differences. It's not the hops, malt, or even the yeast. It's all in the water. The Bohemian pilsener is brewed with soft water, while the German version is brewed with hard water.

Beers brewed with hard water tend to be drier than those brewed with soft water. And because there is less residual malt sweetness in the beer, the hop bitterness comes through stronger. The moral of the story: German pilsners are hoppier than the Bohemian versions, making them the hoppiest of all the traditional pale lager styles. (I say traditional because American versions with American hops can be way hoppier.)

Like the pilsener, much else is the same. The beer is straw-colored with just a little malt sweetness. It's clean, and the hop aroma is distinctively German: spicy or flowery rather than citrusy or fruity.

In the glass: Brilliant light gold, super bubbly, large white head

In the nose: Fresh hay, dried flowers, and graham crackers

In the mouth: Zesty citrus, fresh grass, bitter herbs, and water crackers

In one word: Crisp

Pour it into this: Pilsner glass

Drink instead of: Adjunct lagers, vodka gimlet, or sauvignon blanc

Pair with: Spicy cuisines such as Thai, Indian, and Mexican; shellfish; pork products such as sausage, ham, and bacon; grilled fish and veggies; fried things; pizza; and mildly sharp and pungent cheeses like cheddar, Humboldt Fog, and muenster

Brief history lesson: The first German brewery to attempt a pilsner-style beer was Aktienbrauerei Zum Bierkeller of Radeberg, which is now known as Radeberger Brewery. As opposed to the helles, the German Pilsner was created as a direct replica of the Bohemian pilsener but used German ingredients and higher-sulfate water.

Interesting fact: The French love the German Pils. In fact, when it was first created, France was the largest export market for this style.

Try it: Radeberger Pilsner (the original), Jever Pilsner, Trumer Pils, Spaten Pils, König Pilsner, Pinkus Organic Ur Pils, Harpoon Bohemian Pilsner

DORTMUNDER EXPORT

Golden yellow, super balanced, good carbonation; the booziest of the pale lagers.

BJCP Stats

SRM: 4–6   IBU: 23–30   ABV: 4.8–6.0 percent   OG: 1.048–1.056

My two cents: The Dortmunder Export is the baby bear of the pale lagers. Not as sweet as the helles (mama bear) but not as bitter as the pilsner (papa bear), for some it's juuuusst right. Its defining characteristic is probably its alcohol content, which is higher than all the other pale lagers. It is also the darkest in color and the richest of lagers.

Honestly, this style is hard to come by. That's mostly because it lacks the reputation and popularity of the other pale lager styles. If you can find a Dortmunder-style lager from a brewery that has actually done the style justice, it will be well worth every penny.

Just like its brethren, it's a brilliantly clear beer with a fluffy white head. However, since the malt character is ramped up, you'll often notice the color is more of a true golden than the lighter beers. It also may have a light touch of dimethyl sulfide (DMS), which is to say it may have a touch of a creamed-corn note in its aroma, but there will be no yeasty esters.

In the glass: Deep yellow, clear with lots of little bubbles, big white head

In the nose: Toasted bread and fresh cut grass

In the mouth: Bready, floral, and grassy

In one word: Smooth

Pour it into this: Pilsner glass

Drink instead of: Vodka tonic or chenin blanc

Pair with: Hearty traditional German foods such as sauerbraten, spätzle, and bratwurst; comfort foods like stews, chicken pot pie, and mashed potatoes; and mild soft cheeses like havarti, gouda (especially smoked), and colby jack

Brief history lesson: The lesser known of the light-colored lagers, the Dortmunder Export is another pilsner-inspired style from Germany. It originates from the industrial town of Dortmund. This version was brewed with slightly more alcohol to make it more ideal for export.

Interesting fact: The Dortmunder Export wasn't always a recognized style. In 1969, Fred Eckhardt wrote in his published handbook "A Treatise on Lager Beers" that the Dortmunder Export is a distinctive enough pale lager to be classed as a separate beer style. And thus it was.

Try it: Dortmunder Union Export, Great Lakes Dortmunder Gold, Thirsty Dog Labrador Lager, Ninkasi Oktoberfest Dortmund-Style Lager, 3 Floyds Jinx Proof

The Weird Weissbier (aka Hefeweizen)

Although Americans are more familiar with the term Hefeweizen, the Germans refer to the style as the Weissbier or Weizenbier. And it is one odd style of beer to come out of Germany. It's predominantly brewed with wheat and it's fermented with ale yeast at relatively high temperatures. And why is that weird, you ask? Because Germany is the country known for creating a law (the *Reinheitsgebot*) against brewing with adjuncts like wheat. And as you've seen on the last few pages, it's also the country responsible for perfecting the lager. So even though the Hefe might seem like something that came out of Belgium, we'll go ahead and take a look at it here alongside its fellow Germans.

HEFEWEIZEN/WEISSBIER

Hazy pale yellow, bubble gum, orange peel, banana bread, spicy, very effervescent, and dry .

BJCP Stats

SRM: 2–8   IBU: 8–15   ABV: 4.3–5.6 percent   OG: 1.044–1.052

My two cents: Super yeasty and loaded with lots of fruity esters (mainly banana and bubblegum) and phenolics, Hefeweizens are very closely related in flavor and aroma to Belgian ales yet are still very much German in nature. By that, I mean that the style is more regulated than wheat beers brewed elsewhere.

According to German law, beers that bear the name Weissbier (or equivalent) must be brewed with at least 50 percent malted wheat, but most are actually made with 60 to 70 percent malted wheat. The rest is, of course, malted barley.

Many people classify the Hefeweizen as a chick beer (you know, a style consumed mostly by women). I'm not sure when and where this stereotype came to be, but something tells me it has to do with the inappropriate fruit garnish that often accompanies this style. Please pardon my rant, but these are two issues that we need to address.

First, taste has no gender and, therefore, no style of beer is more favorable to one sex over the other. Second, fruit garnishes are almost always inappropriate when it comes to serving beer. I say almost always because there are a few brewers out there like Shaun O'Sullivan of 21st Amendment who encourage fruit garnishments (in his case, a wedge of watermelon on the High or Hell Watermelon Wheat beer). However, unless the brewer intends for there to be a fruit garnish, it is absolutely inappropriate. And trust me, I'm not the first (or last) person in the craft beer industry to rant about either of these subjects. But, moving on . . .

In the glass: super cloudy, straw yellow, large fluffy white head

In the nose: banana, bubble gum, clove, and orange peel

In the mouth: banana bread, vanilla, lemon bars

In one word: Fluffy

Pour it in this: Weizen glass

Drink instead of: Sangria, piña colada

Pair with: Highly carbonated with soft flavors and little to no bitterness, Hefeweizens are a good match for lighter fare—like fresh seafood, chicken, salads, and fruit desserts—and of course, German cuisine. I like pairing Hefeweizens with beet salads, goat cheese, cocktail shrimp, crab cakes, pretzels with mustard, sausages, lemon gelato, strawberry shortcake, or bananas foster.

Brief history lesson: The Weissbier actually has a pretty interesting story. Scientists have been able to date the brewing of wheat beers back to the Bronze Age—which started around 3300 BC. This really isn't too much of a surprise, considering most ancient "beer" was brewed with a smorgasbord of grains. Light wheat beers, however, didn't come "to be" until advances in kilning made pale malts accessible. But, before the Weissbier would come into existence, it would have to clear one great big hurdle—the *Reinheitsgebot*.

Long story short, the *Reinheitsgebot* attempted to end all wheat beer brewing in Germany (Bavaria at the time), but a few medieval Dukes in Bavaria were able to obtain exclusive brewing rights (not without a price, though) to maintain the production of wheat beers. It eventually became a huge source of revenue for Bavaria, which was pretty much a war state at this point.

The popularity of the Weissbier saw a huge fall in the late 1700s, but was revived in 1856 when the Schneider Family bought the legal rights to brew the style. As with all styles, Prohibition took a hit on the Weissbier, but it regained strength again in the 1960s and has been a very popular style since.

Try it: Weihenstephaner Hefeweissbier, Schneider Weisse Weizenhell, Paulaner Hefeweizen, Sierra Nevada Kellerweis, Two Brothers Ebel's Weiss Beer, Widmer Hefeweizen.

CLASSIC (PREMIUM) AMERICAN PILSNER

Fizzy yellow beer brewed with adjuncts such as corn and rice; pale, lackluster yet consistent.

BJCP Stats

SRM: 3–6   IBU: 25–40   ABV: 4.5–6 percent   OG: 1.044–1.060

My two cents: Oh, you seriously thought I was going to talk about the yellow fizzy corn beers in my book? Ha! If you've never tasted a macro lager, I commend, if not envy, you. We've all been down this road, whether it be in high school (shhhh) or college. These beers, when made by the two or three large breweries famous for them, are typically similar to their German counterparts in appearance, but their aroma and taste is noticeably different. They're often made with 20 to 30 percent flaked maize or rice in combination with six-row barley. They have a grainy, corn flavor if you really try to taste them. There is hop bitterness, but never hop aroma. In general, they are not much more than fizzy beer-like water, and they are best served ice cold.

In the glass: Yellow and fizzy

In the nose: Stale Cheerios with hints of grass that may or may not have been peed on

In the mouth: Biodegradable corn cups

In one word: Fizzy

Pour it into this: Pint glass or from the can

Drink instead of: Water

Pair with: Hot dogs, beefy jerky, boxed mac and cheese, frozen pizza, and pretty much anything you would find in a ballpark or football stadium

Brief history lesson: As previously noted, the classic American lager was a pilsner-inspired style brewed in the United States. Pre-Prohibition, the style was a bit hoppier and less adjunct-riddled. Post-Prohibition, the IBUs dropped, alcohol dropped, and adjuncts became a definitive characteristic of the style.

Try it: Coors Banquet, Pabst Blue Ribbon, Budweiser something—why are you doing this to yourself? Seriously, why?

Feeling adventurous? Try a Radler—the German version of the Shandy. The drink is essentially a concoction made of various types of German beers, usually a light lager, mixed with lemonade or soda. It's very popular in the summer months and for good reason. See page 228 for my recipe.

Note: Many American craft brewers have put their own twist on traditional pale lagers. These lagers don't typically fall under the "classic American lager" category because most are brewed with traditional ingredients, not adjuncts. Some stick to traditional recipes, some use adjuncts like corn and rice, some have Americanized them with American-grown hops, and some have even gone as far as to imperialize them (brew them at double, sometimes triple strength). And now, there is even a style known as the India pale lager (IPL) rapidly emerging. Those crazy Americans.

I say skip the mass-produced, get crazy, and try one of these nonconventional Americanized pale lagers: Dogfish Head My Antonia, Base Camp In-Tents IPL, Flying Dog UnderDog Atlantic Lager, Jack's Abby Hoponius Union, or Odell Double Pilsner.

KÖLSCH

Brilliant pale gold, thin head, soft hay and grass aromas, faint hints of fruit (typically apple), super crisp, refreshing.

BJCP Stats

SRM: 3–6   **IBU: 25–40**   **ABV: 4.5–6 percent**   **OG: 1.044–1.060**

My two cents: When it comes to the specs (aka color, bitterness, alcohol etc.)—the Kölsch and the German Pilsner are nearly identical. Both are (typically) brewed with pilsner or pale malt and noble hops. The fundamental difference is yeast. Technically speaking, the Kölsch is a German pale ale (despite its remarkable semblance to a pale lager). A Kölsch is fermented with ale yeast—but done so at cooler temperatures and then lagered for a month. It's considered a hybrid rather than a pure lager or ale.

However, I consider it more of a lager and here's why: I often joke that anyone can brew a decent IPA or a stout—the real testament of a great brewer is his or her ability to brew an outstanding Kölsch or pilsner. Like the pilsner, the Kölsch is an extremely delicate beer style characterized less for what it is and more for what it isn't. A great Kölsch should be extremely clean, crisp, and balanced—virtually flawless. The Kölsch has no specialty malt flavors to hide flaws behind. And you can't cover up any flaws by adding copious amounts of hops.

Even though the colder fermentation levels prevent most ale esters from forming, it is not uncommon to detect a subtle fruitiness in a Köslch's aroma and flavor. Across the board, a Kölsch should be ultra crisp, clean, and refreshing. No single ingredient should dominate and all flavors should be soft.

In the glass: light gold, brilliant, faint head

In the nose: sweet hay, white bread, whisper of pear

In the mouth: unsalted crackers, hints of apple, clean

In one word: Delicate

Pour it in this: Kölsch glass or pilsner flute

Drink instead of: pinot grigio, vodka

Pair with: I'm a big fan of partnering the Kölsch with sushi, shellfish, and other seafood dishes—but it also goes really well with classic German fare.

Brief history lesson: The Kölsch is kind of an anomaly when you think about it. It was created in Cologne, Germany in the late nineteenth century when pale malts were beginning to make their way into beers. Most German brewers at the time were making pale lagers but, for some reason or another, the crazy kids in Cologne opted to use a local ale yeast strain instead.

As with French wine and Trappist products, the Kölsch is a product with protected geographical indication—which essentially means that only the beers produced in Cologne can bear the name Kölsch. When the style is brewed elsewhere, it's technically not supposed be called a Kölsch—but many American brewers do it anyways (tsk tsk).

Try it: Reissdorf Kölsch, Metropolitan Krankshaft Kölsch, Saranac Kölsch, Alaskan Summer Ale, New Holland Full Circle, Magnolia Kalifornia Kölsch, Calicraft Cali Cöast

chapter three

THE DARKER SIDE OF LIGHT

Amber and Dark Lagers

For some reason or another, people associate the lightness (be it in weight, alcohol, or calories) of a beer with how pale it is. Red, brown, or black beers must be heavier than their über pale counterparts, right? That's like saying red wine is always heavier than white wine. Sure, most of the time that's probably the case, but there are always exceptions to the rules. Just like beaujolais and sauternes are exceptions for wine, nothing debunks the myth about dark beers quite like dark lagers.

How Beer Gets Its Color

The color of beer is directly related to its malts. The fermentable sugar in the majority of craft beer comes from malted barley that has been germinated and kilned. Additional color and malt flavor come from the roasting process. No roast to light roast yields straw and golden colors and biscuit flavors, medium roast yields amber and copper colors and caramel and nut flavors, darker roast yields brown and light black colors and chocolate and coffee flavors, and the heaviest roast yields black color and burnt flavors. (This is discussed further on page 112).

Most craft beers, with wheat beers being the exception, are made up of 75–100 percent base malts, the palest malted barley on the spectrum. Specialty malts make up the next largest amount at 5–15 percent, and black and dark malts typically make up only 1–5 percent of the overall recipe, which means it takes only a small percentage of dark malt to create a darker colored beer. Think of it in terms of food dye; although food dye does not dilute or make up a noticeable percentage of a cupcake recipe, a few small drops go a long way. (The same is true for aroma when it comes to things like vanilla extract.)

Color vs. Alcohol

Don't let color deceive you. There are plenty of full-bodied pale beers with high sugar and alcohol content, just as there are light-bodied dark beers with lower sugar and alcohol content. The difference between a lightweight, lower-calorie beer and a heavy, higher-calorie beer is not color; it's alcohol content.

Although lab tests could give you more accurate results, all you really need to know is that sugar content and calories in beer are in direct correlation to its alcohol content. It takes more sugar, in this case maltose, to make more alcohol. So therefore, in the most basic of conclusions possible, the higher the alcohol a beer has, the more maltose used, and the more calories in the end product.

Note: Mass-produced domestic lagers brewed with adjuncts like corn and rice are the exception to that statement. Many large corporate breweries monopolized on the American obsession with dieting, developing stripped-down, so-called "light" versions of what they claim to be beer, but has more likeness to mineral water, in my opinion.

The moral of the story? Don't be afraid of dark beer! Dark doesn't mean it's heavy. And just because a beer is super pale doesn't mean it's light in other ways. But don't take my word for it, debunk the myth for yourself by trying out one of these darker colored yet lighter-bodied lagers.

SCHWARZBIER (BLACK LAGER)
Darkest lager, virtually black, ruby hues, brilliant tan head, slightly roasty, bitter chocolate, clean.

BJCP Stats
SRM: 17–30   IBU: 22–32   ABV: 4.4–5.4 percent   OG: 1.046–1.052

My two cents: The schwarzbier, or black lager as it's referred to in the United States, is one style that completely defies the stereotype that dark beer is heavier, richer, and more caloric than its pale counterparts. Oh, poor dark beer, always being judged by the color of its malt.

Schwarzbiers are often referred to as the "black pils," and for good reason. Although extremely dark in color, these beers are exceptionally clean, light, and relatively low in calories, much like a pilsner. If you hold one up to the light, you'll often see garnet highlights; they're never truly deep, dark black. They may also have some low roast or coffee-like character, but they'll never have any burnt notes like a stout. Their bitterness is also generally on the low side, and the finish is clean and dry, again much like a pilsner.

Schwarzbier (black lager)

In the glass: Deep brown, ruby hues, big tan head, and brilliant clarity

In the nose: Iced coffee and bittersweet chocolate chips

In the mouth: Bohemian pils spiked with drops of coffee extract

In one word: Magnificent

Pour it into this: Pilsner glass, schwarzbier goblet, stein (when appropriate)

Drink instead of: Pinot noir, dark and stormy

Pair with: Roasted and grilled meats, Reuben sandwich, pumpernickel bread, boar sausage, duck pâté, carne asada tacos, chicken mole, gruyere and muenster cheeses

Brief history lesson: The schwarzbier is a pretty old style. Its roots date all the way back to the ninth century BC—although today's version probably has virtually no semblance to the original. But that is a good thing. Technology for the win!

The style originated from southeastern Germany, an area that included parts of both Bavaria and Bohemia. The style was first documented in 1390 in the city of Braunschweig (what we English-speaking folk call Brunswick).

Try it: Köstritzer Schwarzbier, Kulmbacher Mönchshof Premium Schwarzbier, Samuel Adams Black Lager, Moonlight Brewing Death and Taxes, Sprecher Black Bavarian, Duck-Rabbit Schwarzbier

MUNICH DUNKEL

Dark brown, garnet hues, rich Munich malts, bread crust, nuts, caramel, clean finish.

BJCP Stats

SRM: 14–28   IBU: 18–28   ABV: 4.5–5.6 percent   OG: 1.048–1.056

My two cents: Outside of Germany, this isn't really a popular style. That makes sense since it's like the brown ale or the porter of Germany—both under-appreciated styles for those who worship extreme flavors (super bitter, super sour, high alcohol, and so on).

Yet the dunkel is worth seeking out. I like to think of dunkels as the middle child of the lager family. It's a malt-forward style, which means it has a higher level of perceived sweetness than pale lagers and schwarzbiers. But it isn't quite as malty and rich as the bock family (a category we will discuss in Chapter 8). While dunkels are super malty and toasty, they are also very clean and dry compared to brown ales. Rich Munich malts give it a different flavor entirely from American ales, with hints of chocolate, nuts, caramel, and toffee. The clean lager yeast means you won't have any fruity esters getting in the way of those flavors either.

In the glass: Dark brown, garnet highlights, creamy tan head, sometimes murky

In the nose: Bread crusts, dry crackers, hints of nuts

In the mouth: Perfectly browned toast, nut butter, drizzle of honey

In one word: Friendly

Pour it into this: Pilsner glass, stein (when appropriate)

Drink instead of: Beaujolais nouveau, rum and Coke, Newcastle

Pair with: Hearty comfort foods, beef stews, braised meats, rabbit, bratwurst, BLTs, roasted duck, elk, brussels sprouts, mashed potatoes and gravy, German chocolate cake, and nutty cheeses like fontina, aged gruyere, and swiss

Brief history lesson: This was the first style to feel the fury of the German Purity Law (*Reinheitsgebot*) and, as a result, it was the first "standardized" (codified and regulated) lager. The style originated in the Bavarian villages and countryside and was the quintessential German style of beer before the pale lagers were developed.

Try it: Ayinger Altbairisch Dunkel, Paulaner Alt Münchner Dunkel, Harpoon Dark Gordon Biersch dunkels, Dinkel Acker Dark, Löwenbräu Dunkel, Augustiner Dunkel

VIENNA LAGER

Reddish amber, brilliant clarity, good carbonation, soft, elegant maltiness, slight toast, low bitterness.

BJCP Stats

SRM: 10–16   IBU: 18–30   ABV: 4.5–5.5 percent   OG: 1.046–1.052

My two cents: This style would be virtually extinct if it wasn't for Mexico. Okay, maybe that's an exaggeration, but in all seriousness Mexico is the largest producer of this amber lager despite its German origin. It's sad, but most commercially produced beers in this style also use adjunct ingredients, like corn, so they aren't really true to the style. American versions, as with most styles, tend to be a bit bigger and bitterer.

If you close your eyes and taste this style blind, without looking at the color, you might guess it was a pale lager not an amber lager. This is because, although it is amber in color, it has a slight toasted malt flavor but no caramel notes.

The most well known modern-day Vienna lager is probably Negra Modelo, and I'm not going to lie: For a mass-produced corporate lager, it is a pretty darn tasty beer, what I might call the lesser of the evils. If you ever stumble across it on draft, I highly recommend ordering a pint, especially with spicy food (or even just chips and salsa). The body is fairly thin, as one would expect from a mass-produced lager, but it is a super clean and refreshing beer that has just a kiss of malt sweetness.

In the glass: Brilliant amber, red and copper hues, large off-white head

In the nose: Light toast, hints of biscuit, clean

In the mouth: Lightly toasted bread, simple

In one word: Elegant

Pour it into this: Pilsner glass, stein (when appropriate)

Drink instead of: White zinfandel, piña colada, and any other Mexican lager style

Pair with: Carnitas tacos, chorizo, ham, nachos, roasted chicken, nutty cheeses like aged gruyere and cheddar, pepper jack cheese, pretzels, sausages with sauerkraut and mustard

Brief history lesson: The invention of the Vienna lager is attributed to Anton Dreher. It is considered to be the original amber lager and the prototype to the much more popular Oktoberfest. There are little records about Dreher's beers, but it is assumed that they were amber and brilliant and brewed with Bavarian lager yeast.

Try it: Negra Modelo, Great Lakes Eliot Ness, Olde Saratoga Lager, Devils Backbone Vienna Lager, Dos Equis Amber Lager, Abita Amber

OKTOBERFEST (MÄRZEN)

Brilliant marigold, bright clarity, soft head, clean aroma, light toasted malts, crisp, quaffable, tastes like autumn.

BJCP Stats

SRM: 7–14   IBU: 20–28   ABV: 4.8–5.7 percent
OG: 1.050–1.057

My two cents: I look forward to September for no other reason than the release of this style. If you could bottle autumn, this is what it would look like. Dark gold to deep orange, Oktoberfests radiate a hue that is similar to both changing leaves and an autumn sunset.

Although amberish in color, Oktoberfest has virtually no caramel malt flavors or sweetness. If anything, it has a light toasted, biscuit malt flavor. It is a touch heavier in body than the palest of the lager, but just barely. It's a smooth beer with medium to high carbonation and a mild noble hop flavor. This all adds up to an easy-drinking beer fit for a stein come fall.

I don't know if it's a result of my German heritage or my fondness for the autumn months, but Oktoberfest beers rank really high on my list of favorite beer styles. They have more structure than pale lagers, but aren't quite as heavy on the palate as pale ales. Personally, I think that Oktoberfests are the perfect transition style to go from the warm weather wheat beers, pale lagers, and blonde summer ales to the rich, spiced, roasty, and boozy winter beers.

In the glass: Brilliant deep gold, autumn sunset in a glass

In the nose: Delicately toasted bread, hay, dried leaves

In the mouth: Melba toast, crisp, and effervescent

In one word: Stunning

Pour it into this: Stein (when appropriate), pilsner glass

Drink instead of: Grüner veltliner, Moscow mule

Pair with: Traditional Oktoberfest fare: Bavarian pretzels, wiener schnitzel, *schupfnudeln* (fried potato dumplings), warm German potato salad, spätzle, sauerbraten, and bratwurst with sauerkraut

Brief history lesson: The *Oktoberfestbier* name is one of many protected "Designations of Origin" in the beer world. The only beers allowed to tout the name are those brewed within the city walls of Munich. All other beers brewed in the style must be labeled as Märzens or Oktoberfest-style beers.

The style was originally brewed in March (hence the name *Märzen*), stored in cool caves during the summer months, and then released in the fall. Although brewed since the Middle Ages, the style was first standardized by Gabriel Sedlmayr of Spaten Brewery in 1871, whose variation was greatly inspired by the Vienna lager.

The Oktoberfest tale is one too long and detailed to give it justice in this book. Essentially, it began on October 12, 1810, as a celebration of the marriage between Crown Prince Ludwig (later King Ludwig I)

and Princess Therese of Hildburghausen. It is now the world's largest fair—and the longest beer festival, taking place over the course of 16 days. Even my liver can't handle a festival that long.

Did you know: Only six breweries are allowed to serve beer at Oktoberfest. They are also the only breweries allowed to brew beers under the *Oktoberfestbier* designation. These include: Augustiner-Bräu, Hacker-Pschorr-Bräu, Löwenbräu, Paulaner, Spatenbräu, Staatliches Hofbräu-München

Try it: Ayinger Oktoberfest-Märzen, Hofbräu Oktoberfest, Victory Festbier, Great Lakes Oktoberfest, Spaten Oktoberfest, Paulaner Oktoberfest, Flying Dog Dogtoberfest

STEAM BEER/CALIFORNIA COMMON

Light copper, brilliant, good head, toasted bread, light caramel, woody, minty hops, clean and refreshing.

BJCP Stats

SRM: 10–14   IBU: 30–45   ABV: 4.5–5.5 percent   OG: 1.048–1.054

My two cents: Wait, what? Isn't the good ole' Cal Common an ale? Well, sort of. The best way to describe where this style sits is that it's the opposite of the Kölsch (see page 29). By that, I mean while Kölsch beers are fermented with ale yeast at lager temperatures, steam beers are fermented with lager yeast at ale temperatures—which makes them a hybrid style in the opposite way.

They fit in with other amber and dark lagers as they are malty with notes of caramel and toast, and they're also pretty dry and crisp. If there's a signature departure, it's that the aroma generally has a distinctive woodiness from the use of Northern Brewer hops. Although steam beers might resemble pale ales in color, alcohol, and bitterness, they should be ester-free like lagers (aka no fruity aromas).

In the glass: Light copper, clear, off-white head

In the nose: Toasted bread, light caramel, dried leaves

In the mouth: Whole-wheat toast, agave nectar, woody, clean

In one word: Blasé

Pour it into this: Nonic pint

Drink instead of: Whiskey soda, white wine spritzer

Pair with: I'm a big fan of pairing this all-American style beer with all-American classics like ballpark hot dogs (with all the works), Philly cheesesteaks, burgers, chowder, pizza, and deli-style sandwiches.

Brief history lesson: An all-American style, the steam beer was invented in the late 1800s in northern California. Traditional steam beers (often called California common) were made with "cheap" ingredients and were mostly intended for blue-collar consumption. However, today's steam beers are made with much higher-quality ingredients—as evidenced by the popularity and success of Anchor Steam.

Speaking of Anchor Steam, Anchor Brewing Co. is credited with creating the modern-day "steam beer" (it even owns the trademark on the name). Anchor Steam is considered to be the prototype for this style category, although several brewers have adopted the unique style.

Try it: Anchor Steam, Southampton Steam Beer, Flying Dog Old Scratch Amber Lager, Southern Tier 2x Steam, Baxter Tarnation California-style Lager, Cismontane The Citizen

chapter four

THE IPA AND ITS EMERGING SUBCATEGORIES

The history of the India pale ale is a tale that many beer geeks love to tell and most beer writers have written about at some point or another. There is even an entire book dedicated to this awesome style (*IPA* by Mitch Steele, and it's a great read).

Although the who, what, where, and when is a bit hazy and disputed, the simple and abridged version of the story goes like this: The India pale ale was a highly hopped pale ale, often higher in alcohol, developed by English brewers in the late eighteenth century for export to India.

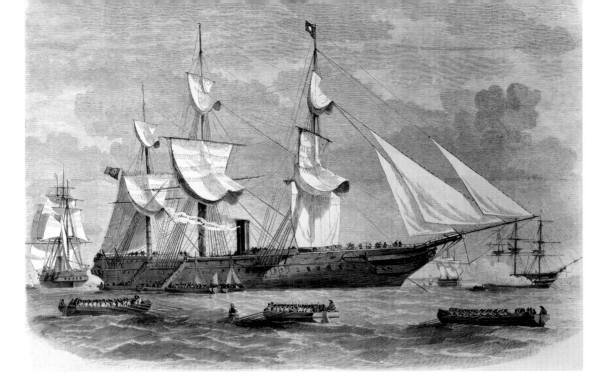

Elaborating on that statement is tough, and most people end up perpetuating a misinformed, yet slightly more glamorous, version of the actual story. The following is my well-researched and, I hope, mostly correct version of the myth, the legend, the India pale ale.

Back in the 1700s, almost everything was shipped by, well, ships. It took most cargo ships anywhere from four to six months to travel from England all the way down and around the entire continent up to India.

At this time, beer was stored, transported, and conditioned in wooden barrels. Conditioning in this particular situation refers to an additional fermentation that occurs after the primary or first round of fermentation. It's a process of maturation and natural carbonation. But we can talk about that later.

Wood is extremely porous, making these shipping vessels highly susceptible to oxygen and bacteria, both being enemies of beer and just about everything perishable. Wet and humid with fluctuating temperatures and constant agitation, old wooden ships were potential breeding grounds for infection but also ideal conditions for conditioning (like that word play?), depending on the style of beer.

Exporting beer from England to other countries was not exactly a new and different practice for English brewers. England's rich history of colonization made beer exportation extremely pertinent. After all, one couldn't let those poor English soldiers and settlers go thirsty, right?

In the late eighteenth century, a brewer named George Hodgson of Bow Brewery made nice with the traders at the East India Company, whose ships were harbored a stone's throw away from the brewery. Hodgson gave the ever-thirsty traders a liberal credit line of eighteen months, which made him quite popular with the crew, to say the least.

Hodgson's relationship with the East India Company allowed him to dominate the beer export market for nearly forty years. Ships transported several styles from Bow Brewery to India, but the most popular, by and large, was his Hodgson's October beer—a style that is now referred to as "old ale" or "stock ale."

Traditionally, October beer was a slightly stronger, highly hopped beer, somewhere between pale and amber in color, made to last anywhere from one to two years. Both alcohol and hops have antiseptic properties that make them sturdy barriers to bacteria, which increases the shelf life and, in this particular case, the ship-life of beer. Since October beers were brewed with more hops and booze, they were also ideal beers for export.

This is where the story tends to get a little fuzzy. Although Hodgson's October beer was the inspiration for what is now known as the India pale ale, it was not invented on purpose, per se, to survive the export to India—a common misperception and the most popular story told.

It is important to note that October beers were not the only beers that survived the export to India. Porters and other brews were also taking the four-month tour around Africa, but it was the October beers that were the most popular. The most likely reason for this is that the rocky shipping conditions expedited the maturation process of the beer, making it taste as if it had been in the barrels for double or triple that amount of time. This probably means this particular beer tasted better when it landed in India than when it left England, hence people loving it.

On a side note, this practice was also common for the aging of fine spirits and wines, like cognac and scotch. There are a few distillers today that still employ the tradition of rapidly maturing barrels of spirits by shipping them around the globe for months throughout the rocky ocean waters. But I digress, where were we?

Oh yes, the IPA. After forty-odd years of exporting beer to India, Hodgson left the brewery in the hands of his sons. The kids got greedy, pissed off the East India Company, and essentially got the boot. This opened the door for other English brewers, specifically those from Burton-on-Trent, to go after the brewery's lost market share.

The Burton brewers borrowed a chapter from Hodgson's book and started brewing their own extra-hoppy pale ales. One key difference is that their versions were more attenuated, meaning drier with less residual sugar, which allowed the bigger hop profile to really shine.

Eventually, the beer-swilling publicans in England found out about these hoppy pale exports, and the IPA soon eclipsed the porter as the hometown favorite style.

Notice the tricky language, because up until this point the style was still not called the India pale ale. The IPA name did not appear in writing or in advertising until 1841—nearly sixty years after Hodgson had first started shipping his hopped-up October beers to India.

IPA Today

Flash forward 170 years or so, and the India pale ale is now the most brewed, drank, and celebrated style of craft beer in the world. I've already discussed the depressing era known as Prohibition—aka the plague responsible for the death of thousands of breweries and dozens of beer styles—and its repercussions that still haunt us today. Needless to say, the IPA was not immune and was lost for several decades.

But now, thanks to today's brewers, it is not only found but also more popular than ever. Today, this illustrious style represents the pinnacle of brewing innovation with its broad spectrum of diverse brands, subcategories, and regional flavor variations, making it one of the most iconic styles of modern-day craft beer.

In a world where innovation only breeds innovation, it's natural that craft beer, an industry born from ingenuity, is ever evolving. Today, there are no laws that dictate how beer must be brewed, and the creative ability of craft brewers is seemingly unlimited. Older styles are continuously being manipulated to create newer styles and subcategories. As a result, style guidelines and categories are constantly changing to keep up with the evolution of craft brewing. Today's most popular style of craft beer, the IPA, is also the most modified, and in the ultra-critical eyes of the beer "purists," bastardized. So we'll start with the classics.

The Three Defined Categories of IPA

Did I say just three? Well, yes, the English IPA, American IPA, and imperial/double IPA are currently the only accepted styles. However, so many brewers and beer judges consider the American Black Ale—often referred to as the Black IPA—to be the fourth defined IPA style, we'll go ahead and include it as its own entry on the pages that follow. After the big four, we'll also take a quick look at the myriad variations.

ENGLISH IP.A

Golden amber, grassy, fruity, caramel, bready, toffee-like, slight hop bite, dry mineral finish.

BJCP Stats

SRM: 8–14	IBU: 40–60	ABV: 5–7.5 percent	OG: 1.050–1.075

My two cents: English-style IPAs can be hit or miss for many American beer drinkers. They tend to be sweeter and English hops just don't have the same punch-you-in-the-mouth bitterness that American varietals boast. As a result, English IPAs can seem dull and less than thrilling to the hop-obsessed American constantly pushing the boundaries of his palate, if not entirely wrecking it.

But, that doesn't mean this style is boring. These beers have a beautiful malt body from traditional English malts. They have unique fruity esters from the English ale yeast. And, because they tend to be balanced, they make an excellent match for many foods, which would otherwise be destroyed by a stiff IPA. Last but not least: the hops! Uniquely herbal hops can appeal to many beer drinkers who just don't care for the smack of citrus or dankness American hops bring to an IPA.

Several American breweries, particularly those on the East Coast, brew English-American IPA hybrids using the traditional English malt blend, English ale yeast, and American hops. These unique IPAs have the caramel and toffee-like sweetness of an English IPA with the resinous pine and bitter citrus bite for which American hops are so well loved.

In the glass: Deep copper, amber hues, sometimes murky

In the nose: Sweet grass, dried pine leaves

In the mouth: Werther's Original

In one word: Classic

Pour it into this: Nonic pint glass

Drink instead of: Scotch and water, oaked chardonnay

Pair with: Fish and chips, bangers and mash, shepherd's pie, burgers, chili, and Indian curry dishes like mulligatawny soup, chicken tikka masala, vegetable korma, and samosas. As for cheese, you can never go wrong with English classics like stilton blue, cheddar, and gloucester.

Try it: Meantime Brewing IPA, Samuel Smith IPA, Goose Island IPA, Yards Brewing IPA, Great Lakes Brewing Co. Commodore Perry IPA,

Did you know? Humans aren't wired to love bitter flavors. Being able to detect bitterness is a survival mechanism in all animals, since bitter tasting substances are historically associated with poisonous foods. So don't beat yourself up if you don't love hoppy beers. Hops are an acquired taste (just like blue cheese, olives, and tannic red wine). So really, hop lovers are just crazy masochists deep down inside. We train ourselves to like, and even love, what we never should (trust me, I know).

AMERICAN INDIA PALE ALE

Golden, effervescent, sometimes cloudy, citrusy, resinous, honey, floral, smack you in the face bitter.

BJCP Stats

SRM: 6–15   IBU: 40–70   ABV: 5.5–7.5 percent   OG: 1.056–1.075

My two cents: Pine. Grapefruit rind. Dank weed. These are all signature aromas of the American IPA. Sound like a beer that's not for the timid? You're right about that, my friend. Perhaps that's why the American IPA is one of my top three favorite beer styles on this planet. (The other two would be pilsners and saisons. But then again, ask me tomorrow and I might choose three completely different styles.) The reason I love American IPAs so much is probably because my first real beer epiphany happened with an American IPA (see page 47). Up until that point, I didn't think I liked beer. Granted, I had not yet been exposed to craft beer at all, so I technically didn't even know what real beer was, but I digress. The moral of the story is that I love American IPAs.

The differences between the American IPA and its British sibling starts with the malt. While British IPAs sport a biggish malt body, American IPAs use malts that stay the heck out of the way. The same goes for the yeast. American IPAs have minimal esters, better to let the hop aroma take center stage. In color they can be light gold to reddish copper, but unlike say an amber ale, the aroma should be all hops, hops, and more hops. East Coast–style IPAs can get a bit British on the malt side, but when you hit the West Coast, pale and bitter is what you're going to get.

In the glass: Gold to copper red, strong head, sometimes hazy (hop haze)

In the nose: Citrus, pine, hay, grapefruit, tropical fruits

In the mouth: Citrus pith, pine sap, lemon peel, fresh grass

In one word: Invigorating

Pour it into this: Nonic pint glass

Drink instead of: Sauvignon blanc, margarita

Pair with: Fried foods, buffalo chicken wings, pizza, jambalaya, lox, sausage, cured meats, blackened fish, Indian curries, Mexican food, fried pickles, carrot cake, cheesecake, and even sushi. When it comes to cheese, think sharp, funky, and aged—the more pungent the better.

Brief history lesson: Brewed to celebrate the bicentennial of Paul Revere's historic ride, Anchor Brewing's Liberty Ale is often revered (how is that for play on words) as the first American IPA. Sierra Nevada Celebration Ale is a close second, with roots back to 1981.

Try it: Russian River Blind Pig IPA, Ballast Point Sculpin IPA, Bell's Two Hearted Ale, Bear Republic Racer 5, Dogfish Head 60 Minute IPA

IMPERIAL (DOUBLE) INDIA PALE ALE

Golden amber, often hazy, abrasively bitter, citrus pith, pine, boozy, light malt sweetness, dry finish.

BJCP Stats

SRM: 8–15   IBU: 60–120   ABV: 7.5–10 percent   OG: 1.070–1.090

My two cents: The invention of the double IPA is most commonly attributed to Vinnie Cilurzo, owner and brewmaster of Russian River Brewing Company. He first developed his double IPA recipe, the prototype

for Pliny the Elder, in 1994 at Blind Pig Brewery in Temecula, California. According to beer legend, it was an accident: Vinnie added 50 percent too much malt to the mash tun and tried to correct the mistake by adding 100 percent more hops. His oops moment turned into our super win.

Nowadays, Blind Pig is the name of Vinnie's regular IPA, while Pliny the Elder is his ever-coveted double IPA. While I love Blind Pig, anyone who knows me—or even sort of knows me from the Internet—knows that Pliny the Elder is, hands down, one of my favorite beers on this planet.

No matter what imperial IPA you're sipping, expect an extra-hoppy and more alcoholic version of the India pale ale. The color, like an IPA, can range from golden to reddish copper. Some will be clear while others sport a hoppy haze. Due to the increased malt, you may also notice a bit of additional sweetness. However, some brewers get around that by drying out the beer with sugar. Sugar? Wouldn't that make the beer sweeter? Nope. As it turns out, yeast can pretty much completely convert corn sugar to alcohol, so there is less residual sweetness in a fermented beer than if the brewer used all malt.

In the glass: Sunset yellowish orange, excellent lacing

In the nose: Pine cones, grapefruit, grass, cat pee, honey

In the mouth: Boozy heat, tree sap, Sour Patch Kids

In one word: Intense

Pour it into this: Snifter

Drink instead of: Shots of tequila, fernet

Pair with: This style is a doozy to pair with food, as it can easily numb the tongue, preventing it from tasting any other flavors, or completely overwhelm the flavors in a dish. The bolder the food, the better—super pungent blue cheeses, extra sharp cheddars, really stinky barnyard cheeses. Spicy food works well, but only to a point. Whereas hops can act as a cooling agent, alcohol only exacerbates the burn. So take heed when paring ultra-spicy foods with high-alcohol imperial IPAs; it can hurt more than help.

Sometimes, the simplest of pairings are the best. Case and point: Russian River Brewing Co. Pliny the Elder and Pliny Bites—a wood-fired pizza crust topped with a house blend of cheeses and jalapeños served with a marinara dipping sauce. The fat from the cheese and the heat from the jalapeños cut right through the bitterness of the beer. The hop flavor really shines through, the alcohol is softened, and each sip of beer tastes better and better with every bite.

Try it: Russian River Pliny the Elder, Avery Maharaja, Stone Ruination, Firestone Walker Double Jack, Alchemist Heady Topper, 3 Floyds Dreadnaught IPA, Weyerbacher Double Simcoe IPA, Bell's Hopslam

BLACK IPA/AMERICAN BLACK ALE
Very dark to black, roasty, strong hop aroma, chocolate, coffee, light caramel, citrus, pine, bold bitterness.

BJCP Stats
SRM: 35+   IBU: 50–70   ABV: 5–6 percent (some may be higher)   OG: 1.056–1.075

My two cents: A rose by any other name applies here. The name and origin of this style has been greatly debated by brewers all over the United States. Those who live in or around the Cascadian watershed call these beers Cascadian Dark Ales or CDA for short. And pretty much everyone else in the country calls these beers Black IPAs. Many East Coasters credit Greg Noonan from Vermont Pub and Brewery as the inventor of the style, but the Pacific Northwest folks might tell you otherwise.

Technically, the style has officially been named and defined by the (American) Brewers Association as the American-style black ale. It is essentially an IPA brewed with the addition of dark specialty malts, resulting in a dark brown to black IPA with a hint of roasted malt flavor (the roasted malt should be present and noticeable but not too pronounced). Hop character should still shine through, despite the addition of roasted and caramel malts. All in all, these beers should be pretty balanced.

In the glass: Blackish brown to jet black, fluffy tan head

In the nose: Pine, caramel, plum, lemon zest

In the mouth: Dark chocolate, grapefruit, fig newtons

In one word: Rebellious

Pour it into this: Nonic pint or snifter (for higher alcohol versions)

Drink instead of: Malbec, Amaro, dark and stormy

Pair with: Burgers, grilled steak, barbecued ribs, chili, jerk chicken, blackened catfish (or red snapper), roasted or grilled portabella mushrooms, smoked gouda, gorgonzola, aged cheddar, white pizza, dark chocolate, tiramisu

Try it: Stone Sublimely Self-Righteous Ale, 21st Amendment Back in Black, Southern Tier Iniquity, Deschutes Hop in the Dark Cascadian Dark Ale, Lagunitas NightTime, New Glarus Black Top, Odell Mountain Standard Double Black IPA

The "Other" IPAs

Although those are the only styles of IPA that are defined and judged, the spectrum of IPA subcategories is not limited to three. Essentially, outside of changing its color, there are two ways that brewers manipulate the style: (1) take an IPA base recipe and ferment it with an atypical yeast strand; (2) take a different style of beer and hop it as if it were an IPA.

This is just a brief attempt to name and describe some of the not-yet-defined subcategories of IPA emerging in the marketplace. Please note that as with most experimental beer styles without official guidelines, these subcategories are still a bit ambiguous and open to interpretation. They are an attempt by breweries to describe what you're about to taste as much as anything else.

BELGIAN-STYLE IPA

Take an IPA base recipe and ferment it with a Belgian yeast and you've got yourself a Belgian-style IPA. Most of these have a similar appearance, malt content, hop aroma, and flavor profile as an IPA, but with noticeable fruity esters and flavor characteristics of a Belgian yeast. What yeast the brewer chooses and what hops he or she pairs it with can create dramatically different beers.

WHITE IPA

This riff on a Belgian-style IPA is its own thing. Brewers take a Belgian witbier, which has a wheaty malt base and a distinctive yeast, and hop it like an IPA. So expect the same color, body, and esters as a witbier but with noticeable hop aroma, flavor, and bitterness.

INDIA SESSION ALE/SESSION IPA

India session ales provide all of the hop goodness of an IPA, but at a more sessionable (aka lower) alcohol level. These are beers designed for the hopheads who want a great hoppy beer to drink over a long period of time.

BRETTANOMYCES/WILD IPA

Wild IPAs can be made with a wide variety of cultures for a wide variety of flavors. Currently, the most popular thing to do is use Brettanomyces for primary or secondary fermentation of a classic IPA recipe. Some strains will make the beer more tropical, with hints of pineapple, while others will be more like what you'd expect if you made an extreme version of a beer like Orval. They can change significantly over time.

RED IPA

Once an IPA malt bill goes too extreme, you basically have an American red ale brewed at a higher strength and hopped like an IPA. Typically, redder in color than an IPA, with deep ruby hues, this beer is for fans of American IPAs that want more malt character but not the substitution of ingredients you find in an English IPA.

RYE IPA

Rye IPAs are similar to Red IPAs in that they're mostly a showcase for a different malt body than you'd find in a traditional IPA. Besides wheat, rye is one of the most popular nonbarley brewing grains, and many brewers and beer drinkers like the way it amplifies hops.

SPICED/HERBED IPA

This catchall category is for any IPA brewed with the addition of spices, herbs, or flowers. Some brewers use ingredients like grapefruit peel or blood orange to amplify the citrusy American hop profiles, while others will use something completely different than what you'd ever get using hops alone. For example, Elysian brews a very popular IPA with jasmine.

As you can imagine, the potential for subcategories of subcategories becomes exponential when these styles are combined. As more and more brewers step outside of the traditional style guidelines, expect to see more variations of the IPA style to appear in the marketplace.

My First IPA

I can still smell the Centennial hops like it was yesterday. It was Labor Day in Columbus, Ohio. I was a ripe twenty-three years of age, fresh out of college, studying to be a sommelier with an intense passion for wine and little to no experience drinking beer, let alone craft beer.

My knowledge for wine and experience in the restaurant industry landed me a management position in a farm-to-table concept in downtown Columbus. I found myself on a bus with my new employer and the entire restaurant team headed to a local organic farm, where we sourced a good amount of our produce.

With us we brought all the fixings for a proper picnic, including beer. I watched in awe as my new co-workers unloaded case after case of beers I had never heard of. The packaging was colorful, artistic, and the beer names were weird and intriguing—much different from anything I had seen before.

As soon as the boxes were busted open, I noticed that everyone seemed to be drinking one beer in particular: Bell's Two Hearted Ale.

Two Hearted will always hold a special place in my heart. It was my first IPA and my memories from that day are still vivid. I had never experienced anything like it. Citrus and pine aromas, wickedly bitter taste, super dry finish—it was flavorful and intense. It smacked me in the face over and over again, with each sip, but still had me begging for more.

From that moment on, I became obsessed with hops and started seeking out any and every IPA I could get my lupulin-addicted hands on. Traveling, trading, and even working for beer, I became a relentless IBU chaser, constantly seeking the intoxicatingly bitter thrill of hops.

chapter five

THE OTHER HOPPY BEERS

Although the IPA is the most famous hoppy ale today, it wasn't always the most popular or even the most brewed style. The popularity and prevalence of the American IPA only came about in the late 1990s. Before that, other hoppy styles like pale ales, browns, and amber, were more common. Although English brewers were one of the last to embrace hops as an ingredient (Germans, Dutch, and Flemish being the first), they were the first to truly develop beer styles to showcase the flavor and bitterness of hops. For many people, some of these hoppy styles serve as gateway beers to the big, powerful, and almighty IPAs.

Real Ale (Cask Ale)

Real ale is a term coined by the Campaign for Real Ale (CAMRA), and it refers to unfiltered, cask-conditioned beer. What does that mean? After the wort undergoes its normal primary fermentation in tanks, it is transferred into casks instead of kegs. These casks, sometimes called firkins, house the beer while it conditions. The yeast is still active, so it's often fed a small dose of sugar to help give the beer a natural, albeit very low, level of carbonation.

Other ingredients can also be added to the cask. Traditionally, most brewers will only add dry hops or fining agents, like isinglass or carrageenans. The former will alter the taste of the beer while the latter are added to help clarify the beer by settling out the yeast and hop particles. Even so, some cask beers still pour slightly hazy.

Once the beers are hopped, fined, and carbonated to the brewer's satisfaction, the beers are ready to be served—directly from the cask, of course. It's important to note that there's no addition of nitrogen or carbon dioxide as a gas, which is the common practice for keg beer. That's why you'll see cask beers at breweries or bars served with special equipment to pump the beer from the cask. It's the traditional method of serving English beer and a tradition that CAMRA is actively fighting to preserve.

Cask Beer vs. Keg Beer

According to the folks at CAMRA, the main difference between cask-conditioned beer, which they call real ale, and kegged beer is that the former is a natural "living" product and that the latter is not. They are correct in that the yeast is still alive and present in cask beers, whereas most kegged beers have had the yeast removed through filtration prior to packaging. According to CAMRA, removing the yeast from beer makes it sterile and, therefore, not "real."

British beer purists and real ale advocates will probably both nod their heads in disgust and agreement when I say that Americans just don't appreciate real ale as much as they should. But to our defense, most breweries and bars aren't set up for cask programs. And although it's an admirable and much treasured form of brewing history, cask beer is an extremely time consuming and often expensive tradition for breweries and bars without the proper tools in place. Also, many craft breweries do not filter their beers. This means the beers they serve from a keg fall somewhere in between what CAMRA considers real ale and the filtered beers that CAMRA looks down upon. There is often additional yeast character in craft beer even if it's not used to serve the beer.

English vs. American Styles

When referring to hoppy beers, it is important to note that the words *English* and *American* are not only adjectives that define the country of origin for each style, but they are also adjectives that can help to differentiate between two seemingly similar styles.

When placed before the name of a style (i.e., brown ale), the word *English* usually implies that the beer style was brewed using English hops and English ale yeast. Conversely, when the word *American* appears before a style category (i.e., amber ale), the word usually implies that the beer was brewed using

American hops and an American ale yeast strain. It is just important to know that the modifier *American* before a beer style often means the beer will be a hoppier, less malty version of the style. The modifier *English* followed by a style name almost always means you'll find a maltier, less hoppy version of the style.

The Bitter Family

Bitter is an English term for pale ale. It represents a category of English-style pale ales separated by alcohol content. The ordinary bitter is the lightest (3.2–3.8 percent ABV), followed by the special/best bitter (3.8–4.6 percent ABV) and the extra special bitter, aka ESB (4.6–6.2 percent ABV). Bitters are almost always served from a cask, with the exception being American interpretations. Bottled versions are typically labeled as English Pale Ales.

I'm only going to talk about the ordinary and the ESB in depth. This does not mean that the special/best bitter isn't important; it's just not as common as the other two styles and isn't really as distinct as them either since it falls somewhere in between the two. It is deeper in color and stronger in alcohol, body, and flavor than the ordinary, but it is still lighter and weaker than the ESB. If you were to blend an ordinary bitter with an ESB, you'd get a pretty good understanding of what a special/best bitter looks and tastes like.

ORDINARY BITTER (SESSION ALE)

Pale copper, clear-ish, low carbonation (cask versions), grassy nose, clean, and earthy hop bitterness.

BJCP Stats

SRM: 4–14   IBU: 25–35   ABV: 3.2–3.8 percent   OG: 1.032–1.040

My two cents: The ordinary bitter is the lightest of the bitters, clocking in less than 4 percent ABV. If you're in England or another country that serves a good amount of the stuff, it is usually just referred to as a bitter. Maybe that's because there's nothing ordinary about it. Although one of the lesser-known beer styles on this side of the pond, the bitter is one the most enjoyable styles out there. It's super low in alcohol, very refreshing, and just really damn drinkable. You'll find most are close to light copper in color with brilliant clarity. You'll taste and smell some complex fruity esters from British yeast, as well as some floral, earthy, or resiny hops. You'll also notice that there's hardly much head on this style of beer, but that's due to its traditionally low carbonation. Only slightly spritzy, it goes down smooth.

The bitter is considered to be the original session beer—a low-alcohol, strong-flavored category of beer rapidly growing in popularity among craft beer drinkers. While you might see different names used here in the United States, where nonstyle styles like Session IPA are the norm, many of these "new" beers have their roots in the classic bitter. It makes a lot of sense that our brewers would look to the bitter when crafting low-alcohol recipes, considering our own country's dominant brewing style for that strength of beer: the light lager.

It is almost impossible to find a true English bitter in the United States. And this isn't because Americans aren't fans of the style; it's mostly because these beers just don't travel well. Another major factor is that most American bars (yes, there are exceptions, but few and far between) aren't equipped with the proper tools or knowledge for tapping and serving cask beer. If English cask beer does make it over the pond, its quality can vary a lot depending on how it was transported and stored. The best rule of thumb for drinking cask beers at a bar is to choose the freshest, most local option.

In the glass: Straw colored, cask versions are flat, kegs have more fizz

In the nose: Dried hay, water crackers, dried apricots

In the mouth: Biscuit, grassy sweetness, bitter, crisp, light

In one word: Quaffable

Pour it into this: Nonic pint

Drink instead of: Vodka and soda, pinot grigio, PBR

Pair with: Another pint! Bitters also pair nicely with lighter fare like salads; fresh, raw seafood; ceviche; sushi; crab; goat cheese; feta; spring rolls; and roasted chicken.

Brief history lesson: All pale-colored English ales, including the IPA, were created around the same time—the mid-1600s. Advances in kilning gave brewers pale-colored malts, creating a new category of beers. While the new style was being labeled as pale ales in marketing and print, the publicans would refer to them as bitters when ordering at the bar (they were more bitter than other draught beers like milds and porters).

Try it: Bitters are traditionally found only on cask, but some American brewers have put a version in the bottle: Goose Island Honkers Ale, Surly Bitter Brewer, Anchor Small Beer, John Smith's Extra Smooth, Samuel Smith Tadcaster Bitter.

EXTRA SPECIAL BITTER (ESB)

Deep copper, caramel, molasses, dried leaves, yellow raisin, chewy, bitter, smooth.

BJCP Stats
SRM: 6–18   IBU: 30–50   ABV: 4.6–6.2 percent   OG: 1.048–1.060

My two cents: The extra strong/special bitter (ESB) and the English pale ale are synonymous. The term ESB was originally a brand name owned by Fuller's Brewery, which launched the beer in 1971; but that doesn't stop Americans from using the name.

Color and flavor-wise, this style actually shares more in common with the American amber ale than it does the American pale ale. In the glass, they're a golden to deep copper color with low carbonation. There are a lot of caramel and toffee notes, but the beer is not really sweet. There is a substantial hop presence and often a substantial hop aroma as well. I like to think of the ESB as a baby English barleywine.

Diacetyl—a butter-flavored compound—is often present in this style, albeit in low concentrations. It's not necessary, but it is an acceptable characteristic of this style and of some other English beers.

Note: Diacetyl is the chemical used to produce the buttery flavor and smell in microwave popcorn, margarine, some candies, baked goods, and even pet food. It is a natural by-product of fermentation that is typically reabsorbed by the yeast, when given enough time. If you ever receive a beer and it tastes buttery, you now know the problem and its name. If it's more than a touch and you're not drinking something like an ESB, send that beer back.

In the glass: Deep copper, clear, off-white head, low carbonation (cask)

In the nose: Toffee, dried leaves, roasted pecans, toast

In the mouth: Werther's Original, golden raisins, lemon rind

In one word: Smooth

Pour it into this: Nonic pint

Drink instead of: Chardonnay, old fashioned, well whiskey

Pair with: Fish and chips; sweeter pork dishes like roasted pork loin, ham, pulled pork, and BBQ ribs; beef stew; zucchini bread; biscuits and gravy; roasted duck; farmhouse cheddar; Somerset camembert; cheshire cheese

Brief history lesson: This is the strongest ale in the bitter category. It is often interchangeable with the English Pale Ale (although, all bitters are technically English pale ales).

Try it: Fuller's ESB, Wychwood Brewery Hobgoblin, Grand Teton Bitch Creek ESB, Shipyard Old Thumper, Alaskan ESB, Anderson Valley Belk's ESB, Redhook ESB

The American Ale Family

Early in my beer-drinking days, I had a mentor tell me that there was virtually no difference between the three classes of American ales—the pale, the amber, and the brown. The only difference, he said, was color. A few years later, I casually repeated this lesson to a local brewer, who then scolded me for not only believing it, but also for propagating the false information.

To my defense, if you look at the stats on paper, there is no major difference between the three styles, except for SRM and maybe a slight difference when it comes to IBUs. Alcohol and gravity are just about identical throughout; however, each style is its own unique little snowflake with its own flavors as well as color.

AMERICAN PALE ALE

Golden, effervescent, pine, citrus, fresh cut grass, honey, biscuits, crisp, dry.

BJCP Stats

SRM: 5–14   IBU: 35–45   ABV: 4.5–6.2 percent   OG: 1.045–1.015

My two cents: This American pale ale is probably the style most responsible for igniting the craft beer revolution in the United States. It has a moderate to strong hop aroma with signature notes like citrus and pine, but nothing over the top or to the level of an IPA. Clean malt character supports the hops, and the style is known for its balance. It has a medium body, but the firm bitterness and dry finish keep it really drinkable.

In the glass: Bright, golden, effervescent, strong head

In the nose: Fresh cut grass, lemon peel, pine, and honey

In the mouth: Grapefruit pith, pine needles, dried hay

In one word: Fresh

Pour it into this: Nonic pint

Drink instead of: Sauvignon blanc, gin martini, tonic water

Pair with: American hops like salty, fried, and fatty foods—the citrus hops just pop. Think mac and cheese, garlic fries, pepperoni pizza, fresh seafood (especially mussels and clams), fried calamari, and miso soup (trust me on the last one). Hops also work well with spicy food, as they help to cool the burn. Pair the American pale ale with buffalo chicken wings, pepper jack cheese, Mexican food, Indian curries, and sushi dipped in wasabi.

Brief history lesson: Oh my, this is a tough one. The style was definitely born in northern California—this much I can say with great confidence. The who, what, where, and when is a bit complicated. Jack McAuliffe of New Albion Brewing Company and Fritz Maytag of Anchor Brewing are often credited for inspiring the American pale ale, both having brewed hop-forward ales using American-grown Cascade hops in the late 1970s.

American Pale Ale

But if there has to be one grandfather of the style, it is Ken Grossman of Sierra Nevada Brewing Company. And, to this day, Sierra Nevada Pale Ale is still considered to be the standard American pale ale—the one that all others hold in comparison.

Try it: Sierra Nevada Pale Ale, 3 Floyds Zombie Dust, Oskar Blues Dale's Pale Ale, Stone Pale Ale, Deschutes Mirror Pond Pale Ale, Odell Brewing St. Lupulin

Did you know? The Belgians make pale ales, too, but their versions are significantly less hoppy and way fruitier than English or American pale ales. They are most commonly found in the Flemish provinces of Antwerp and Brabant, and considered easy drinking, everyday beers. Commercial examples include: De Koninck, Speciale Palm, Russian River Perdition, and Ommegang Rare Vos.

AMERICAN AMBER ALE

Copper, effervescent, pine, citrus, fresh cut grass, caramel, balanced, clean.

BJCP Stats

SRM: 10–17   IBU: 25–40   ABV: 4.5–6.2 percent   OG: 1.045–1.060

My two cents: Like the British bitter, the American amber ale is often a single-word order: "I'll have an Amber." It's often a gateway style for craft beer newbies, and for that reason it's a brewpub staple. In the glass, it's a cousin of the American pale ale with less hop aroma and a bit of increased malt character.

The secret behind the popularity is, in a word, *balance*. While you can certainly find examples with lots of hop aroma, most have just enough to keep things interesting. The same goes on the malt side; just a touch of crystal malts provide some caramel flavor but not too much. American ale yeast keeps the finish clean and much less fruity than a British yeast would. When it's brewed well, the beer is anything but boring and often the perfect pint for a variety of pub foods.

In the glass: Amber, copper, effervescent, strong head

In the nose: Caramel, fresh cut grass, pine

In the mouth: Dark honey, lemon peel, apricot, resin

In one word: Balanced

Pour it into this: Nonic pint

Drink instead of: Tequila Sunrise, moscato

Pair with: Pizza, pizza, PIZZA! No, really, the American amber ale is often revered as the go-to style for pizza. (Another reason it's a brewpub favorite, no doubt.) I also like it with sweeter barbecue sauces, pulled pork, Reuben sandwiches, BLTs, Manhattan clam chowder, baby back ribs, burgers, carnitas tacos, asiago, and havarti cheese.

Brief history lesson: Also called red ale before the style had a name, the American amber ale was essentially made by modifying the American pale ale. Ambers are brewed with a touch more caramel and specialty malts than pale ales. The invention of this style isn't really attributed to one person or one brewery, though they were born in the Pacific Northwest (that much is known). At one point, amber ales were one of the most popular styles of beer for craft brewers and for good reason: They are extremely well balanced, smooth, and quaffable.

Try it: New Belgium Fat Tire amber ale, Bell's Amber Ale, Ithaca Cascazilla, Full Sail Amber

AMERICAN BROWN ALE

Brown, off-white head, toasty, nutty, light chocolate, citrus, grass, dry.

BJCP Stats

SRM: 18–35   IBU: 20–40   ABV: 4.3–6.2 percent   OG: 1.045–1.060

My two cents: The American brown ale is a hoppy brown beer; however, it's not quite a porter when it comes to roastiness and not quite a pale ale when it comes to hoppiness. It's a tricky style with considerable variation from brewery to brewery.

The key to it is similar to the amber ale: balance. It doesn't go all out in any one direction. It's a light to dark brown color, rather than black, and it has sweet, rich malt aromas, including caramel, chocolate, nuts, and toast. It can have substantial bitterness, though typically not quite up to IPA levels. And unlike British ales, the signature citrus and sometimes dank hop aromas are present in this brown ale.

In the 1990s, hoppy brown ales were pretty much a standard in most brewers' portfolios, not unlike the IPA today. Most first- and second-generation craft brewers had (and still have) an American Brown in their lineup. This includes the likes of Sierra Nevada, Anchor Brewing, Brooklyn Brewery, Bell's, Avery, Dogfish Head, Rogue, New Holland, North Coast, Lost Coast, and the list goes on.

Although it is no longer a quintessential style today, many third-generation breweries are turning out fantastic American brown ales, perhaps even challenging consumer perception about the style. Sixpoint Brownstone and Surly Bender are two great examples of these more modern browns.

Despite their sometimes dull color (it's hard to get excited about brown) American browns are far from boring. Personally, I prefer the malt structure and flavors of American browns to that of American ambers. Give me toast and nuttiness over caramel sweetness any day.

In the glass: Brown, transparent, off-white head

In the nose: Hazelnut, citrus, hints of cocoa powder

In the mouth: Caramel, nuts, semi-sweet chocolate, pine

In one word: Nutty

Pour it into this: Nonic pint

Drink instead of: White Russian, chianti

Pair with: American browns love nutty cheeses like aged gouda or gruyere, jarlsberg, manchego, and tête de moine. Brown ales are also a good match for dark meats, especially grilled red meats, lamb, and sausages. They also pair nicely with hearty, autumnal cuisine like beef stews, pot pies, chili, butternut squash, mashed potatoes and gravy, roasted turkey, stuffing, and roasted root veggies.

Brief history lesson: In 1986, American craft beer pioneers Pete Slosberg and Mark Bronder released Pete's Wicked Ale, a hopped-up version of the English brown ale that is largely responsible for establishing the American brown ale as a commercial beer style and category for beer competitions.

Try it: Avery Ellie's Brown Ale, Dogfish Head India Brown Ale, Big Sky Moose Drool Brown, Lost Coast Downtown Brown, Bell's Best Brown, Smuttynose Old Brown Dog Ale

chapter six

THE DARKER SIDE OF ALE

Dark ales all share two things in common: They are typically the darkest in color, and they tend to have more malt-forward flavor and aromas than most styles. But that is where the similarities end. The range of flavors in dark ales is quite impressive. Some can be syrupy sweet with pronounced notes of caramel and toffee. Others can be bone dry with intense flavors of dark chocolate and coffee. Bitterness, body, and alcohol content all vary with each style.

It might be hard to believe, considering the prevalence and popularity of light lagers today, but dark-colored ales (porters, brown ales, milds, oh my!) used to be all the rage. Heck, even our US of A forefathers preferred brown beers.

These days dark beers often get a bad rap because they are so misunderstood. People seem to fear dark beer, something I have never been able to understand. Dark beer probably has more in common with the foods we love than pale beer, after all. Chocolate, coffee, caramel, nuts, toasted bread, toffee, molasses, brown sugar—all great flavors, wouldn't you agree? And just because a beer might be dark, it doesn't mean that it's heavy. Many dark-colored types of ale are actually quite light in body, alcohol by volume, and calories. Dry stouts are one of the lightest beers out there.

ENGLISH MILD

The lightest of the dark beers. Light amber to mahogany brown, small head, toffee, molasses, plum, toast, sweet finish.

BJCP Stats

Pale Mild	SRM: 17–34	IBU: 10–24	ABV: 2.8–4.5 percent	OG: 1.030–1.038
Dark Mild	SRM: 12–18	IBU: 10–24	ABV: 2.8–4.5 percent	OG: 1.030–1.038

My two cents: The mild is an underappreciated, often ignored beer style. Like the bitter, the mild is a classic session beer. Extremely low in alcohol with great, rich malt flavor, milds are a great style for occasions that require prolonged periods of drinking, like family barbecues, camping, and watching sports. Milds are sometimes referred to as "tavern ales."

Technically speaking, there are two subcategories of English Milds: pale milds and dark milds. The original gravity, IBUs, and alcohol by volume of both styles are virtually identical. The major difference between the two is color and, to some extent, malt flavor.

In the glass, pale milds tend to be light to dark amber in color, while dark milds range from dark reddish to brown. They're generally pretty clear, but they're usually not filtered. There's little to no hop presence and generally the malt flavor and some yeasty esters dominate the aroma. Nuts, chocolate, caramel, toffee, molasses, plum, and toast are all possible depending on the malts used to create the beer. Some milds finish sweet while others can be quite dry.

In the glass: Hazy mahogany brown, low head retention

In the nose: Porridge, walnuts, cocoa, caramel

In the mouth: Plum, toffee, toasted bread, chocolate

In one word: Friendly

Pour it into this: Nonic pint

Drink instead of: Jack and ginger, Bud Light, beaujolais nouveau

Pair with: Bar snacks like pretzels, mixed nuts and marinated olives, chips and dip, beer cheese soup, french onion soup, beef stew, chili, and hot dogs

Brief history lesson: Milds got their name for the same reason bitters got theirs—patrons used it as a way to differentiate between the two styles at pubs. They would either order the bitter (the hoppy pale ale) or the mild (the less hoppy, less alcohol and therefore more "mild" ale).

Try it: Milds are almost always found on draught; classically they're cask-conditioned as well. It's hard to bottle beer with this low of an ABV and keep it fresh, but some bottled versions do exist: Moorhouse's Black Cat, Surly Mild, Bar Harbor Lighthouse Ale, and Goose Island Mild Winter.

PORTER

Deep brown with ruby hues, fluffy off-white head, very roasty, nutty, toffee-like, chocolate, low bitterness.

BJCP Stats

Brown	SRM: 18–35	IBU: 20–30	ABV: 4–5.4 percent	OG: 1.040–1.052
Robust	SRM: 22–35	IBU: 25–50	ABV: 4.8–6.5 percent	OG: 1.048–1.065

My two cents: In brewing competitions, porters are often divided into two subcategories: the brown porter and the robust porter. The brown porter tends to be lighter in color, slightly lower in alcohol, and less roasty than the robust porter, which is significantly darker, stronger, and hoppier. English porters tend to have a stronger yeast presence (fruitiness) than American versions. As with all styles, American porters tend to be hoppier.

All porters will be medium brown to dark brown in color, making them not only roastier but also darker than styles like the American brown ale. They have a strong malt aroma as well, and hops, when present, shouldn't be all that noticeable. If a porter gets too hoppy, chances are the beer is more of a Black IPA (see page 44). The malt itself is often a mix of chocolate, roast, caramel, nuts, and coffee, making this beer a favorite among chocolate lovers and coffee fiends alike.

In the glass: Brown with ruby hues, thick off-white head

In the nose: Chocolate, toasted bread, roasted hazelnuts

In the mouth: Cocoa powder, toffee, licorice, lightly burnt bread

In one word: Velvet

Pour it into this: Nonic pint

Drink instead of: Dark and stormy, rum and Coke, malbec

Pair with: Anything covered in brown or sausage gravy like biscuits, meatloaf, and mashed potatoes; game meats like quail, venison, and rabbit; lamb; beef stew; shepherd's pie; roasted, smoked, and grilled meats; burgers topped with cheddar and bacon; carne asada tacos; Cahill's Irish Porter Cheddar; cheese fondue

Brief history lesson: The name *porter* was first used around 1721 as a catchall name for stronger brown beers. The first porters were brewed from 100 percent brown malt, which was cheaper than pale malt. London brewers eventually discovered that brown malt was actually less efficient—the brewers could get more sugars using less pale malt, but then the beer wouldn't be brown. But the public adored its brown beer (kind of odd to think about now considering the popularity of light lagers).

The game-changing moment came in 1817 with the invention of black patent malt. Like food dye, a little black patent malt goes a long way. This invention allowed brewers to successfully make a brown porter using 95 percent pale malt and 5 percent black patent malt. Technology, FTW!

Did you know? Before 1700, English brewers sold very young beer to the distributors or bar owners, who were then responsible for aging the beer until it was in proper condition to serve. Porters were the first English beers to be matured at the brewery before they were sent to bars.

Try it: Deschutes Black Butte Porter, Great Lakes Edmund Fitzgerald, Alaskan Smoked Porter, Maui CoCoNut PorTer, Duck-Rabbit Porter, Ballast Point Black Marlin

= Stouts =

The darkest of the dark ales, jet black to deep brown, garnet hues, coffee, dark chocolate, roasty, bitter.

BJCP Stats

| Average SRM: 30–40 | IBU: varies | ABV: 4–12 percent | OG: 1.036 - 1.115 |

My two cents: I cannot, for the life of me, understand why people are afraid of stouts. Out of all the dark beers in the world, stouts are my favorite. And for good reason: They taste like espresso-flavored dark chocolate.

When people tell me they don't like stouts, I sometimes wonder whether they've never tasted a stout or if they're misinformed about the style. And so, I put them to the test:

Do you like coffee? *Yes.*

How do you take it? *Black.*

Light, medium, or dark roast? *Dark.*

And espresso? *Stronger the better.*

You like coffee and you don't like stouts? Are you f***ing kidding me? Barley and coffee beans all start the same—green. Then they are roasted to varying degrees. Coffee is roasty and astringent. Stouts are roasty and astringent. Stouts are essentially carbonated, alcoholic, caffeine-free coffee (well, unless they are actually brewed with some coffee, which does happen).

Not a coffee fan? Let's try another angle:

Do you like chocolate? *Yes.*

White, dark, milk? *Dark.*

Stouts are essentially liquid dark chocolate without sugar and carbonation.

Do you like grilled foods?

Do you like red wine?

Do you like steak?

Yes, yes, yes. You freaking like stouts so just suck it up. Stouts are awesome. Case closed.

Stouts are typically broken down into one of six categories, listed below. Although they might range in alcohol, bitterness, and sweetness, all stouts are deep brown to jet-black with garnet hues and all have pronounced roasted malt characteristics reminiscent of coffee and dark chocolate.

In the glass: Black as night, garnet, ruby, sparkling

In the nose: Cocoa powder, espresso, burnt

In the mouth: Dark chocolate, coffee, astringent, smooth

In one word: Sultry

Pour it into this: Nonic pint

Drink instead of: Cabernet sauvignon, zinfandel, rye whiskey

Pair with: Oysters—o–m–g oysters and stout, so phenomenal, just do it. Red meat—steak, lamb, burgers—especially grilled or braised, smoky chili, chicken mole, beef stew, french onion soup, stout-baked mac and cheese and stout-braised short ribs (recipes in Section 5), mushrooms, bacon, German chocolate cake, cheesecake, fruit desserts, vanilla ice cream (stout float!)

Brief history lesson: Stout beer originally just meant strong beer and the label was applied to all sorts of styles. Stout porters started to pop up in the 1700s and, eventually, the word *stout* became synonymous with strong porter.

(IRISH) DRY STOUT: Typically a draught beer, dry stouts are lowest in alcohol and the driest. The dryness comes from the use of roasted unmalted barley.
IBU: 30–40, ABV: 4–5 percent

SWEET/MILK STOUT: Stout that has residual sugar in it—typically from the addition of lactose (milk sugar), which isn't fermentable. Many milk stouts, especially those with cocoa added, taste exactly like chocolate milk.
IBU: 30–40, ABV: 4–6 percent

OATMEAL STOUT: Stout brewed with the addition of oats, which give it a fuller, creamier mouthfeel and chocolate-milk-like flavor. IBU: 25–40, ABV: 4.2–5.9 percent

FOREIGN EXPORT STOUT: Higher alcohol stouts originally brewed for export to the tropical market (Virgin Islands, Jamaica, and so on) and sometimes called "tropical stouts." Similar to the dry or sweet stout, just more booze.
IBU: 30–70, ABV: 5.5–8 percent

AMERICAN STOUT: Similar to the foreign export stout except it has a bolder roasted malt character and bolder hop profile, typically from the use of American hops.
IBU: 35–75 (it can get up there). ABV: 5–7 percent

RUSSIAN IMPERIAL STOUT: The biggest, bitterest, most alcoholic stout.
IBU: varies ABV: 8–12 percent

OTHER (LESS COMMON) VARIATIONS

Chocolate stout: Stout brewed with some form of chocolate whether it be cocoa powder, nibs, or even candy bars

Coffee stout: Stout brewed with, you guessed it, coffee

Oyster stout: Stout brewed with oysters. Some brew with only the shells, while others opt to brew with the entire oyster, shell and all.

Try it: Avery Out of Bounds Stout, Maine Beer Co. Mean Old Tom, Sixpoint Diesel, Bison Chocolate Stout, Modern Times Black House, Anderson Valley Barney Flats Oatmeal Stout, High Water Campfire Stout, Alpine Captain Stout, Oakshire Overcast Espresso Stout

SCOTTISH ALES

Dark copper, creamy tan head, sticky sweet, caramel, dried fruit, earthy, slightly peaty.

My two cents: Some of the caramel flavors in Scottish ales actually come from the addition of crystal malts, and some of it comes from a process where a portion of the wort is boiled a tad longer than normal, which allows barley sugars to caramelize in the kettle.

Much like English ales, Scottish ales are classified by alcohol strength. For Scottish ales, you'll most commonly find Light (60 Shilling), Heavy (70 Shilling), and Export (80 Shilling). All are almost identical in color with similar bitterness levels and malt flavors. The only real difference is the amount of alcohol. All of them are deep amber to dark copper with a creamy tan head. You'll find light fruitiness, caramel notes, and sometimes a low to moderate peaty aroma that is sometimes perceived as earthy, smoky, or very lightly roasted. Malt dominates the flavor, and this is not one for the hopheads. Hop flavor and bitterness is low to none.

Average SRM: 9–17
Average IBU: 10–30

Light Scottish Ale ABV: 2.5–3.2 percent
Heavy Scottish Ale ABV: 3.2–3.9 percent
Export Scottish Ale ABV: 3.9–5 percent

In the glass: Dark copper, creamy tan head

In the nose: Caramel, smoke, golden raisins, dried herbs

In the mouth: Toffee, honey, dried apricots, mushrooms

In one word: Sticky (sweet)

Pour it into this: Nonic pint

Drink instead of: Cognac, rum and Coke, Moscow mule

Pair with: Cock-a-leekie soup, kippers, smoked salmon (cream cheese and bagels), black pudding, chicken tikka masala, haggis, neeps and tatties, Canadian bacon, duck pâté, Scotch eggs, roast beef, Dunlop cheese, Lanark Blue cheese

Brief history lesson: Like many English beers, Scottish ales were priced out and categorized by alcohol strength—the more alcohol, the higher the shilling number (cost of the beer). Today, the styles typically get lumped together under the title Scottish ale. Confusingly, Scotch ale is typically perceived to mean wee heavy, the strongest of the Scottish beers.

Try it: Thirsty Dog Twisted Kilt Scotch Ale, Innis and Gunn Original, Long Trail Hibernator, Odell 90 Shilling Ale, Orkney Brewery Dark Island, Sun King Wee Mac

IRISH RED ALE

Deep reddish copper, caramel, buttered toast, toffee, little to no hop presence.

BJCP stats

SRM: 9–18   IBU: 17–28   ABV: 4.0–6.0 percent   OG: 1.044–1.060

My two cents: I hate this saying, but it is what it is. The Irish red ale is one of the most average beer styles on the planet. Everything about it is either moderate or medium. Perhaps the most signature thing about it is the color. It's a brilliant deep reddish copper.

That doesn't mean the beer isn't worth drinking. It has plenty of fans and in the hands of an expert brewer it can be an enjoyable pint. It tends to have moderate caramel flavor and sweetness, with some buttered toast and toffee aroma. There's not much for the hop lovers here: low bitterness and no hop aroma to speak of.

In the glass: Deep amber, thin off-white head

In the nose: Caramel, toast

In the mouth: Toffee, buttered toast

In one word: Average

Pour it into this: Nonic pint

Drink instead of: White zinfandel, vodka

Pair with: Classic Irish foods like soda bread, black pudding, cottage pie, Irish stew, bacon and cabbage, and corned beef and mashed potatoes

Brief history lesson: Like the style, the history of the Irish red ale is kind of boring. It originated in the town of Kilkenny in 1710 and was, essentially, an Irish knockoff of the English pale ale.

Try it: 3 Floyds Brian Boru Old Irish Red Ale, Great Lakes Conway's Irish Ale, O'Hara's Irish Red Ale, Smithwick's Irish Ale, Boulevard Irish Ale, Harpoon Hibernian Ale, Cigar City Hornswoggled

chapter seven

MEANWHILE, IN BELGIUM . . .

If ales are from Venus and lagers are from Mars, Belgian beers are from another galaxy. Okay, maybe that is a tad bit of an exaggeration, but Belgian beers are unlike any of the others. That's largely because the star ingredient in Belgian beer is not hops or even malt—it's yeast.

It is important to note that the Belgians love their pale lagers just as much as the rest of the world. In fact, Belgium-based Stella Artois is one of the best-selling light lagers in the world. However, the most interesting Belgian styles—the classics—are brewed with native Belgian ale yeast.

Belgium is best known in the US beer geek world for its Trappist and Abbey ales, some of which are arguably the best beers in the world. Belgium is also the origin of spontaneously fermented, sour beers, but we will discuss those in their own chapter.

Trappist vs. Abbey Beers

The name *Trappist* is a protected trademark reserved only for products produced by Trappist monasteries. Today, there are more than 170 Trappist monasteries in the world, but only 10 of them have active breweries. Six are in Belgium, two are in the Netherlands, one is in Austria, and one is in the United States.

Monastic beers brewed at non-Trappist monasteries are referred to as Abbey ales. The use of the word *Abbey* is fairly regulated as well. Any beers brewed in the Trappist or Abbey style must be labeled as such. For example: Abbey dubbel vs. Abbey-style dubbel.

Note: Just about every beer brewed in Belgium has its own glassware, specifically designed for showcasing the beer in the best way possible. For convenience, I recommend pouring these beers into either a tulip-shaped glass or Belgian-style beer goblet of sorts. When in doubt, or Belgian glassware-less, pour any of these styles into a wine glass (especially a big red wine glass, if you have it).

Pouring Bottle-Conditioned Beers

Many Belgian beer styles are bottle-conditioned, meaning they undergo a secondary fermentation in the bottle. It is important to store these bottles upright and, if the bottles have been agitated in transit, to let them settle for at least an hour if not a day before consuming.

Bottle-conditioned beers are under a lot of pressure from the extra CO_2 released during secondary fermentation, so be careful when popping the cork (or the cap). To prevent crazy amounts of foaming, make sure the beer is completely chilled down before opening.

To pour, tilt your glass at a 45-degree angle and slowly pour the beer down the side of the glass. As the glass fills, slowly tilt it toward right side up. Stop pouring when the yeast starts to move and there is about a half inch of liquid left in the bottle. For most styles, *do not* pour the yeast into the glass.

Shooting the yeast: While you shouldn't pour the yeast into the glass, don't dump it down the drain either. The residual yeast is loaded with all sorts of nutrients, like Vitamin B. Pour the yeast into a separate glass and shoot it like a shot of liquor.

Belgian Lace

Most beer styles are capable of leaving lacing on the glass, but none leave behind rings of foam quite like Belgian beers.

What is lacing? Lacing refers to the white ring of bubbly residue that remains on the glass after the head dissipates. Belgian beers tend to be highly carbonated, and that bigger and "rockier" head tends to leave better lacing than other styles of beer.

Beware, head lovers, as oil kills foam and prevents lacing. Glassware that has not been properly cleaned and rinsed can significantly impact the amount and duration of head and lacing, hence the old keg party trick of using nose grease to reduce the foam quickly.

BELGIAN BLONDE ALE

Deep gold, brilliant, dense white head, perfumy, spicy, lemon peel, honeysuckle, super bubbly.

BJCP stats

SRM: 4–7   IBU: 15–30   ABV: 6–7.5 percent   OG: 1.062–1.075

My two cents: Belgian blondes are super clean, easy drinking beers. The less fruity versions can be slightly pilsner-like since the malt base is quite similar to pilsners. You'll taste that signature-smooth sweetness underneath the esters. They're also generally quite clear, which is not true of all Belgian styles. The yeast itself is often perfumy, and you might smell honey, orange, or lemon notes, but not the signature citrus of American hops. These beers have strong carbonation, which creates a large pillowy head.

Belgian blondes make a great gateway beer for anyone who is looking to graduate from mass-produced domestic lagers to something more flavorful but isn't quite ready to jump into more aggressive styles like IPAs and stouts. They are also great beers for enjoying during the hotter months—on the beach, by the pool, on the golf course, at a barbecue, anywhere you go!

In the glass: Bright yellow, super bubbly, strong head

In the nose: Orange blossom, fresh baked bread, spice

In the mouth: Honey, lemon peel, crackers

In one word: Effervescent

Pour it into this: Tulip or goblet

Drink instead of: Riesling, gin and tonic, yellow fizzy lagers

Pair with: Mussels, lobster, crab, clams—heck, all shellfish—fried foods (especially fish), green curry, spicy sausage, salads, brie, and camembert

Brief history lesson: The Belgian blonde is a newish style developed to entice pilsner drinkers, or so I've been told. It is a house beer for several Abbey and Trappist breweries in Belgium, designed to be consumed on a daily basis—as opposed to the much higher alcohol styles that those breweries are most known for.

Try it: Leffe Blond, Affligem Blond, New Belgium Spring Blonde, La Trappe Blond, Kasteel Blond, Val-Dieu Blond

BELGIAN TRIPEL

Deep yellow, super effervescent, huge head, fruity, lemon peel, orange, banana, clove, dry.

BJCP stats

SRM: 4.5–7   IBU: 20–40   ABV: 7.5–9.5 percent   OG: 1.075–1.085

My two cents: The Belgian tripel is probably the most seductive beer style in the world. It is deviously pale and dangerously effervescent. Since it's smooth, fruity, and deceptively light, this style goes down way too easy considering the amount of alcohol it contains.

Trappist tripels will always trump American versions because, well, they just do. I can't explain it; they have a certain *je ne sais quoi* that makes them amazing. It could be the romantic history I suppose. I will never forget the exact date, location, approximate time, and the people I was with the first time I tasted Westmalle Tripel—the original. But I digress.

This style should always be poured slowly into a glass. It produces a big, billowy, long-lasting head that leaves thick lines of lacing on the glass with every sip. Tripels fill the nose with a complex blend of spicy phenols, fruity esters, and sugar cookie-like malt aromas. Yeast profile varies considerably brewery by brewery, but most tripels have pronounced aromas of clove or banana. They should be highly carbonated with a soft, barely noticeable alcohol warmth and a bone-dry finish.

In the glass: Pale blonde, billowy white head

In the nose: Banana, clove, orange peel, honey

In the mouth: Lemon meringue pie, sugar cookies, banana, baking spice

In one word: Exquisite

Pour it into this: Tulip, snifter

Drink instead of: Champagne, chablis, corpse reviver

Pair with: Lobster, seared scallops, mussels, seafood bisques, triple crème cheese, washed-rind cheeses, yellow curry, tikka masala, duck à l'orange, fettuccine alfredo, brown butter and sage sauce (over pasta), pumpkin bread, cheesecake

Brief history lesson: Just like British ales, Belgian beers were originally labeled by strength—in their case, single (3 percent), dubbel (6 percent), and tripel (9 percent). The first tripels were brown because pale malt wasn't available until the late 1600s. Westmalle released the first pale Belgian tripel in 1934, and it has been the standard in the style ever since.

Try it: Westmalle Trappist Tripel, Unibroue La Fin du Monde, Victory Brewing Golden Monkey, Allagash Tripel, Bruery Trade Winds Tripel, Gouden Carolus Tripel, Flying Fish Exit 4

BELGIAN DUBBEL

Dark copper (brown), large dense head, raisins, figs, chocolate chip cookie dough, chewy.

BJCP stats

SRM: 10–17   IBU: 15–25   ABV: 6–7.6 percent   OG: 1.062–1.075

My two cents: In my opinion, the Belgian dubbel is one of the few beers that almost makes you do a double-take: Is it in fact beer? Putting your nose into a glass of Belgian dubbel is like walking into a bakery— hints of fresh-baked cinnamon raisin rolls, chocolate chip cookie dough, banana bread, and fig jam.

Like fine wine, this is one style of beer that truly gets better with age. The dark stone fruit flavors concentrate with a hint of oxidation. So luscious, so smooth, so freaking good: to me they can be reminiscent of a port wine—if you were to carbonate one, of course.

These beers are dark amber but generally clear. Like other Belgian beers they tend to have big fluffy heads with strong lacing, though dubbels' heads are more off-white than a pure white cloud. The malt aroma can vary significantly by brewery, with chocolate, caramel, toast, and stone fruit. However, all examples will have a rich and complex malty sweetness, medium-low bitterness, and very low hop flavor.

In the glass: Brownish with red hues, large frothy head

In the nose: Plums, figs, currants, clove, banana bread

In the mouth: Raisin bread, caramel, cookie dough, toast

In one word: Luscious

Pour it into this: Belgian-style goblet, tulip glass

Drink instead of: Pinot noir (burgundy), tempranillo, Manhattan, side car

Pair with: Seared duck, duck confit, Peking duck, duck à l'orange, foie gras (did I mention duck?), cherry and figs sauces and reductions, washed-rind Trappist cheeses, brie, gouda, goat cheese, suckling pig, pulled pork, candied bacon, chocolate desserts, bread pudding, figs wrapped with prosciutto, nuts, fruit pies, banana nut bread

Brief history lesson: The origin of the modern-day Belgian dubbel is, once again, attributed to the Trappist Abbey of Westmalle. The style was first created in 1856, but then revised to be stronger in 1926.

Try it: Westmalle Dubbel, St. Bernardus Pater 6, Chimay Red, Maredsous 8, Trappist Rochefort 6, Allagash Lost Abbey Lost and Found Dubbel Ale, Lost Abbey Lost and Found Abbey Ale

Belgian Strong Ales (a Brief Mention)

Belgian strong ales can be divided into two groups: golden and dark. Belgian golden strong ales are similar to Belgian tripels but paler, lighter in body, crisper, drier, and they are hopped aggressively. Great examples of this style include Duvel, Russian River Damnation, and Piraat. Belgian dark strong ales are kind of a catchall category for dark Belgian beers higher in alcohol than the dubbel. They are sometimes referred to as quads and have a lot of the same complex malt and dark dried-fruit character that Belgian dubbels have—just with more booze. Great examples include Westvleteren 12, Rochefort 10, St. Bernardus Abt 12, Chimay Grande Reserve (Blue), and Lost Abbey Judgment Day.

WITBIER

Pale straw yellow, hazy, mousy head, orange zest, lemon peel, coriander, honeysuckle, angel food cake.

BJCP stats

SRM: 2–4	IBU: 10–20	ABV: 4.5–5.5 percent	OG: 1.044–1.052

My two cents: The witbier is called many things. You might find it labeled as a Belgian wit, Belgian white ale, blanche bière, or even just simply "wit." I think it is one of the most refreshing, approachable, food-friendly styles out there. Witbiers remind me a lot of angel food cake—light, airy, fluffy, sweet but not too sweet, and they taste delicious with berries and whipped cream.

In my opinion, there aren't enough witbiers in the world. And no, Blue Moon does not count. In the glass, most are a very pale, straw gold color with a milky appearance. The mousy head has good retention and laces down the glass. It also helps deliver those big floral, spicy, herbal aromas to your nose. After you take a sip, expect a delicate sweetness with layers of flavor. While there's honey, vanilla, coriander, and other spice, there's also often orange or lemon notes, which may be a reason that some brewers pair the beers with a slice of fresh orange or lemon.

In the glass: Very pale, super hazy yellow, fluffy white head

In the nose: Orange peel, honeysuckle, coriander, pie crust

In the mouth: Sugar cookie, orange blossom honey, lemon zest, spice

In one word: Elegant

Pour it into this: Weizen glass (witbier glass), tulip

Drink instead of: Prosecco, gin and tonic, piña colada

Pair with: Mussels and clams—especially mussels and clams steamed in witbier, Thai curries, shrimp, lobster, cod, halibut, mahimahi (pretty much all white fish), sushi, spicy foods, goat cheese, feta, fresh summer salads with citrus dressings, ceviche, fruit salsas, pancakes, angel food cake, whipped cream, berries, and lemon meringue pie

Brief history lesson: Although witbiers date back to the 1500s, the rapidly increasing, widespread popularity and demand for pale lagers (especially after World War II) nearly forced the style into extinction. In 1966, Pierre Celis, a former milkman turned brewer, opened Brouwerij Celis in his hometown of Hoegaarden with the single goal of reviving the town's beloved witbier style.

In addition to the traditional brewing ingredients (water, barley, hops, yeast), Celis brewed his witbier with wheat, coriander, and dried Curaçao orange peel. This recipe has become the standard for the style.

Try it: Hoegaarden Wit, Allagash White, Blanche de Bruxelles, Ommegang Witte, Avery White Rascal, Unibroue Blanche de Chambly, Hitachino Nest White Ale, Jolly Pumpkin Calabaza Blanca, Alaskan White

SAISON (FARMHOUSE)
Pale orange, hazy, effervescent, Meyer lemon, peppercorn, clove, shortbread, funk.

BJCP stats

SRM: 5–14   IBU: 20–35   ABV: 5–7 percent   OG: 1.048–1.065

My two cents: I freaking love saisons. It alternates with a good West Coast American IPA as my all-time favorite style. To me, saisons have everything I look for in a really great wine: they're often fruity but not sweet; earthy and slightly bitter but not astringent, the alcohol is in check; and they have a ridiculously dry finish. It's no coincidence saisons are one of the most food-friendly beverages on planet Earth.

While all Belgian styles vary a good amount from brewery to brewery, nowhere is this truer than with saison. That said, most have a pale orange color with complex fruity esters in the aroma. The malt character is interesting, often with a variety of grains not found in other beer styles for added complexity. Some styles will have a slight tartness, and some brewers will also use wild yeasts like Brettanomyces for even more unusual rustic aroma. The finish is almost always extremely dry and refreshing.

In the glass: Pale orange, hazy, thick, lasting head

In the nose: Lemon peel, shortbread, pepper, clove

In the mouth: Sweet hay, Meyer lemon, dried flowers, honey

In one word: Majestic

Pour it into this: Tulip

Drink instead of: Gewürztraminer, gin-based cocktails (Aviation, Corpse Reviver II)

Pair with: Everything under the sun. Saisons are particularly fantastic with anything from the sea: shellfish; oysters; mussels; clams; crab; lobster; raw seafood such as sashimi, poke, ceviche, tartar; smoked salmon; fried cod; and so on. Thai curry and saisons are a mind-blowing experience. Saisons are also great with mushrooms, spicy foods, funky cheeses, creamy cheeses, smoked cheeses, raw milk cheeses, aged cheeses—did I say cheese?

Brief history lesson: Saisons were originally a seasonal style of beer, hence the name (*saison* is French for "season"). They were brewed at the end of the winter season for storage and consumption in the warmer months, especially spring.

Saisons were created during a time when water was virtually undrinkable. Back then, people didn't really understand how to properly dispose of wastewater, and it was often mixed with regular water. Sewage and water treatment and all that stuff didn't exist, and things were especially bad in the countryside.

Needless to say, water had a lot of bacteria in it and it would make people sick. But since humans need water to survive, they had to figure out ways to stay hydrated, especially while slaving away on the farm during the hot summer harvest months.

The solution was low-alcohol beer, which was boiled to the point of sterilization. These beers served a function-over-fashion purpose (the function being hydration, not intoxication), though it is rumored that farm workers were allocated up to five liters each workday as a way to stay hydrated. Early saisons were kind of kitchen-sink recipes. Brewers made the beers with whatever grains, herbs, and flowers were available.

Saison (farmhouse)

Try it: Saison Dupont, Pretty Things Jack D'or, Bison Brewing Saison de Wench (shameless plug), Fantôme Printemps, 21st Amendment Sneak Attack Saison, Lost Abbey Red Barn Ale, Ommegang Hennepin, Boulevard Tank 7 Farmhouse Ale

BIÈRE DE GARDE

Golden, amber or brown, hazy, big head, caramel, toffee, pear, dried flowers, toasted bread, smooth.

BJCP stats

SRM: 6–19	IBU: 18–28	ABV: 6–8.5 percent	OG: 1.060–1.080

My two cents: OK, so technically this style isn't Belgian; it's French. I know, I know—then why is it in this chapter? Well, the bière de garde shares a lot in common with the saison, which is also a style with some French crossover. Both are farmhouse beers and both are characterized in great part by the native yeasts originally used to create them. But, as alike as the two may seem, there are distinctive differences between the two in taste and color. Bière de gardes are typically maltier and sweeter with less spice and hop bitterness.

There are three main variations of this style—blonde, amber, and brown—so the color ranges from gold to reddish to chestnut. Most have a light to moderate toasty character and some caramel notes are acceptable. In fact, the malt flavor's toasty, toffee-like character is one key difference from a saison. With a low-hop bitterness and moderate alcohol, these are smooth beers that drink more like a lager than saisons do.

Bière de Mars ("beer of March") is a variation of the bière de garde. It was originally brewed in winter for consumption in March and typically does not age well. The Bière de Mars has a similar taste profile to the bière de garde with a significantly lower alcohol content (usually between 4.5–5.5 percent ABV).

In the glass: Gold, red, brown—it's a chameleon!—hazy, big head, strong lacing

In the nose: Caramel, pear, fresh dough, red wine, must

In the mouth: Toffee, grapes, lemon peel, dried flowers

In one word: Distinctive

Pour it into this: Tulip, wine glass

Drink instead of: French wine, Mai Tai, whiskey soda

Pair with: Roasted duck, lamb, venison, grilled or roasted chicken, mussels, escargot, carbonade flamande (beef and onion stew with beer), chicon au jambon (gratin of Belgian endives with ham), lapin aux pruneaux (rabbit with prunes), brie, aged gouda, asparagus, artichokes, bread pudding, waffles

Brief history lesson: *Bière de garde* translates to "beer for keeping." It is from the Nord-Pas-de-Calais region of France, which is located directly across the English Channel and linked to the UK by the Eurotunnel.

Like saisons, bière de gardes were traditionally brewed in farmhouses during the winter and spring and then kept in cold cellars for consumption during the warmer months. Its signature "cellar" character comes from indigenous yeasts and sometimes molds, making it an extremely difficult style to recreate both at the small-scale homebrew level and at the larger-scale commercial level.

Try it: Two Brothers Domaine DuPage French Style Country Ale, 3 Monts Flanders Golden Ale, Southampton Biere de Mars, Lost Abbey Avant Garde, Hill Farmstead Biere de Norma, Brasserie Castelain St. Amand

What's So Special about the Maproom in Chicago on May 31, 2008, around 9 p.m. CST?

That's the exact date I tasted my first saison and tripel, and perhaps most important, the first time I tasted Orval, arguably the best beer on the planet.

Orval is an extremely intriguing beer. It is unique among Trappist beers in that it gets dry-hopped, and it is the only Trappist beer to get spiked with the wild yeast Brettanomyces upon bottling. As a result of being bottle-conditioned with wild yeast, Orval is constantly evolving inside of the bottle. No two bottles of Orval are the same.

If you drink Orval fresh, it tastes very similar to an English pale ale—spicy, floral, slightly bitter, and very dry. But if you taste it after the five-month mark, you will find yourself drinking an entirely different beer. And the more age it has, the more unique it becomes. The wild yeast starts to make it tart and funky. The older it gets, the weirder it gets (much like people).

No two Orvals taste alike. Each bottle has its own extremely unique character. Orval is the snowflake of beers. If you can, I challenge you to find multiple vintages of Orval—at least one "fresh" bottle (within five months of bottling) and two older versions. Taste them all side by side and tell me what you think.

chapter eight

BIG, BOLD, AND BRAZEN

For the most part, the alcohol tier system looks like this: Spirits and liqueurs have more alcohol than wine, and wine has more alcohol than beer and cider, which tend to share a similar alcohol range. The exception to this rule of thumb is fortified and distilled wines, like cognacs and ports, and high-gravity beers.

In a nutshell high gravity means high alcohol. The word *gravity* speaks to the amount of fermentable sugars created during the brewing process before fermentation. The higher the original gravity—the amount of fermentable sugars in the wort—the higher the potential alcohol content of the beer.

Lots of sugar equals lots of alcohol equals high-gravity beer.

Everyone draws their own line, but I like to classify high-gravity beers as those with an ABV of 8 percent or higher. Beers in this ABV range aren't exactly new: the Brits, Belgians, and Germans have been brewing somewhat boozy beers for hundreds of years as brewers learned that increasing the sugar and alcohol in beer made beer more stable for storage and export.

Modern-day brewers are constantly pushing the boundaries on just how high they can go—with the alcohol level. There are now well-made beers in the 12 to 18 percent range, such as Dogfish Head World Wide Stout and Goose Island Bourbon County Stout. Some breweries also try to outdo each other for the "world record" of strongest beer. Perhaps the most attention-getting of these efforts is BrewDog's The End of History, a super rare and immensely alcoholic beer clocking in at 55 percent ABV. Most of these beers are excellent candidates for cellaring (see page 141).

When in Doubt, Imperialize

There has been a recent trend to increase the alcohol level of many traditionally lower-alcohol styles of beer. When the term *imperial* is placed before a style of beer, it essentially translates to a stronger version of the style. Sometimes, such as with an IPA, you will see the word *double* instead. But double IPA and imperial IPA are indeed the same style of beer.

When it comes to imperial, there are some traditional styles. For example, many breweries release a seasonal Russian imperial stout or have an imperial IPA as part of their standard lineup. Brewers are constantly introducing new subcategories of styles by making them stronger as well, which we'll call imperialization. No style is safe when it comes to this trend. Imperial pilsners, imperial saisons, imperial witbiers—you name it and it's either been imperialized or is in the process.

To make things extra confusing, not all strong beers can be identified with the word *imperial,* though. Barleywines, bocks, Baltic porters, and more are all also high-gravity beers we'll discuss on the pages that follow.

A Word on Food Pairings

When it comes to high-gravity beers, food pairings can be slightly difficult to design. This is because these styles can be so powerful and rich that they have the ability to overwhelm most foods. Since these styles share a lot of characteristics in common with port, sherry, cognac, and other dessert wines, high-gravity beers make great pairings for desserts and cigars. And if you are like me, many of these beers might actually be the dessert (why eat dessert when you can drink it, right?).

When in doubt, pair these big, bold, and brazen styles with strong and pungent cheeses, grilled meats and game, roasted mushrooms and root vegetables, and chocolate desserts. See page 155 for more comprehensive pairing information.

ENGLISH BARLEYWINE

Deep brown, ruby hues, strong caramel aroma, light bitterness, thick, rich, and boozy with notes of toffee and molasses.

BJCP stats

| SRM: 10–22 | IBU: 30–60 | ABV: 6–9 percent | OG: 1.060–1.090 |

My two cents: Like its name suggests, barleywines can be as alcoholic as some lower alcohol wines. As with any English vs. American style, the British version is far less bitter and hoppy than its American counterpart. In fact, English barleywines are pretty close to an extreme version of the ESB.

Barleywines epitomize the flavor of caramel malt—rich, sweet, and slightly syrupy. They're famous for their intense, complex maltiness with nutty, toffee aromas as well as molasses and dried fruit character. While flavors do vary brewery by brewery, age also plays a role. Barleywines can change and evolve over as much as two decades. As time goes on, the alcohol burn and hop bite softens, both eventually disappearing with time, and the malt flavors begin to oxidize, developing pronounced dried and stone fruit characteristics (like dried plums, figs, and apricots).

In the glass: Deep garnet, thin tannish head, legs for days

In the nose: Molasses cookies, toffee, maple syrup

In the mouth: Dried yellow raisins, brown sugar, dried leaves

In one word: Sticky (sweet)

Pour it into this: Snifter

Drink instead of: Brandy, cognac, side car

Pair with: Strong cheeses like English stilton, foie gras, pâté, cured meats, olives, roasted nuts, roasted root vegetables, chicken masala, dark chocolate, pecan pie

Brief history lesson: As with many English beer styles, the barleywine wasn't a new invention as much as it was an evolution of already existing styles. The English have been brewing strong beers for centuries, but it wasn't until the nineteenth century when the term *barleywine* emerged. The Burton brewers, specifically Bass & Co., were the first to coin the barleywine. At first, the term didn't really designate a particular style; it was kind of a catchall category for strong ales that were typically of higher quality than the rest of the beers in a brewer's portfolio.

As I understand it, the Beer Judge Certification Program was the first institution to really define the parameters of the barleywine and turn it into an actual style.

Try it: J. W. Lees Vintage Harvest Ale, Firestone Walker Sucaba, Weyerbacher Blithering Idiot, Flying Dog Horn Dog Barley Wine Style Ale, Deschutes Mirror Mirror, Heavy Seas Below Decks

AMERICAN BARLEYWINE

Deep copper, ruby highlights, citrusy, pine, dried apricots, honey, toffee, abrasively bitter, boozy.

BJCP stats

SRM: 10–19	IBU: 50–120	ABV: 8–12 percent	OG: 1.080–1.120

My two cents: The "Americanized" version of the English barleywine is exactly what you'd expect. It's bigger on hops and often on alcohol as well. You know our brewers: Go big or go home, right? Younger versions tend to be big, bold, and abrasively bitter. Aged versions tend to be milder and boast sherry-like oxidized fruit characteristics.

Even though American beers are known for hops, and the American IPA does pack a fair amount, it is still a malt-driven style at its roots. The full-bodied, chewy character of the malt is what separates many of the big American barleywines from imperial IPAs, after all. Make no mistake, even with all the IBUs, these are rich, malty beers meant for slow sipping by the fire.

Note: Some American brewers have experimented with making wheat beers at barleywine strength—aptly referring to the substyle as "wheat wines." These beers tend to be lighter in body than barleywines as a result of adding a substantial amount of wheat to the grist. Some also add honey, which lightens the body even more. Wheat wines aren't typically hopped like barleywines, so they tend to be less bitter and a little sweeter. But take heed: There is still a considerable amount of malty sweetness and alcohol warmth in this style. Want to give it a try? Seek out The Bruery's White Oak, Founders Sweet Repute, and Perennial Artisan Ales Heart of Gold.

In the glass: Deep amber, ruby hues, off-white head, low carbonation

In the nose: Grapefruit, prunes, honey, roasted nuts

In the mouth: Orange rind, dried apricots, pine, toffee, booze

In one word: Audacious

Pour it into this: Snifter

Drink instead of: Scotch, old fashioned, sherry, cabernet sauvignon

Pair with: Blue cheese, prosciutto, figs, grilled steak, foie gras, cigars, sardines, roasted duck, glazed ham, mushroom risotto, olives, fresh walnuts, crème brulee, dark chocolate

Brief history lesson: The resurgence of the barleywine is often attributed to the early pioneers of American craft beer. In 1975, Anchor Brewing released Old Foghorn Ale, which is considered to be the first modern American barleywine. It was introduced around the same time as the first American IPAs.

Try it: Sierra Nevada Bigfoot, Dogfish Head Olde School Barleywine, Bell's Third Coast Old Ale, Avery Hog Heaven Barleywine, Victory Old Horizontal, Rogue Old Crustacean

BALTIC PORTER

Deep reddish brown, thick tan head, rich malty aroma, toffee, licorice, plums, raisins, dark chocolate, boozy.

BJCP Stats

SRM: 17–30   IBU: 20–40   ABV: 5.5–9.5 percent   OG: 1.06–1.090

My two cents: Although it's often overlooked by a lot of beer lovers—especially compared to Russian imperial stout—I think that the Baltic porter is a pretty damn awesome style. And why, you ask? As much as I enjoy the fruity esters of a great ale, I also really love clean beers—beers with little to no yeast profile. These beers really allow the hop or the malt profile, in this case, to really shine through.

More often than not, the Baltic porter is considered to be a lager, which might sound weird considering the name *porter* refers to a style of ale. However, since the style is brewed with ale yeast at lager temperatures it is really a hybrid of sorts. Cooler fermentation means that fruity yeast character should not be present in Baltic porters. They should be big, bold, and malty—but still clean.

Baltic porters are dark, reddish brown with a thick and persistent tan head. The rich malt aromas mingle with dried fruit esters. Notes of caramel, toffee, licorice, plums, prunes, cherries, currants, and chocolate are all common. The roast character is smooth, never burnt. Just as with Russian imperial stout, there is often noticeable alcohol warmth, though the beer shouldn't come off as hot.

In the glass: Deep ruby brown, billowy tan head, good carbonation

In the nose: Plums, chocolate, currants, toffee

In the mouth: Clean, roast coffee, prunes, caramel, booze

In one word: Baroque

Pour it into this: Snifter

Drink instead of: Port, dark rum, Negroni

Pair with: Oysters; smoked fish; pickled, fried, or smoked herring; grilled meats; blood pudding; pork sausages; Swedish pancakes; trotters; game; pierogis; chanterelles; bilberry pie; brownies; chocolate

Brief history lesson: As the name might suggest, the Baltic porter is a direct descendant of the English porter. It was originally developed as an export style, much like the Russian imperial stout and the India pale ale. This stronger version of the English porter was first brewed in late 1700s for export to the countries surrounding the Baltic Sea (Finland, Sweden, Poland, and so on). As with many styles, the Baltic porter lost its luster during Prohibition and the world wars. It only just made a comeback in the 1990s and is still one of the least brewed styles in the United States.

Try it: Victory Brewing Baltic Thunder, Sixpoint 3Beans, Alaskan Baltic Porter, Nøgne Ø Porter, Foothills Brewing Baltic Porter

RUSSIAN IMPERIAL STOUT
Jet black, ruby, tan head, complex aroma, espresso, dark chocolate, prunes, slightly burnt, boozy.

BJCP stats
SRM: 30–40	IBU: 50–90	ABV: 8–12 percent	OG: 1.075–1.115

My two cents: The first use of the word *imperial* in brewing originated with this style, whose name resulted from its popularity with the Russian Imperial Court. It set the precedent for many modern-day brewers who now use the word *imperial* before a style name to designate a higher gravity or stronger version of the original. Most American brewers drop the "Russia" part of the name and simply refer to this style as the imperial stout.

Mirror, mirror on the wall, who's the strongest beer of all? My jury of one is out on this matter as I think that both the barleywine and the RIS are equally potent. Personally, I think that the RIS is smoother and sexier (probably because of the roasted malts), while the American barleywine is more abrasive and zanier (due to its intense hop profile). Both are great candidates for barrel-aging and cellaring.

Did I really just say sexier? I did, but pour one yourself and you'll see why. RISes pour jet black, and you'll immediately get a hit of roasted grain mingling with fruity esters, hops, and a touch of alcohol. One sip and you'll either love or hate the rich, deep, complex flavors of chocolate, coffee, dark fruit, caramel, burnt bread, raisins, and plums. Hop and malts both contribute to a strong bitterness, but it's balanced by a velvety smooth body. Take a few sips and feel the warmth. The finish can actually be dry or sweet, depending on the brewery.

In the glass: Black as night, garnet hues, thin tan head

In the nose: Espresso, burnt toast, dried figs

In the mouth: Chocolate-covered raisins, iced coffee, booze

In one word: Velvety

Pour it into this: Snifter

Drink instead of: Barolo, bordeaux, rye whiskey, Manhattan

Pair with: Roquefort, gorgonzola, aged gouda, bacon, braised short ribs, lamb, grilled steak, black and blue burgers, roasted portabella mushrooms (stuffed with cheese = yum), anything with chocolate, vanilla ice cream, caramel, tiramisu

Russian imperial stout

Brief history lesson: The history of the Russian imperial stout is very much a chicken vs. the egg sort of tale. Like the IPA, the RIS was a stronger, more aggressively hopped beer designed to survive a long export. But whether or not it was specifically designed for export to Russia is debatable.

What we do know is that lower alcohol beers are susceptible to infection and contamination during long voyages. And we also know that lower alcohol beers are more likely to freeze during extended trips across cold areas—like say the chilly countries surrounding the Baltic Sea and the frozen tundra of Russia.

Stronger versions of English porters and stouts were already being exported to the Baltic region by the time the Russian royals got their hands on them. So technically, the "imperial stout" was not originally created for the Russian Imperial Court because they already existed. However, the Russian Imperial Court is responsible for popularizing the style and essentially putting it on the map.

This bigger, bolder version of the English stout designed for export to the Baltic region was ultimately dubbed the Russian "imperial" stout (*stout* being the word for "bigger" and "high-gravity" back then) because it was extremely popular among the Russian royals. Naturally, the name didn't exactly hurt sales. In fact, it was a great move from a marketing perspective.

The two Russian figureheads most associated with the RIS are Peter the Great and Catherine the Great. They both became enamored with dark English beer during trips to England, and Catherine was even known to brag about how much of the stuff she could drink—which was apparently more than most English men.

Try it: Stone Imperial Russian Stout, North Coast Old Rasputin, Oskar Blues Ten FIDY, Great Divide Yeti Imperial Stout, Brooklyn Black OPS, Surly Darkness, De Struise Black Albert, Foothills Sexual Chocolate

The Bock Family

Strong dark lager, light to deep brown, super smooth, malty sweet, prune, plum, clean, soft alcohol warmth.

BJCP stats
SRM: 14–22   IBU: 20–27   ABV: 6.3–7.2 percent   OG: 1.064–1.072

My two cents: Some of my worst/best nights have involved bocks. You may have experienced the same thing if you drank more than one beer ending in –ator, as in Celebr-ator, Optim-ator, Salv-ator, etc.

That –ator naming trend originated from the monks of Paulaner, who essentially developed the first dopplebocks. They called their strongest beer "Salvator" after "the Savior." Other Munich breweries were quick to follow suit and many American craft brewers continue the tradition today.

Bocks go down super smooth, even though they're a family of strong German lagers. (In fact, they are the strongest of all recognized categories when it comes to lagers.) The traditional bock is light copper to brown with a large creamy, off-white head. It has a strong malt aroma and drinks clean with little to no hop aroma or fruity esters. Complex malt flavors with notes of caramel and toast and a very clean lager character are hallmarks of the style, but there are numerous variations:

MAIBOCK (HELLES BOCK): The quintessential spring beer, the maibock is a moderately hoppy golden amber lager that is refreshing, yet strong and flavorful. Boasting plenty of booze and hops, the maibock is the boldest of the amber-hued lagers (which include the Oktoberfest and Vienna lager). 6.3–7.4 percent ABV.

DOPPELBOCK (DOUBLE BOCK): Some people refer to beer as liquid bread—and no beer style best embodies liquid bread quite like the doppelbock. In fact, this style was developed by German monks as a form of liquid bread to be consumed during times of fasting, which is quite brilliant when you think about it. The doppelbock is essentially a double strength bock, hence the "double" part in the name. Speaking of names, breweries often call their doppelbock something that ends in -ator (e.g. Celebrator). The style boasts strong notes of chocolate, dark fruit, and toasted malt. However, like all lagers, it still finishes super smooth and clean. 7–10 percent ABV.

EISBOCK: This substyle is made through a freezing process, not unlike ice wine. Essentially, the beer is frozen and then the ice (water) is removed, concentrating both the alcohol and the malt flavors in the beer. These are the most intense of the lagers and one of the most malt-forward beer styles out there. Rich, sweet, chocolatey, toasty, and very, very boozy with a full, yet smooth, mouthfeel and slightly syrupy finish. 9–14 percent ABV.

WEIZENBOCK: The name says it all—this style is a wheat bock, which is sort of an imperial version of a wheat beer. (Technically, they are wheat beers brewed to bock strength.) Unlike the rest of the bocks, these beers are brewed with ale yeast—so they are probably closer to being an imperial version of the weissbier or hefeweizen. Give one a try and you'll find a creamy, fruity, rich, and boozy beer with pronounced caramel malt notes and a slightly spicy, clove-like flavor. 6.5–8.0 percent ABV.

In the glass: Clear dark brown, ruby highlights, large off-white head

In the nose: Caramel, roasted nuts, brownies, zero fruit

In the mouth: Rum raisin ice cream, cocoa powder, toasted bread

In one word: Luscious

Pour it into this: Stemmed pokal beer glass (German bock glass), snifter, or tulip

Drink instead of: Riesling, Jägermeister, kir royale

Pair with: Bockwurst (duh!), roasted lamb, beef stew, venison, wiener schnitzel, aged or smoked gouda, limburger (cheese), apfelstrudel, Belgian waffles, German chocolate cake, vanilla or coffee ice cream, fresh berries

Brief history lesson: The first bocks were developed in the mid-1400s in northern Germany in the city of Einbeck, a major player in the international trading realm. Einbeck's most prized export was, naturally, its strong dark beers made from wheat and barley. One of the greatest customers of this strong beer was the House of Wittelsbach—the ruling family of Wittelsbach—and they are rumored to have imported and drank so much of the stuff that it started to impact the local Munich economy.

So the Bavarians did what many businesses do when they realize how much money they are losing on outside expenses: they took the project in house. By the late 1500s, Munich brewers were starting to brew their own versions of the bock. In fact, the famous Munich brewery Hofbräuhaus was built solely for the purpose of brewing this new style of beer. These beers quickly replaced the original from Einbeck.

Ultimately, several styles of bock beers would emerge, driven mostly by the season or time of year in which they were brewed and consumed. The most common derivative we see today is probably the maibock, the spring bock brewed for enjoyment during the colder spring months (like May).

The Bavarian monks also had a well-known love affair with the bock. In fact, the Paulaner monks can be attributed to creating what is now referred to as the doppelbock (slightly stronger version of the traditional bock). They were rumored to sustain themselves on this "liquid bread" during long fasts. Over the years, these beers got progressively stronger, ultimately morphing into what is now known as the doppelbock. I'm going to go out on a limb here and say that fasting in Munich didn't suck.

On a side note, there are several theories on the origin of the "bock" name. The most likely theory is that the word *bock* was derived from its city of origin, Einbeck. In German, *ein bock* translates to "one bock." Other stories point to the goat. Bock also translates to "billy goat" in German, hence why many bock-style beers have goats on the label. Some theories suggest that bocks were named such because the style was traditionally brewed in the winter under the zodiac sign Capricorn (the goat).

My favorite tale involves a drinking contest between a Bavarian duke (who was also a brewer) and a knight from Brunswick. They were each supposed to drink a cask of beer from the other's store. After a few drinks, the knight was the first to topple onto the floor. He tried to blame his misfortune on a goat that for some weird reason had come into the courtyard where all this lollygagging was taking place. The Bavarian brewer responded with jest, "The bock that threw you over was brewed by me."

Try it: Anchor Bock Beer, New Glarus Back 40 Bock, Ayinger Celebrator, Tröegs Troegenator Double Bock, Spaten Optimator, Salvator Doppel Bock, Hofbräu Maibock (Urbock), Sprecher Mai Bock, Moonglow Weizenbock

OTHER HIGH-GRAVITY STYLES DISCUSSED ELSEWHERE:
Strong Scotch aka wee heavy (page 64)
Imperial IPA (page 43)
Belgian dubbel, tripel, quad (starting on page 70)

chapter nine

SOUR AND BARREL-AGED BEERS

Although the styles in this chapter vary drastically, there is one thing in common that they all share: They're all weird. Or perhaps I should say they're all unique in a really beautiful way. Each of them is produced through an unconventional fermentation process. In the case of sour beers, wild yeast and bacteria are used in place of or in addition to traditional brewer's yeast. In the case of barrel-aged beers, beer is allowed to age in barrels after its initial fermentation.

Sour Beers

Depending on how you look at it, sour beers are either the most natural form of beer or they are infected. And really, both arguments are true. Like natural wine, sour beers are made with native or indigenous yeast. But unlike natural wine, many sour beers are also exposed to other less predictable microflora (also known as bacteria).

Technically, sour beers are created through one of two different processes: either via spontaneous fermentation in the open air or a controlled, yet still wild culture based, fermentation. The difference is between the two is control. Whereas wild yeast will always have a certain *je ne sais quoi* about it, some strains have been isolated and studied in depth and can thus be purposefully inoculated to create specific flavors in beer.

Lambics (from Belgium) make up the majority of 100 percent spontaneously fermented beers in this world. While a few modern-day sour brewers are dedicated to making spontaneously fermented beers, most control the brewing process as much as they can by choosing specific strains of wild yeast and bacteria and then carefully inoculating beer with them.

Lambics

In my personal opinion, lambics are among the most fascinating and interesting styles of beer. Ales and lagers are both meticulously fermented with cultivated strands of brewer's yeast using tremendous control. On the other hand, lambics are produced through a process called spontaneous fermentation.

Although it is impossible to confirm the origin of the word *lambic* (*lambiek* in Flemish or Dutch), its most likely origin is the small town of Lembeek ("Lime Creek"), a municipality close to Brussels. Today, lambic production is still concentrated around that area in the western part of Brussels and in the nearby Pajottenland.

Lambic wort is usually comprised of 60–70 percent barley malt and 30–40 percent unmalted wheat. Unlike many other styles of beer, hops are used more for their preservative qualities than as a flavoring agent. Since the beers sour naturally, there is even little need for the traditional bittering role of hops. For that reason, lambics are typically brewed with hops that have been aged, as many as three years in some situations. Since the flavor, aroma, and bitterness of hops deteriorate with time, lambics have virtually no detectable hop presence.

The physical brewing process of lambics is one of the most time consuming of any beer style. Lambic beers use a variety of mashing regimes, some being very lengthy and elaborate (e.g., running two different mashes at the same time with varying temperatures). Unlike most beer styles, which usually boil for an hour to an hour and a half, the lambic boil lasts anywhere from three to six hours.

After the boil, conventional beers are usually cooled in a heat exchanger. Lambics are not. Instead, lambic wort will spend the night in a coolship—shallow cooling vessels—where it is allowed to cool naturally in the night air.

As the wort cools, it is exposed to all sorts of local yeast, bacteria, and other microbial flora. The wort can be inoculated with as many as 80–120 different single-celled microorganisms, all of which will assist in the spontaneous fermentation of the beer. The next day, this bacteria and yeast-infused wort is pumped into oak barrels or oak tanks, where the fermentation process begins.

As you can imagine, spontaneous fermentation is a lengthy process. The microorganisms involved in the creation of lambics must work in a specific sequence. Each microorganism depends on the metabolized products of its predecessors. It takes about two to three years for the entire process to be completed and to produce a mature lambic. That's quite an investment of time when you consider even the strongest ales usually finish their fermentation in just a few weeks.

Second Runnings

There is a surprisingly large amount of sugar in grains that needs to be extracted, and brewers extract as much of that sugar as possible during the mashing phase. Once the wort (sugar water) is separated from the grain husks, it's transferred to the boiler.

The first batch of wort is the strongest, the sweetest, and the most sugary. As the liquid continues to be rinsed with hot water for additional wort, it is watered down and becomes weaker. Ultimately, when the sugar level of the wort in the boiler is on par for the particular style, the brewer stops the transfer, and they stop collecting wort.

Most brewers don't use all of the sugars that are extracted from the mash not only because it's not necessary, but also because you can run the risk of over-extracting, which gives the resulting beer a harsh quality. However, various brewing traditions blend different runnings to make different beers. Some may choose to make a strong beer from the first runnings, then take what is known as the second runnings and make a "small" beer, which will be a lower alcohol beer, from it. They can be quite interesting and elegant in their own special way—if you can find them.

The majority of lambics are found in bottles these days; however, some American interpretations can be found on draft. There are technically five subcategories of lambics, but only two—the gueuze and fruit lambics—are easily found outside of Belgium. These subcategories include the following:

Straight lambic: Cloudy, noncarbonated (almost still), unsweetened, unblended, straight lambics are almost entirely found on draft. They are extremely hard, if not impossible, to find outside of Belgium.

Faro: Faro is a blend of old and new lambic that has been sweetened with dark candy sugar and, on occasion, flavored with spices. Faros tend to be light murky brown in color and are sweeter than all the other lambics (the exception being artificially sweet fruit versions). Lindemans Faro lambic is an example of this style that's relatively easy to find in the United States.

Mars (Bière de Mars): Typically the weakest of the lambics, this style was created using the second runnings (sometimes third runnings) of a normal-strength lambic. Its name literally translates to "March Beer," and it was apparently popular at one point, although now the style is technically "extinct" (no longer in production) in Belgium. However, some American and French breweries have kept the dream alive by brewing interpretations of the styles in recent years. Jolly Pumpkin, Ommegang, and New Belgium have all made one in recent years.

Fruit: Fruit lambics are essentially young lambics (roughly six months old) that have fruit of some sort added to the barrels during fermentation. The addition of the fruit sugars sparks a new fermentation, which can last for another eight to twelve months. The fruit lambic is then filtered and bottled. In some circumstances, additional fruit juice or sugar is added, which kicks off yet another fermentation inside the bottle. The most common flavors include sour cherry (kriek), raspberry (framboise), peach (pêche), blackcurrant (cassis), strawberry (aardbei), or apple (pomme). In the United States, you might be able to find Lindemans Framboise, Cantillon Kriek, Drie Fonteinen Oude Kriek, Lindemans Cassis, Oud Beersel Oude Kriek Vieille, and Upland Raspberry Lambic (an American interpretation).

The potency of flavors in fruit lambics can vary from producer to producer. Some can be extremely fruity, while others might have a more subtle fruit character. Some can be very acidic and tart, while others might be more sweet and syrupy. Color can also range from blush pink and peach to bright red, pink, and deep purple.

Fruit lambics make excellent pairings for a variety of desserts and salads—and even some sweeter meats like duck and pork. I am particularly fond of pairing them with chocolate, cheesecake, fruit tarts and pies, vanilla bean ice cream, beet salad, goat cheese (drizzled with honey), roasted nuts, duck, and barbecued pulled pork.

Gueuze: This last category of lambic gets a full entry, as it can be tracked down stateside and it's one of my all-time favorite styles. But keep in mind that the world of sours does not end with lambics. This is merely the tip of the iceberg. Several other traditional and even more non-traditional styles of beer use wild yeast and bacteria in the fermentation process. But we will get to the rest of those after we discuss the great gueuze.

GUEUZE

Spontaneously fermented, tart, funky, yogurt-like, barnyard, sweet hay, fruit.

BJCP stats

SRM: 3–7	IBU: 0–10	ABV: 4.2–5.4 percent	OG: 1.04 –1.056

My two cents: One of my top five favorite styles of beer, the gueuze is made by blending young lambic (six months to one year old) with more mature vintages (two to three years old). It is then bottled with sugar, where it undergoes a secondary fermentation not unlike that of champagne (also known as the *méthode champenoise*). As a result, gueuzes are highly carbonated. They are tart, but not overly so, and remind me a lot of plain yogurt and raw kombucha.

In the glass: Straw yellow, bubbly, brilliantly clear

In the nose: Sweet hay, lemon zest, apple, horse blanket

In the mouth: Raw kombucha, plain yogurt, Meyer lemon

In one word: Avant-garde

Pour it into this: Flute glass

Drink instead of: Champagne, cider, gin fizz

Pair with: Because of their high acidity and barnyard nature, gueuzes are a great match for young and stinky cheeses, briny shellfish, and high-acid foods. I especially enjoy pairing gueuzes with oysters, mushrooms, mussels, crab cakes, ceviche, fish tacos, salsa, pickles, caprese salads, and other salads dressed with vinaigrettes. This beer also plays nicely with salty, fatty foods like sausages, charcuterie, sardines, and butter sauces. The acidity helps cut through some of the fat as well as counter the saltiness in those foods.

Try it: Boon Geuze, Cantillon Gueuze, Hanssens Oude Geuze, Lindemans Cuvée René, Drie Fonteinen Oude Geuze, Cantillon Lou Pepe, Bruery Rueuze (American interpretation)

FLANDERS RED ALE
Deep burgundy, clear, super fruity, dark cherries, plums, hints of vanilla, vinous and tart.

BJCP stats
SRM: **10–16**
IBU: **10–25**
ABV: **4.6–6.5 percent**
OG: **1.048–1.057**

My two cents: If there was ever a style of beer comparable to red wine, the Flanders red ale is it. Like most red wines, Flanders reds spend a significant amount of time maturing in oak barrels, where they oxidize (in a good way) and develop distinct wood characteristics. This style is typically aged for up

Gueuze

to two years in these barrels, which are also riddled with wild yeast and bacteria, something that differentiates them immensely from wine. As with lambics, these wild yeasts and bacteria give the Flanders red ale its distinct, almost vinegar-like, tartness.

However, Flanders reds do not get their color from grapes. Like all red-hued beers, the color comes from its blend of specialty malts, which includes a base of Vienna or Munich and a blend of caramel malts. As with its fellow sour beers, hops are used sparingly and have virtually no presence in this style.

In my opinion, many Flanders reds taste like well-aged balsamic vinegars that have been slightly diluted and force carbonated. I've never gone as far as attempting to make said concoction and try it side by side with the beer, however, that does sound like a fun experiment.

In the glass: Deep red, good clarity, pale tan head

In the nose: Black cherries, ripe plums, vanilla and chocolate

In the mouth: Balsamic vinegar, dried cranberries, orange zest

In one word: Fancy

Pour it into this: Tulip glass

Drink instead of: Pinot noir, fruit ciders, strawberry daiquiris

Pair with: The dark vinous nature of these beers makes them an excellent pairing for darker meats with higher fat content—like beef, pork, and duck—as well as rich desserts and pungent cheeses. Try pairing Flanders red ales with roasted duck, figs, prosciutto, smoked cheeses, lobster, fried calamari, blue cheese, sweet pork sausage, pan-seared steak, mushrooms, dark cherries, chocolate-raspberry cake, and cheesecake.

Brief history lesson: Although Belgium is one country, it is technically divided into two different regions: Flanders in the north (they speak Dutch) and Wallonia in the south (they speak French). Obviously, the Flanders red originates from the northern part of Belgium, which borders Germany and the Netherlands.

Try it: Rodenbach Grand Cru and Duchesse de Bourgogne are easy to find imports. A variety of US breweries are also known for the style, including New Belgium La Folie, Monk's Café Flemish Sour Ale, Lost Abbey Red Poppy, and Bruery Oude Tart.

FLANDERS OUD BRUIN (BROWN ALE)

Dark reddish brown, good clarity, raisins, figs, toffee, orange zest, lightly tart, chocolate.

BJCP stats
SRM: 10–16   IBU: 10–25   ABV: 4.6–6.5 percent   OG: 1.048–1.057

My two cents: Oud bruins are often referred to as the slightly maltier cousin of the Flanders red. They are sweeter, with more pronounced notes of stone fruit and caramel malts, and significantly less sour. Unlike its red cousin, oud bruins typically don't spend much time in oak or take on as much oak character, although they are aged for several months, if not a full year.

Oud bruins are typically fermented with a combination of both Saccharomyces (regular brewer's yeast) and Lactobacillus (yogurt bacteria). Their brown color comes from the addition of darker caramel malts as well as a hint of roasted or black malt. As with other sours, hops are used in the brewing, but don't play a large part in the overall tasting experience. Oud bruins are not as popular or as easy to find as Flanders red ales.

In the glass: Deep red, good clarity, pale tan head

In the nose: Figs, dark cherries, orange zest, caramel

In the mouth: Sweet-and-sour sauce, toffee, prunes, cocoa

In one word: Provisional

Pour it into this: Tulip glass

Drink instead of: Red table wine, sherry, Manhattan

Pair with: The rustic roots of oud bruins make them a great match for classic peasant fair.

Try it: Petrus Aged Pale, Liefmans Goudenband, Petrus Oud Bruin, New Glarus Thumbprint Enigma, Ichtegem Old Brown

LEIPZIG-STYLE GOSE

Straw gold, effervescent, lemon zest, lemon juice, yogurt, saltwater, spice.

BJCP stats

SRM: 3–9   IBU: 10–15   ABV: 4.4–5.4 percent   OG: 1.036–1.056

My two cents: What makes the gose (pronounced goes-uh) most unique and unlike any other beer style is its slightly saline character. It is brewed with a blend of pale malts and wheat and can be spiced with both coriander and hops, but it gets the saline character from the addition of salt to the brewing water. Although traditionally spontaneously fermented, modern versions undergo a more controlled fermentation with both ale yeast and Lactobacillus. The result is a tart, fruity, spicy, and crisp ale with a slightly salty finish.

In the glass: Brilliant, straw yellow, bubbly white head

In the nose: Lemon peel, the ocean

In the mouth: Plain yogurt with a squeeze of lemon and sprinkle of salt

In one word: Zesty

Pour it into this: Tulip, flute glass

Drink instead of: Vodka soda, mimosas

Pair with: The light tartness and slight saltiness of the gose makes it a wonderful partner for anything from the sea and many fresh milk cheeses. I'm a big fan of pairing a gose with anything from a raw bar or sushi bar—oysters, shrimp, sashimi, crab, you name it. Other great pairings include seaweed salad, steamed mussels, ceviche, feta, Humboldt Fog (cheese), citrus vinaigrettes, yellow beets, chicken kabobs with tahini sauce, and fruit desserts.

Brief history lesson: Although most commonly associated with the town of Leipzig, the gose was first brewed in the early sixteenth century in the town of Goslar, where it gets its name from the river Gose that flows through the town. In 1826, the city council of Goslar actually abolished gose brewing altogether. If it weren't for the brewers of Leipzig, the style would have been lost forever.

Because the gose was so popular in Leipzig, they started to brew it themselves (as opposed to importing it from Goslar) in the early 1700s. By the early 1900s, it was the most popular style in the town as well as many parts of northern Germany. Production of this style declined during the world wars and then it stopped altogether during the Cold War. Luckily, gose production resumed when the Berlin Wall came down, but sadly, it was no longer the popular style it had once been.

Today, only three breweries in Germany brew a traditional gose. Luckily, many American craft breweries have revived this almost-extinct style, adding their own unique twists to the traditional recipe.

Try it: Leipziger Gose; Westbrook Gose; Almanac Golden Gate Gose; Portsmouth Gose; Marin Duck Goose Gose; Anderson Valley The Kimmie, The Yink & The Holy Gose

BERLINER WEISSE

Very pale yellow, effervescent, sour lemon candy, yogurt, kombucha, tart, super light.

BJCP stats

SRM: 2–3   IBU: 3–8   ABV: 2.8–3.8 percent*   OG: 1.028–1.032*

*American versions are typically stronger

My two cents: Much like the terms *champagne* and *bordeaux* are exclusive to wines produced in those respective regions of France, the term *Berliner weisse* is highly regulated in Germany, only to be used by beers brewed in Berlin. Today, many American breweries have adopted the style and actively use the Berliner weisse name in labeling German-style Berliner weisse beers.

The style is a tart, highly effervescent, and low alcohol ale fermented with Lactobacillus. Because it is most often brewed with pale malts and 25–30 percent wheat and bottle conditioned, the Berliner weisse tends to be moderately hazy and pale yellow in color. Traditionally, the Berliner weisse was served with a shot of raspberry or woodruff-flavored syrup to balance its sour taste. Although still served this way in Germany, Americans typically drink it straight.

In the glass: Super pale gold, somewhat hazy, bubbly

In the nose: Sourdough bread, lemon juice and zest

In the mouth: Lemon yogurt, raw kombucha

In one word: Snazzy

Pour it into this: Flute glass

Drink instead of: Lemonade, mineral water, moscato

Pair with: Like the gose, the Berliner weisse makes a great match for fresh and raw seafood and fresh cheeses. I also like to partner it with citrusy vinaigrettes, fresh fruit salads, and salty fried foods. Try a Berliner weisse with goat cheese, fried sardines, scallop ceviche, tuna poke, fried pickles, melon salads, fresh heirloom tomatoes, fish tacos, and strawberry shortcake.

Brief history lesson: As its name would suggest, the origin of the Berliner weisse is most commonly attributed to Berlin, Germany. Although beer experts debate the exact location and date of its origin, the first evidence of weisse-making in Berlin dates back to 1642. Upon discovering the Berliner weisse in 1809 while occupying Germany, Napoleon himself has been rumored to refer to the highly effervescent style as "the Champagne of the North."

It was the most popular style of beer in Germany by the nineteenth century, being brewed by nearly 700 different breweries. However, by the end of the twentieth century there were only two breweries left in Berlin and a handful in the rest of Germany producing the style.

Try it: The Bruery Hottenroth, Dogfish Head Festina Peche, Night Shift Ever Weisse, Golden Road Berliner Weisse, Bell's Oarsman

Wild Beers

The terms *wild* and *sour* are usually used interchangeably, but there is a difference. Beers are soured by introducing acidifying bacteria (Lactobacillus and Pediococcus being the most common) to fermenting beer. Wild beer is generally used to describe any beer that displays the earthy characteristics of Brettanomyces yeast strains—often shortened to Brett— regardless of whether the beer is a light golden ale or a strong dark stout. Often, these styles receive all three of the bacteria to blend a funky, sour character that many beer geeks have developed an affinity for.

Color varies from light to dark, super effervescent, funky, earthy, sometimes fruity, very dry. This style category is literally a free for all. Fruit, no fruit, light malt, dark malt—these beers can range in color from super pale in color to pink, to red to orange, purple and deep brown. Bittering units and alcohol contents also vary.

Pair with: Wild beer loves cheese—and the funkier and stinkier, the better. Aged brie, sharp cheddars, and aged blue all pair nicely with wild sour beers.

Try it: The Commons Flemish Kiss, Crooked Stave L'Brett d'Or, Anchorage Galaxy White IPA, Russian River Sanctification, Trinity Brewing TPS Report

Barrel-Aged Beers

The process of maturing beer in oak barrels is not novel. Before stainless steel kegs were invented, wooden barrels and bottles (and jugs) were the most common modes of transporting beer from one place to another. All sorts of beers, from pale ales to porters and stouts, were transported in oak barrels. Cask beers were traditionally served from, you guessed it, wooden casks. It's what they had back in the day. However, the concept of aging beers in previously used spirits and wine barrels is a modern addition to brewing.

Wooden barrels are extremely porous, which essentially means that they allow a certain amount of oxygen to pass through. As with most perishable things, oxygen in the barrels expedites the aging process of beer. Many brewers (wine makers and distillers) refer to this process of intentional oxidation as maturation. Some brewers dose the barrels with a layer of nitrogen gas before plugging up to limit the oxidation of barrel-aging beers—but there is no way to prevent it completely.

As beer ages, many chemical changes occur that change the flavor of beer. The end result varies depending on a variety of factors that include, but are not limited to, the style of beer that is being aged, the type and age of the barrel, the length of the barrel-aging period, and the temperatures at which the barrels are kept.

THE POWER OF THE BOURBON BARREL

The most common types of barrels used by brewers are neutral oak barrels—often charred but unadulterated and spiritless—and bourbon barrels. These two types of barrels are the easiest to find and also produce some of the most desirable results.

Note: Whiskey makers and wine makers can use their barrels repeatedly—although many winemakers will release barrels after a few years of use. However, by law, bourbon producers can only use their barrels once. Each batch of bourbon must be aged in fresh, untainted barrels. This is the reason why bourbon barrels are the most abundant variety of liquor barrels available to brewers.

While neutral barrels can provide more of a blank canvas, bourbon is known for its distinct vanilla, oak, and toffee flavors—all of which can be infused into beer with just a few months of aging inside of bourbon barrels. Most brewers put big, boozy, rich, and malty beers, like imperial stouts and barleywines, into bourbon barrels for aging. The result can be some highly sought-after beers, like Founders Kentucky Breakfast Stout.

It's not uncommon for a beer's alcohol content to increase a percentage point or two while sitting in the barrels. Sometimes a new layer of alcohol heat and booziness is added from the residual bourbon inside the walls of the barrels. However, most brewers drain and rinse spirits and wine barrels prior to the first use, and thus very little is actually left in the barrel. This is usually done as a precautionary method as a way to remove any undesirable matter that might be inside. In the case of bourbon barrels, this helps to remove any loose pieces of char from the barrel.

Yet as beer ages in a barrel, the water in the beer gradually evaporates, which gives the beer a slight bump in alcohol. The longer a beer ages, the more water that evaporates. Most beers go up 1 percent in alcohol while in the barrels, but it is not unheard of for them to increase as much as 2–3 percent while aging.

Most barrel-aged beers spend between six months and a year in the barrel. A few brewers will age the beers in barrels for several years, blending multiple vintages and even styles of barrel-aged beers to produce an entirely new and unique beer.

OTHER TYPES OF WOOD

Some brewers who might not have enough space or access to oak barrels opt to add neutral or liquor-soaked oak chips or spirals directly to the fermenters or bright tanks post-fermentation. Instead of aging a beer for months inside of barrels, they allow the beer to condition inside the tanks with oak chips or spirals for a few weeks instead. This method expedites the "oaking" process, producing oak-infused beers in a much shorter timeframe than if they were aged in barrels due to the increased surface area of the chips.

In addition to neutral oak and bourbon barrels, craft brewers all over the world have been experimenting with every type of barrel you can imagine. Red wine barrels, chardonnay barrels, brandy barrels, cognac barrels, tequila barrels, gin barrels, whiskey barrels, sherry barrels—you name it and it's either been done or aging as we speak.

Commercial examples of barrel-aged beers: Goose Island Bourbon County Stout (imperial stout aged in bourbon barrels), Russian River Consecration (sour dark ale aged in cabernet barrels with blackcurrants), Russian River Temptation (sour blonde aged in chardonnay barrels), Founders Kentucky Breakfast Stout (imperial stout aged in bourbon barrels), Captain Lawrence Golden Delicious (apple brandy barrel-aged Belgian tripel), Odell Fernet Aged Porter (imperial porter aged in fernet barrels), Half Acre Gin Barrel Aged Pony Pilsner, The Bruery Black Tuesday (imperial stout aged in bourbon barrels), Almanac Brandy Barrel Pêche

SECTION two

BECOMING AN EXPERT

The Brewing Process, Brewing Ingredients, Evaluating Beer, and Respecting Beer

chapter ten

BREWING AND BEER INGREDIENTS

While it might seem like magic, and takes years to master, the brewing process can be summed up in a way that's easy to understand. It's like cooking: if you gather all the right ingredients and you follow the instructions, you can brew beer in the comfort of your own home (or garage). If it weren't easy to get started, there wouldn't be millions of homebrewers in the world.

Notice I didn't say it was easy to be a *great* brewer, or even a good one, though. There are degree programs and schools for that, and there are also brewers who have just put in the years and learned the tricks of the trade on the job. The point is, brewing can quickly get as complex as you'd like it to be, but the basic process and ingredients? Surely we can all get up to speed on that.

The Brewing Process

Before we go through things in a little more detail, let's run through the nutshell version as quickly as possible.

Yeast is like a five-year-old hyperactive kid who loves candy. When it gets into sugar water, yeast goes completely insane, eating the sugar and spitting out alcohol and carbon dioxide and some other stuff we can talk about later. But the problem is, malted barley keeps its sugar under lock and key. In order to get the yeast to magically turn barley into booze, you have to get malt to release its sugar.

The sugars in barley are locked inside the husks, so those need to be cracked open. Then the brewer needs to steep the vulnerable little grains in hot water. Hot water helps to suck the sugars out, and what brewers end up with is sort of a flavored sugar water (made from maltose instead of sucrose). Then brewers take that hot sugary solution, and they boil it to remove some of the water and further concentrate the sugar. They also flavor the syrup with hops, so that it is bittersweet instead of pure sweet.

The deliciously flavored syrup, called wort, is then cooled and pumped into a fermenting tank, where the yeast is thrown in to attack it and turn it into beer. Once the yeast has had enough time to work its magic, the brewers can package and serve the beer.

That's it! Well, that's it at its most basic of basic. Now, let's get into a little more detail. We won't go anywhere near an actual how-to-brew book, but we will take a brief look at the big steps of brewing: mill, mash, lauter and sparge, boil, cool and transfer, ferment, and package.

MILL

When the brewing malts hit the brewhouse, they are dry little pieces of barley. The husks are hard and virtually impervious, protecting all the sweet, sweet sugars inside. In order for sugar to be extracted from the grains, they need to be cracked first. To accomplish this, the grain is either hand milled (bags are lifted over the shoulder and poured into the mill) or it is sent from silos to the mill with machinery, where it is roughly cracked, but not finely ground like flour. It is important the grain isn't milled too finely, otherwise it could gum things up down the line once it's mixed with water. And a stuck sparge is about as much fun as it sounds like—trust me.

MASH

After the grain is cracked, it is mixed with hot water. *Mashing in* refers to the stage when the grain comes into the mash tun, the vessel where the mashing occurs. The *mash* itself is the word for the mixture once the cracked grain is mixed with hot water. The grain then soaks in the hot water at a specific temperature (for most beers it's in the 140s or 150s Fahrenheit), which allows the enzymes in the malt to break down the starch in the malt into sugar. The sugar water produced during the mash process is called wort.

LAUTER AND SPARGE

The *lautering* process happens in three phases. First, the temperature of the mash is often raised, typically through the addition of more hot water, which stops the mashing conversion. Then, the wort runoff gets recirculated—the liquid is pulled from the bottom and then added back to the top. As the wort moves back toward the bottom, the leftover grain husks act as a sort of filter.

The last step is the *sparge*, or the rinsing of the grain. For most brewers, as the wort is slowly removed from the bottom of the mash tun and transferred to the brew kettle, a very light trickling of water is sprayed over the grain bed, rinsing additional sugars from the grain.

BOIL

If you love hops like I do, this is where things get fun. Once the wort has been transferred to the brew kettle, it is brought to a boil. Hops are added during the boil at multiple stages. Hops used for bittering are typically added at the beginning of the boil (between 60 and 90 minutes). Hops used for some additional bitterness and for flavoring hit around 15 to 20 minutes before the end of the boil. Last, hops used for aroma are added right before the end of the boil.

All sorts of fun chemical reactions take place in the boil: The wort is sterilized (no more icky bacteria), the enzymatic processes completely stop (no more conversion of starch into sugar), hops alpha acids are isomerized (hop bitterness, flavor, and aroma compounds are released), and the sugars in the wort become concentrated (as with any reduction). DMS precursors (see page 135 for more information) are also released during the boil.

COOL AND TRANSFER

Once the boil is finished, it is important to remove all the leftover hop solids and any other herbs or spices that may have been added in the boil. The process involves swirling the wort in either the brew kettle or a separate whirlpool tank, forcing solids in the wort to collect in the middle and fall into a cone in the bottom of the tank where they are then removed.

After the hop sludge is removed, the hot wort is sent through a heat exchanger, which rapidly chills down the wort to fermentation temperatures. The cooled wort is transferred into a fermentation tank and gets introduced to the yeast.

FERMENT

Once the wort hits the fermenters, the yeast is pitched in and starts to do its thing, eating up the carbohydrates and converting them into alcohols and carbon dioxide. Most modern-day brewers use stainless steel cylindro-conical vessels—tall thin fermenting tanks with a cone bottom. Some breweries, mostly in Europe, use open fermentation vessels as well.

Most commercial beer takes roughly one to two weeks to ferment, depending on the style, and then another week or two to condition (some styles can take six weeks or longer, though). Hop-forward styles have additional hops added right in the fermenting tanks—which is known as dry hopping—toward the end of fermentation or in the conditioning process. Dry hopping greatly enhances hop aroma in beer, but does not add any hop bitterness.

PACKAGE

Once the beer has converted most of the sugars from the wort, the temperature of the fermenting tank is dropped to a lower temperature, which forces most of the yeast to go dormant and drop to the bottom of the tank. The yeast sludge is removed first, and then when the beer starts running clear, it can be sent to another tank to clarify. Some brewers will filter the beer on the way to this tank, which is referred to as a "bright tank."

Once the beer is finished clarifying and maturing, it is carbonated to the brewers' liking and sent to the bottling line or kegging machine. Some brewpubs serve beer directly from the bright tank, connecting the taps to the tanks.

Ingredients

Although brewers brew with all sorts of ingredients these days—like herbs, spices, and flowers—nearly all beer starts with the four core brewing ingredients: malt, hops, yeast, and water.

Each of the four main ingredients in beer plays an important role in every beer style, but sometimes one ingredient plays a stronger role than all the others. This might seem obvious when comparing a hoppy beer to a malty one. Even the most infrequent of beer drinkers probably know stouts are characterized by their malt while IPAs are all about hops. Yeast and water also play a big enough role to define beer styles. For example, the characteristic banana and clove flavor in a hefeweizen comes entirely from its yeast. And while the malt, hops, and yeast used in both the Bohemian pilsener and the German pilsner are essentially the same; the major difference in water between the two (soft vs. hard) results in two different beers.

Malt

Malt is arguably the most important ingredient in beer. It's the largest component by weight besides water, and it contributes the precious sugar needed to make beer what it is. Other forms of sugar water such as apple juice, pear juice, or grape juice don't make beer. They make cider, perry, and wine, respectively. For beer to be beer, you need that precious malt. Thus, it's understandable that malt has a huge impact on not one, but four key components of beer: alcohol, flavor, color, and mouthfeel.

The alcohol content of beer is directly related to the amount of sugars extracted from the malts used to make the beer. The color of beer is also extracted from the malt, which gets roasted and toasted to varying degrees. Pale beers are made with lighter malts that have little to no toast. Amber-colored beers are made with some caramel-colored malts. And the dark beers are made with at least a malt or two—if not many—that have been roasted to a dark brown or black color.

Barley also contains 9–12 percent protein, and during the malting process around 38–42 percent of that becomes solubilized. It consists of simple amino acids, crucial for yeast nutrition and beer flavor as well as Maillard reactions for specialty malt production and beer flavor. Medium-sized polypeptides are responsible for beer foam, and large proteins are responsible for that signature beer haze.

The roast of the malts also has a huge impact on the flavor of beer. Lighter malts produce toasty and biscuit flavors, caramel malts are toffee-like, and roasted malts yield flavors that range from nutty to chocolatey to burnt. Malts also affect mouthfeel, which is essentially a combination of the texture, weight, and body of a beer. Beer can range from flat, thin, and weak to dense, heavy, and viscous, and it's largely due to the type of malts and the quantity of malts used.

MAKING MALT

Malting is the process of converting barley (or other grains) into malt. Once the barley gets to the malthouse, it is dried, usually on a malting floor. Next comes the germination process: The barley is soaked in water for roughly two days, then it's drained and kept in a constant 60-degree environment for five days.

During those five days, the barley begins to sprout. As the grains sprout, enzymes break down the starches in the barley into simpler sugars. After day five, the sprouting barley is thrown into a kiln for about a day and a half, which halts the germination process and locks in all the sugary goodness. The kilned malt is then roasted to varying degrees, depending on the final goal of the maltsters (the people doing the malting).

MALTS USED IN BREWING

Most beer styles are produced with 80 to 90 percent pale malt, also referred to as base malt or just two-row. This malt is kilned the lightest and doesn't add any significant caramel or roasted flavors to beer. The smaller portion of the beer recipe—which on the malt side is referred to as the grain bill, malt bill, or grist—is made up of a combination of specialty malts.

Note: Beer is generally built upon a base of malted barley, but can also be brewed with a combination of barley and other malted cereal grains—like wheat, rye, and oats.

Specialty malts are typically named either for the flavors or colors they impart on the beer or the region of origin. The most common caramelized malts include carapils, Munich, crystal, and caramel. Biscuit, chocolate, and black are the most common roasted malts. Then there are also smoked malts, rye malts, and various types of wheat malts.

Although there are a growing number of small micro-maltsters in the world, the majority of brewing barley is malted by a handful of larger maltsters, including Briess, Cargill, and Country Malt in North America and Bairds, Castle, and Weyermann in Europe. Although many of the malts that these companies produce are virtually identical to those made by others, many of them have trademarked names to help differentiate their malts from those of competitors. A rose by any other name and all that jazz.

BASE MALTS

Base malts have a name that says it all; these malts typically make up the majority of the malt bill for most styles of beer. As such, none have an extreme amount of color or flavor. Rather, they're like coating a canvas in a neutral wash before you paint a picture. They each have their own character they add to a beer. (If you need proof, just ask your local brewer if he or she could make a great pilsner with British pale malt.)

Two-row: Sometimes called pale ale malt, two-row malt is American-grown and the main base malt for most American beer. It contributes a light straw color and a clean, sweet, and mild malty flavor. Most of the beers you drink from American craft brewers are built on two-row. The name comes from a time when brewers had just two choices for domestic base malt: barley that came from plants with two rows or six rows. (The six-row malt is used only as a base malt by the massive breweries, who pair it with ingredients like rice and corn.)

Pale malt: The British equivalent of American two-row, pale malt tends to have more biscuit and bread character. Some brewers say it's heavier on the palate as well. If your local craft brewer specializes in British ales, they may very well import their favorite maltster's version of pale malt. Some brewers are passionate about specific heritage varieties, such as Maris Otter or Golden Promise, which are still floor-malted the traditional way by hand.

Pilsen malt (pilsner malt): This is the lightest colored base malt available. If British pale malt is a heavier two-row, you can think of pilsen or pilsner malt as the lighter version of two-row. It produces beers with very light color and clean, crisp flavor. For that reason, it's the main malt in pale lager styles, but it is also used in many pale ales. Brewers bent on recreating traditional pilsners typically swear by the German maltsters' version of this malt, though domestic maltsters try to recreate it.

Vienna malt: This malt is typically used in Vienna, Oktoberfest, Märzen, Alt, and other dark lagers. It contributes golden and light orange hues and has a slightly malty, light biscuit flavor.

Munich malt: This is a highly kilned "lager malt" that contributes a golden color with orange to amber hues. It can be used for up to 100 percent of the grain bill in many darker and amber-colored lagers like dunkels and bocks.

CARAMEL, CRYSTAL, AND CARA MALTS

One of the main classes of accent malts—caramel, crystal, and cara—are essentially the same thing. They are just labeled differently depending on the company and country that makes or sells them.

Crystal and caramel malts are actually not kilned, like most brewing malts. Instead, maltsters take the green malt and stew it in a very wet oven of sorts. When this process starts converting the grain's starch to sugar, the temperature is lowered and, as a result, the sugar is crystallized in the hull. The malt is then dried over heat. The degree to which it is heated greatly affects the resulting malt.

On the extreme light end, there are dextrin malts. These malts add unfermentable sugars, which contribute body and a thicker mouthfeel to beer without adding color or flavor. Many maltsters have their own trademarked brand names for certain malts: CaraFoam® (Weyermann®), Carapils® (Briess), Caramel Pils, and Dextrin Malt are all different names for very similar malts.

Crystal and caramel malts in the middle tend to offer varying degrees of sweet caramel flavor. The subcategories of crystal malts are usually labeled based on color. Many are labeled according to the Lovibond color scale (Caramel 60 L, Crystal 120 L, etc.). The lower the number, the lighter the color; the higher the number, the darker the color (of the malt).

On the dark end, crystal malts such as Special B®, Extra Special Roast, and Extra Dark Crystal can add a wide variety of flavors that may include burnt sugar, raisin, prune, cherry, or other dark dried fruit. However, even in dark beers crystal malts are an accent flavor. The main chocolate, roast, and coffee flavors come from roasted malts.

ROASTED MALTS

Roasted malts are just that: highly roasted malts responsible for giving dark beers, like stouts and porters, their rich brown to black color and wide variety of roasty flavors. They are powerful and often used sparingly—a little goes a long way. The most common flavor characteristics of roasted malts include burnt toast, roasted coffee, espresso, and dark chocolate.

Chocolate malt: Adds a bittersweet chocolate flavor and deep ruby color to beer. Used in small amounts for brown ale and extensively in porters and stouts.

Black patent malt: The blackest of the black malts, black patent contributes a burnt bread, char-like flavor and deep brown to black color to beer. It should be used very sparingly.

Roasted barley: Technically, roasted barley is not considered to be a malt because it doesn't get malted. It is unmalted barley that has been lightly roasted. It is known for adding a distinct coffee taste and dryness to stouts.

A Close Look at Common Crystal Malts

Cara-pils: This malt is very light in color and gives a light sweetness to beer. It is used in a variety of styles from pale ales to stouts to improve head retention and give beer a smoother body and more rounded mouthfeel.

Cara-Munich (Dark Munich): Somewhere near the middle of the scale in color, Cara-Munich gives beer a caramel-like sweetness. It increases body and mouthfeel.

Special B: This fairly dark caramelized malt gives beer a unique flavor similar to burnt caramel.

Crystal/caramel malts: The lighter in color the malts are, the less caramel aroma and flavor. Nut-like aromas are present with the darker malts. The most commonly used are:

> **Caramel/Crystal 10:** Adds a light honey-like sweetness and a soft body to beer.

> **Caramel/Crystal 40:** Adds a light caramel sweetness and a smooth body to beer. Used in pales ales and amber lagers.

> **Caramel/Crystal 60:** Perhaps the most commonly used caramel malt. Adds full caramel taste and body to beer. Used in many English-style beers like pale ales, bitters, porters, brown ales, and even stouts.

> **Caramel/Crystal 80:** Adds a lightly bittersweet caramel flavor. Used in many red styles of beer.

> **Caramel/Crystal 120:** Adds a strong bittersweet caramel flavor. Used in small amounts in barleywines, old ales, and doppelbocks.

OTHER GRAINS AND ADJUNCTS

In addition to barley, several other grains are used to make beer. These grains are often referred to as adjuncts, meaning ingredients used to supplement or replace barley, the main fermentable ingredient in beer. In some cases, these adjuncts are used to add flavor, increase foam retention, or create body and texture. These "good" adjuncts include oats, rye, and wheat.

Unfortunately, the majority of adjuncts used in beer on a large commercial scale are used to reduce the costs of production and lighten the flavor and color of beer. The two main culprits of this are rice and corn, which are known to produce "watered-down" styles like American and imported light lagers.

Wheat: Brewing wheat can either be unmalted or malted. Unmalted wheat tends to give a more potent wheat flavor to beer. It is a common ingredient in most wheat beer styles, especially American wheats, Belgian wits, and lambics. Malted wheat is made and used much like malted barley. Some wheat beer styles, like the hefeweizen, use up to 60 percent malted wheat. Wheat gives beer a distinctive haze as well as imparts a notable dryness.

Oats: Brewers use all types of oats—whole, steel-cut, rolled, flaked—depending on the system and the desires of the brewer. Some like to toast the oats before using them, some just use them as is. Oats are predominantly used in oatmeal stouts, but they have appeared in other styles. Oats give beer a smooth, creamy mouthfeel.

Rye: Rye gives beer a nice head as well as a distinctive dryness and slightly spicy flavor. Like oats, rye comes in several forms—rolled rye, roasted rye, flaked rye, malted rye, and regular old rye berries. Rye typically makes up 10 to 20 percent of the grain bill, but some brewers have used up to 50 percent. Rye is most commonly found in pale ales, amber ales, and IPAs.

Corn: The principal adjunct used in American light lagers, it can add a subtle corn sweetness if used in excess, but it's typically just used to lighten the color and body of beer. It is significantly cheaper than the other grains, which makes it an ideal ingredient for mass-produced beers.

Rice: Rice is the other main adjunct used in American and Japanese light lagers. Rice adds little flavor to beer. Like corn, rice is super cheap.

Gluten-free grains: Some brewers are experimenting with gluten-free grains like buckwheat, millet, sorghum, and even quinoa. The jury is out on whether or not gluten-free beers can or will ever be able to shine a light to their barley-based counterparts.

BRINGING IT ALL TOGETHER

The malts covered in this chapter are just a glimpse into the hundreds of varieties of malt a brewer has to choose from. Recipe creation is thus a large part of a brewer's job, and many breweries establish house flavors with their combination of certain malts and yeasts.

Before we move on, let's take a look at the malt bill of three different homebrew recipes to see malt in action:

GERMAN-STYLE PILSNER

Malt: 100 percent German pilsner malt

Pilsners are among the lightest in color and malt flavors—which is why they are brewed with 100 percent pale malts.

AMERICAN STYLE IPA

Malts: 80 percent Two-Row, 7 percent Crystal 20, 5 percent Munich Malt, 5 percent Carapils, 3 percent Wheat

IPAs are generally golden to copper in color, which is why you will typically see a small percentage of crystal or caramel malt in them. They also tend to have a bigger, yet drier, mouthfeel. The wheat helps with that in this recipe.

IRISH DRY STOUT

Malts: 67 percent Two-Row, 12 percent Munich, 8 percent Caramunich, 6 percent Chocolate Wheat, 4 percent Carafa, 3 percent Roasted Barley

Stouts are the darkest of the dark and their recipes demand a significant blend of some of the darkest of roasted malts—like Chocolate and Carafa. Caramel malts are also added to increase body and mouthfeel. Oh, and that small but powerful amount of roasted barley is essentially a requirement for all stouts (it's what truly differentiates this style from porters).

Hops

Hops are technically the flowers of the Humulus lupulus plant. When it comes to brewing, we're just talking about the female flowers. They serve two main purposes in beer. First, they provide bitterness, flavor, and aroma to beer. Second, and just as important, back in the early days of hop usage, they aid in preservation (often referred to as stability). Despite those benefits, brewing beer with hops is kind of a new thing when you think about them in context of the entire timeline of beer.

Beer dates back to 5000 BC, but hops didn't become widely used in brewing until 1100 AD. Before then, all sorts of herbs, flowers, and spices were used to flavor beer. Hops ultimately won the standards

The Color Spectrum of Beer

As I noted before, beer's color is greatly impacted by the color of the malt used to make it. The process responsible for giving malt its color is called the Maillard reaction. It is a chemical reaction that happens between amino acids and sugars in the presence of a lot of heat.

In simple words, it's the reaction that gives food its brown color and toasted, roasted, and caramelized flavors. Toasted bread? Maillard reaction. Seared and browned meats? Maillard reaction. Roasted coffee? Maillard reaction. Chocolate, maple syrup, golden brown french fries, roasted peanuts—all created by the Maillard reaction. And the Maillard reaction is responsible for both the flavor and color of roasted barley.

When it comes to measuring the color of beer, the most common scale used by brewers and beer judges today is the Standard Reference Method (SRM). (Many maltsters use Degrees Lovibond, but we won't really talk about that here).

How the SRM is determined is a bit above my head. There is a mathematical formula for calculating SRM, but let's not kid ourselves here—none of us has the tools nor patience for calculating said number. Lucky for us, there are cheat sheets, I mean SRM charts, that we can use to figure out the scientific color of beer.

SRM/EBC COLOR CHART

SRM	1	2	3	4	5	6	7	8	9	10	11	12	13	14	15
EBC	2	4	6	8	10	12	14	16	18	20	22	24	26	28	30

SRM BEER STYLE COLOR CHART

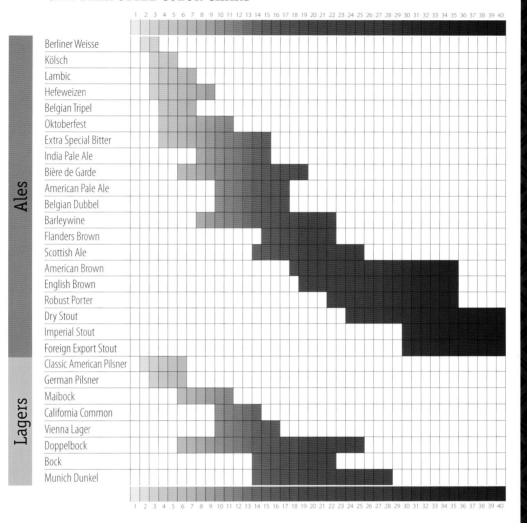

war. Not only did they give beer a unique flavor, they also made beer better. Beer with hops proved more stable, lasting longer and tasting what people thought of as "good" even when shipped long distances.

Note: Having trouble sleeping? Prescribe yourself a super hoppy IPA before bed! Seriously though, hops are a natural sedative. Before they were used in beer, they were predominantly used for medicinal purposes, like treating anxiety and insomnia.

Hops are classified similar to wine: Old World vs. New World. In this context, Old World pertains to Europe (mainly England and Germany), and New World means mainly North America, New Zealand, and Australia. European hops varietals tend to be earthy, spicy, floral, and lower in alpha acids, while American hops tend to be citrusy, piney, tropical, and higher in alpha acids.

What the heck is an alpha acid? Essentially, it's the compound in hops that makes them bitter. The higher the alpha acid content, the more bitterness a brewer can extract from the hop. IBUs—International Bittering Units—measure the amount of alpha acids in a beer. The higher the IBU number, the more alpha acids in the beer. (This is important when deciding if a beer is too bitter for you, as most good bars and brewers will clearly indicate the IBUs of their beers.)

Have you ever tried a beer so hoppy that it left you with a slightly numb and super dry, cottonmouth feeling? Like you just licked tree bark or sand paper? That, my friends, is the alpha acids talking. There is a reason that imperial IPAs are often described as being "palate wreckers" and "abrasive": They temporarily strip your tongue of all moisture and sensation.

Just because a beer has a high IBU doesn't guarantee it will have a high level of perceived bitterness. A lot of high alcohol, malty beers can have higher IBUs, but the alcohol burn and malt sweetness may detract from our ability to perceive the bitterness. Think of it like cooking: A teaspoon of pepper may blend right into a sweet pasta sauce but make a chocolate pudding taste spicy. (That said, higher IBU numbers are generally a good indicator of bitterness.)

There is also a cap on our ability to detect IBUs in beer. Humans can taste up to only a certain level of bittering units and, after that point, it's all the same. The magic number is around 100 IBUs, though some people might argue that they can taste up to 120.

I'm not going to go into each single varietal, but I will tell you a bit about the most common and popular hops you will find in beer on the pages that follow. If you're already hop-obsessed and this isn't enough, there are books dedicated solely to the subject of hops (check out *For the Love of Hops* by Stan Hieronymus).

HOP CATEGORIES

Noble hops are the old-school European hops, typically named for the region in which they were found. They tend to be aromatic hop varietals, yet low in alpha acids (bitterness). The four traditional varietals of noble hops are Tettnanger, Spalt, Hallertauer, and Saaz. These hops are predominantly used in German and Czech-style beers like pilsners and other lagers. They are most commonly described as being earthy, woody, herbal, and spicy.

Next we have the almost-but-not-quite-there noble hops—the native English varietals. These include English Fuggles, East Kent Golding, (Hallertauer) Hersbrucker, and Styrian Goldings. Like the noble hops, these varietals are also highly aromatic, yet low in alpha acids.

North American hops tend to be much higher in alpha acids than their European counterparts. They are often described as being citrusy (lemon, grapefruit, tropical fruits), resinous (pine-like), and dank (pot-like). Some are even likened to cat pee. The most common varietals are the "four Cs": Cascade, Centennial, Columbus, and Chinook. Some of the sexy newish varietals include Simcoe, Citra, Amarillo, and Mosaic.

Note: Hops are a close cousin of the marijuana plant, which explains why the two look very similar and share a lot of the same aromatics. In fact, several brewers use the word "dank" (a marijuana term) to describe some Pacific Northwest hop varietals.

We are now seeing a surge in the popularity of Australian and New Zealand hops, which rival the American varietals when it comes to alpha acids and bitterness. These varietals tend to be citrusy and very tropical (passion fruit). The popular ones include Galaxy, Topaz, Nelson Sauvin, Pacific Gem, and Rakau.

A CLOSE ~~LOOK AT~~ SMELL OF AROMA HOPS

So maybe you have some idea now that you like noble hops, or that you're like me, obsessed with pungent, super vibrant, and citrusy American hops. But what ones do you really like? Why is that IPA your favorite IPA? Let's take a close look at some of the most popular aroma hops and find out. (All the hops that follow are American until you get to the Much Loved Imports.)

CITRUS BOMBS

CASCADE

Alpha acids: 4.5–7.0 percent

In some ways, Cascade is the original American hop. While European and British brewers shied away from the American hops, brewers like Anchor and Sierra Nevada added them by the handful. The result, as we now know, is perhaps the world's most popular pale ale: Sierra Nevada Pale Ale. That beer is still a great showcase for Cascade, which is known for its citrusy character, with hints of grapefruit and floral notes.

CENTENNIAL

Alpha acids: 9.5–11.5 percent

In hop catalogs, you'll often see Centennial described as a super Cascade. While that's a little misleading, since the two have their own unique characters, it's not altogether wrong. The alpha acids in Centennial are higher, and ounce per ounce it tends to have more aroma than Cascade as well. Bell's Two Hearted IPA is currently made using only Centennial hops, so pick one up to see if you like the hop or not.

SORACHI ACE

Alpha acids: 10.0–16.0 percent

Unlike Cascade and Centennial, Sorachi Ace has a citrus character all its own. Most brewers describe it as having lemon and dill notes rather than grapefruit and flowers. While beers with too much Sorachi can offend some nostrils, Brooklyn Brewery's Sorachi Ace has proven popular. It's the best bet to see where you stand on this controversial hop.

FRUITY FAVORITES

AMARILLO

Alpha acids: 8.0–11.0 percent

While Amarillo could be considered together with Centennial and Cascade as it has a citrusy character, it also stands apart from those hops with tropical notes. Before Citra became commercially available, Amarillo was the go-to tropical hop. Nowadays, it's more often used in combination with citrusy hops and dank hops for a complex aroma profile.

CITRA

Alpha acids: 11.0–13.0 percent

Melon, lime, lychee, passion fruit—the intoxicating aroma of Citra hops is hard to pin down. The intense and unique tropical bouquet of Citra has made it an instant favorite with American brewers for big IPAs. While some nationwide IPAs use a bit of Citra, your best bet for trying a single-hop version is with the seasonal release of Lagunitas Sucks or at a local brewery. Unless you're lucky enough to live near 3 Floyds, the maker of the popular Citra beer Zombie Dust.

NELSON SAUVIN

Alpha acids: 12.0–13.0 percent

Nelson Sauvin is likely the most popular hop from the Australia/New Zealand hop-growing regions, though other hops like Galaxy and Pacific Jade are increasingly finding their way into US brews. As you might expect from a hop with "Sauvin" in its name, this hop has a unique wine-like character that has made it popular in a wide variety of beers. Sure, it's tasty in an IPA, but brewers like New Belgium have used it in pale lagers like Shift as well with tasty results.

DANK SAUCE

COLUMBUS/TOMAHAWK/ZEUS

Alpha acids: 14.0–16.0 percent

With a high alpha acid content and an attractive dank aroma with hints of citrus, these hops are some of the most popular and readily available to small craft brewers. Unlike proprietary hops like Simcoe and Citra, which are grown by a single company, the three hops referenced here—often referred to by brewers as CTZ—are all more or less the same hop grown under different trade names by different companies. You probably won't find a single-hop beer made with them, but they're in the blend of many popular IPAs made by Lagunitas.

CHINOOK

Alpha acids: 12.0–14.0 percent

While it's not as straight-up dank as Columbus or Simcoe, Chinook is a staple hop and well-known for its distinctive pine aroma and sharp bitterness. Together with Simcoe, it's responsible for the phenomenon of the Pacific Northwest style of IPA. Many say Stone's Arrogant Bastard has a large amount of Chinook, though Stone has that information "classified."

SIMCOE

Alpha acids: 12.0–14.0 percent

Piney, earthy, citrusy, and definitely dank when it's at its best, Simcoe is the closest thing there is to a signature hop for West Coast IPAs. Brewers beware though, some crops of Simcoe can have a cat piss–like aroma! Weyerbacher makes a seasonal called Double Simcoe that features the hop in a big way.

EAST KENT GOLDING (UK)

Alpha acids: 4.0–6.0 percent

Compared to American hops, East Kent Golding (EKG) hops and Fuggles both have a mild character. While Goldings are also grown in the United States, EKG is specific to East Kent and for good reason. Unlike the American counterpart, EKG has a beautifully distinctive bouquet. It's floral, famously tangerine, but with sweet honey and lemon character. Like an herbal tea, it has a trademark spice quality that you have to taste and smell to identify.

FUGGLE (UK)

Alpha acids: 3.5–6.5 percent

Compared to East Kent Goldings, Fuggles are the black sheep. The brewers that love them really love them, but others would be fine never touching the stuff (or drinking a beer made with them). That's because Fuggles have a much different, famously earthy aroma: Many describe them as dirty or tasting like pipe tobacco. They likely wouldn't make a very good IPA, but they can be a crucial part of a delicious British bitter.

HALLERTAU (GERMAN)

Alpha acids: 3.0–5.5 percent

Hallertau is one of the most widely used noble hops, even here in the United States. While it could best be described as herbal or spicy, the real selling point is its smooth bitterness and delicate aroma, which combine to make it the preferred hop for many classic lagers. Macro breweries tend to buy up most of the yearly yields of Hallertau.

SAAZ (GERMAN)

Alpha acids: 2.0–5.0 percent

While Hallertau and other noble hops are sometimes described as spicy, Saaz is the variety of hops that truly brings the spice. It's zippy and a great fit for hybrid styles like a hoppy Belgian blonde. For a classic beer made with Saaz, try a Pilsner Urquell.

HOPS AND BEER STYLES

As I've emphasized a few times through this section and talk about elsewhere in the book, the category of beer styles impacted and characterized the most by hops is the family of pale ales (which includes ambers and browns in this particular circumstance). Hops also play an important role in pilsners, but not any more or less important than the other three ingredients.

To really drive home the impact of hops, let's take a look at a few different American-style pale ales and IPAs that are brewed almost exclusively with one hop varietal and then take a look at a style that has little to no hop influence:

Example 1: Sierra Nevada Pale Ale is hopped almost exclusively with whole cone American Cascade hops, which give the beer its distinct grapefruit and pine aroma and flavors.

Example 2: Bell's Two Hearted Ale is hopped exclusively with Centennial hops, which give the beer its bold bitterness and strong aromas of citrus and pine. While we can't see the recipe from either brewery, it's safe to say that Bell's uses more Centennial both for bittering and for aroma than Sierra Nevada does for its Pale Ale. If Bell's didn't, the beer wouldn't be as bitter or as aromatic.

Example 3: Kern River Citra Double IPA is hopped almost exclusively with Citra hops, which give the beer its distinct aromas of tropical fruit and citrus as well as a significant level of bitterness. If you drank this side by side with Bell's Two Hearted, it would give you a sense of what happens when you make the same beer style with two different hops.

Example 4: Founders Imperial Stout has a bitterness equal to that of the strongest IPAs; generally, it's about 90 IBUs! While you might think it's the dark malts that give this beer its bite, it's actually still hops. Since little to no hops are used late in the boil, you won't get any hop aroma. However, a significant amount of hops were added at the beginning of the boil to get the beer to the 90-IBU level and balance the residual malt sweetness.

Yeast

Yeast are single-celled organisms that belong to the fungi kingdom—yep, mold and mushrooms are their distant cousins. There are about 1,500 different types of yeast, but the most famous is probably Saccharomyces cerevisiae—the yeast used to leaven bread and to ferment wine and ales.

Saccharomyces cerevisiae loves sugar. Heck, all yeast loves sugar. Fermentation is the process of yeast converting sugar into alcohol and carbon dioxide, after all. In breadmaking, the carbon dioxide stays in the dough, causing it to expand and ultimately lightening the final product. The alcohol produced is cooked off in the baking process. The yeast also die in the oven.

Alcoholic beverages are defined as those that contain ethanol, a psychoactive chemical that is almost exclusively produced through fermentation. All alcohol, even distilled spirits, use yeast at some point in the process. The main two types of yeast used in the production of beer are Saccharomyces cerevisiae—ale yeast—and Saccharomyces pastorianus—lager yeast. Ale yeast is often referred to as "top-fermenting" yeast because they form a bubbly foam on the top of fermenting beer. Conversely, lager yeast are called "bottom-fermenting" yeast.

Another factor that differentiates the two types of yeast is fermentation temperature. Ale yeast are often called "warm-fermenting" yeast because they like warmer fermenting environments, typically between 60 and 70 degrees Fahrenheit. Lager yeast are called "cold-fermenting" yeast because lagers are fermented at cooler temperatures, typically between 45 and 55 degrees Fahrenheit.

Maintaining an ideal and stable fermentation temperature is extremely important with both strains of yeast. Ale yeast will actually go dormant, falling asleep when fermentation drops too cold. Lager yeast is still active at higher temperatures but is more likely to produce undesirable by-products and off-flavors in warm environments.

The exception to the temperature rule are hybrid beers, a class of beers that are either fermented with lager yeast at ale temperatures or ale yeast at lager temperatures. Examples of these include the kölsch and alt (beers fermented with ale yeast at lager temperatures) and the California common (a style brewed with lager yeast at warmer temperatures). These styles are explained in-depth in Chapter 3.

During the fermentation of both styles, the yeast is widely distributed throughout the beer, floating up, down, and all around, eating up all the delicious sugar in the wort and turning it into alcoholic beer. It is important to note that fermentation happens in anaerobic conditions, meaning in the absence of oxygen.

It is also important to note that ideal fermentation conditions—warm, wet, and sugary—are also ideal conditions for the growth of bacteria. Bacteria can infect beer and give it really bad off-flavors. Keeping the brewery in a pristine, sterile condition is extremely important. In fact, it's commonly said that cleaning is 90 percent of the brewing process.

ESTERS

Ale yeast is also known for producing lots of esters—chemical compounds that are most often described as being fruity. Esters are produced under warmer fermentation temperatures, which is why they are typically absent from lagers.

Of all the styles, Belgian ales are often fermented at the warmest temperatures. As a result, they tend to be loaded with esters. One of the most common esters found in Belgian ales is isoamyl acetate—the banana and Juicy Fruit gum ester.

The spectrum of fruity esters is seemingly endless—just think about all the fruits out there! Esters reminiscent of apple, pear, peach, kiwi, raisins, figs, pineapple, orange, apricot, plum, and many more can all be detected in ales.

Fancy Science Name	Smell	Fancy Science Name	Smell
Isoamyl acetate	banana	Ethyl benzoate	fruity
Ethyl acetate	fingernail polish remover	Benzyl acetate	peach
		Methyl butyrate	apple
Ethyl salicylate	wintergreen	Octyl acetate	orange
Ethyl butyrate	pineapple	N-propyl acetate	pear
Benzyl butyrate	cherry	Ethyl phenylacetate	honey
Ethyl propionate	rum	Methyl anthranilate	grapes

All things in moderation, though. Higher concentrations of esters can give off a nail polish-like, rancid or sour aroma.

Undesirable By-products of Fermentation

Balanced alcohol, bright effervescence, yummy fruity esters, and some spicy phenols are all awesome and highly desirable by-products of fermentation. But sometimes things go awry in the tank and yeast produces less than desirable compounds. These by-products are usually produced when the yeast is stressed or bacteria finds its way into the fermentation vessels. We will discuss these yeast off-flavors starting on page 134.

ALE YEAST

Saccharomyces cerevisiae is used to ferment a large spectrum of ale styles. As a result, many different types of Saccharomyces cerevisiae exist. These types are typically named for country, region of origin, or style of production. Examples include California ale yeast, English ale yeast, German ale yeast, Australian ale yeast, Trappist ale yeast, Abbey ale yeast, Bavarian Weizen yeast, Belgian wit yeast, Belgian saison yeast, and so on.

Each ale yeast strain has its own distinctive character, which gives many styles their own distinctive aroma and flavor profile. If you don't brew, it's easy to underestimate the impact of yeast on beer. Sure, we all know by now that yeast is responsible for converting maltose into alcohol and CO_2, but how much flavor could those microscopic little things create?

Well, the majority of flavors and aromas in a hefeweizen are, in fact, the result of its fermentation. Traditional Bavarian hefeweizen yeast is responsible for creating the beer's distinct banana, clove, and sometimes apricot or citrus-like aromas and flavors. In fact, anytime you taste banana or clove in a beer it is always the yeast that created it.

What follows are some of the more common yeast strains with their properties, but keep in mind that there are literally hundreds of types of yeasts used and that just about every style of beer has its own unique strain.

ALE YEAST IN YOUR GLASS

CALIFORNIA ALE YEAST

Can be used in almost any American style, but is known for being used in American pale ales and IPAs

When American brewers decided to use hops with more over-the-top flavor and aroma than their British counterparts, they made another excellent decision at the same time: pair them with a yeast that lets the hops shine. California ale yeast is also sometimes called Chico yeast since Sierra Nevada is considered the original source of the culture most yeast companies use. There are variations and other American ale yeasts out there. Most craft brewers use one of them, but some prefer the next yeast on our list: English ale yeast.

ENGLISH ALE YEAST

English ales, bitters, milds, porters, English stouts

The main difference between English ale yeasts and their American counterparts is that the British yeasts bring a lot more flavor and aroma to the party. Rather than being described as clean, they are described as having a stone fruit or sweet character to them, which varies greatly by the source of the yeast. While this might sound undesirable at first, it's actually a good thing for some types of beer, notably those low in alcohol (and thin in body) to begin with. They tend to make a better British-style bitter or sessionable stout than an American yeast.

KÖLSCH YEAST

Kölsch

If you took an American ale yeast and took it to its extreme, and if you made it as lager-like as possible, you'd have a kölsch yeast. Kölsch yeasts keep taste buds super-focused on the malts and hops in a beer, which is perfect for kölsch-style beers. They're typically built on light pilsner malt and have a restrained use of hops. If you used a yeast with a lot of character, it would overwhelm the flavor. But thanks to the kölsch yeast, they drink a lot like a well-made lager, with just a whisper of fruity yeast on the finish.

HEFEWEIZEN YEAST

Hefeweizen, German wheat beer

While you might be able to get away with switching out varieties of clean American or British yeasts in the same recipe, throw in a hefeweizen strain and your beer just got a whole new flavor. Hefeweizen yeasts are responsible for everything you associate with hefeweizen beer. They're notable in that they're the only strain of Saccharomyces cerevisiae that not only packs esters (the banana and citrus notes) but also phenols (the clove and spice). By manipulating things like fermentation temperature, brewers create their own perfect balance of the two. This strain is also the one you find in the dark version of the hefe, its cousin the dunkelweizen.

BELGIAN WIT YEAST

Belgian wits, wheat ales, spiced ales, specialty beers

While some may think hefeweizens and wits are the same thing, the truth is that they're completely different beers. Both have a wheat malt base, but the different yeasts take them in different directions. Wit yeasts leave the beer slightly tart, and any clove or spice notes are much more restrained than in a hefeweizen.

TRAPPIST ALE YEAST

Belgian ale, dubbels, tripels, high-gravity beers

If you're a fan of dubbels or tripels, you're a fan of Trappist yeast cultures. From brewery to brewery these can have quite a range of flavors, but they frequently produce unique tasting notes—think fruit flavors, especially plum, in dubbels.

SAISON YEAST

Saisons

Just like Trappist ale yeasts, saison yeasts vary considerably by brewery. Some are very peppery and spicy while others are earthy and even slightly sweet. Some share clove or other spice notes with their Belgian cousins, but many do not. One thing they all have in common is their love of sugar: Saison yeasts convert a high percentage of it to alcohol, leaving traditional saisons bone dry.

LAGER YEAST

Lagers

Even though lagers make up the majority of beer brewed and consumed in the world today, they are a relatively new family of beer styles. Ales and beers brewed with various wild strains of yeast and bacteria have been around since the beginning of brewing, but lager beers didn't emerge until the 1400s.

As you might guess, lager-style beers originated in Bavaria, Germany. They didn't know exactly what was happening yet, as yeast would not be discovered for another 400 years, but early lager brewers learned pretty quickly that their style of beers needed to be brewed in cold conditions.

Since refrigeration did not come until the late 1800s, lager brewing was originally limited to the colder months. March typically marked the end of the brewing season. It can be assumed that lagers brewed in the summer were extremely inferior (and probably pretty infected and gross) because in 1553, summer brewing was outlawed in Bavaria. What can I say? German brewers are perfectionists in every sense of the word.

Ultimately, yeast was discovered and refrigeration was invented: two pinnacle moments in the history of lager brewing. Both scientific advances have since lead to the perfection of lager brewing. Now, lagers are the most prolific beer style in the world.

Outside of fermentation temperature, the main difference between lager and ale yeast is that lager yeast does not (and should not) release esters. Yeast aromas and flavors should be completely absent from lagers. The only exceptions would be diacetyl and acetaldehyde—natural by-products from fermentation that are acceptable in extremely low concentrations in Bohemian pilseners and American lagers, respectively. (For more about off-flavors, see page 134)

SPONTANEOUS AND WILD FERMENTATION

Not all beer is brewed with lager or ale yeast; some styles are brewed with a combination of wild yeasts and bacteria. Traditionally, these beers were made through spontaneous fermentation, but nowadays brewers have learned how to cultivate and exert influence over fermentation with these wild strains.

Spontaneous fermentation is exactly what it sounds like: fermentation that occurs naturally. Instead of fermenting beer within a sterile temperature-controlled environment, spontaneously fermented beers are exposed to the local air and environment. Lambics are an entire category of beers dedicated to this unique and lengthy fermentation method (see page 88).

Some brewers use coolships—vessels that I think look like giant cookie sheets—to jumpstart the fermentation process by increasing surface area. As one might guess, coolships are also used to cool the wort via the natural coolness of the night air. The cooling wort is exposed to various bacteria and natural yeast at the same time, and the fermentation process begins. In some situations, the wort is left to ferment in the coolships for several months before being transferred to barrels or bottles for secondary fermentation.

Other brewers prefer to transfer the beer to barrels right away, where they then let the natural yeast and bacteria do their thing. It is important to note that a lot of used wine barrels have wild yeast and bacteria of their own living inside them. For that reason, it is not uncommon for one batch of beer to taste different from barrel to barrel.

During spontaneous fermentation, various bacteria and natural yeast take turns converting the sugars in the wort into beer—all while producing their own unique and interesting by-products. One of the most desirable traits developed during spontaneous fermentation is some sourness, as this is one of the ways sour beer is made.

Sour beer can also be made through a more controlled fermentation environment using wild yeast that have been propagated at the brewery or in a laboratory. Either way, the most common types of wild yeast and bacteria predominantly used to make sour and funky beer are Brettanomyces, Pediococcus, and Lactobacillus.

BRETTANOMYCES

The cool kids simply refer to this family of wild yeast as "Brett." Brett is a total sugar addict. It is typically found on the skins of fruits. Brett is mostly considered to be a fault or defect in wine. It can be impossible to control and can essentially ruin wine, but sour beer brewers love it.

Brett is like the Energizer Bunny of yeast. It will eat and eat and eat and eat until every single molecule of sugar is gone or until it's forced to stop. As a result, Brett can produce extremely dry beers and, on rare occasion in total moderation, it is used to dry out various red wines—most notably those from Burgundy, Rhône, and Piedmont.

The easiest way to slow or stop Brett fermentation (or any fermentation for that matter) is to drop the temperature of the beer to cellar temperatures. Brett prefers higher fermentation temperatures and will go dormant at colder temperatures. Keep in mind, however, Brett won't sleep forever. As soon as the bottles and kegs start to warm up, Brett will wake right back up.

There are hundreds of strains of Brett and each has its own distinct character. (The two most common for brewing sour beers and lambics are Brettanomyces bruxellensis and Brettanomyces lambicus.) Brett can be funky, barnyard-like, tropical, horsey, leather-like, and even floral.

PEDIOCOCCUS

Pediococcus, or Pedio for short, belongs to the lactic acid group of bacteria. It is a probiotic commonly added to fermented foods like yogurt, cheese, sauerkraut, and buttermilk. In both beer and food applications, Pedio converts sugar into lactic acid and makes things taste sour. Unfortunately, Pedio also tends to release diacetyl (the butter compound)—something chardonnay producers might enjoy, but most brewers hate. This is why Pedio is almost always partnered with Brett, which will literally eat anything, including diacetyl.

LACTOBACILLUS

Lactobacillus, or Lacto for short, is kind of like the gang leader of the lactic acid group. It is the primary bacteria used in the production of yogurt, sauerkraut, pickles, cider, kimchi, and other fermented foods. It is also the microorganism responsible for giving sourdough bread its signature sourness. Like its cousin Pedio, Lacto is considered a "good bacteria" and an important probiotic. When used in brewing, Lacto converts the sugar in the wort into lactic acid, giving beer a sour, almost yogurt-like flavor.

The Poetry of Esters

Julia Herz of the Brewers Association—one of my most cherished friends and valued mentors—collected a handful of super creative poems about esters from a few highly respected craft brewers in the United States. She originally published the poems in a CraftBeer.com article post called "The Poetry of Esters" and, with permission, I am republishing those poems here.

TRIOLET ON THE JOYS OF ISOAMYL ACETATE AND HER PALS

By Ethan Cox | president and co-founder | Community Beer Works | Buffalo, New York

Behold the esters of your beer:
banana, peardrop, apple-like
The brewer's charge, an overseer
Behold the esters of your beer:
(restrained, as not to interfere)
roses, honey, solvent-spike!
Behold the esters of your beer:
banana, peardrop, apple-like.

AN ODE TO ESTERS

By Jason Oliver | head brewer | Devils Backbone Brewing Company | Roseland, Virginia

Esters, esters, are good for the beer.
How you ferment is how they'll appear.
Much less in a lager than in an ale,
Swirl your glass around and pleasantly inhale.

O ESTER MY ESTER

By Seth Gross | owner | Bull City Burger and Brewery | Durham, North Carolina

There's something on my mind regarding esters
If I don't let out the thought it just festers

Chemical compounds with nuances of fruit
Aromas expelled when our yeasts toot

If you find your ale a little off or bland
Watch your pitch rates from the corny can

Keep your temperatures proper or at least up high
You'll achieve the flavors that'll make you cry

Tears of joy from apricots, pineapple and banana
Tears of pain if nail polish . . .
. . . Wipe your eyes with a bandana

ESTERS HAIKU ONE

By Seth Wright | brewer | Wachusett Brewing Company | Westminster, Massachusetts

Yeast stress shall dictate
Levels of isoamyl acetate
Brewers salivate

ESTERS HAIKU TWO

By Grant Pauly | owner | 3 Sheeps Brewing Co. | Sheboygan, Wisconsin

Be gone orange slice,
You have no place in my glass,
Esters reign supreme!

In fact, water is arguably the most crucial ingredient in brewing. Beer is made up of around 90 to 95 percent water, by mass, after all. However, it might surprise you that the amount of water it takes to produce beer is far greater than the amount of water in the actual beer itself.

Water is needed in just about every step of the brewing process, not just in the end product (the beer). Brewers often joke that 90 percent of brewing is cleaning and all of that incessant cleaning requires gallons upon gallons of water. Water is needed to clean everything in the brewery—from the kettles to the fermenting tanks to the floor, the bottling line, the keg machine, and so on.

The average brewery uses five to eight gallons of water to produce one gallon of beer. The more efficient and conscientious breweries can use as little as two or three gallons of water, while the less efficient breweries can use up to ten gallons of water for one gallon of beer. For obvious reasons—both environmental and economic—water conservation is a huge topic of discussion for brewers today.

HARD VS. SOFT WATER

Not all water is created equal. Think about your experience with tap water—and not just drinking it, but showering or washing dishes with it. Hard water tends to be rich in minerals like calcium and magnesium. Soap does not lather up well with hard water, and it tends to leave hair and skin feeling dry and dull—and dishes spotty and filmy. Conversely, soft water contains few or no extra elements and soap lathers up really well in it.

When it comes to brewing, some styles work better with hard water, while some styles require soft water. Many styles are actually characterized by the type of water with which they are brewed. The Bohemian pilsener is traditionally brewed with soft water, while German pilsners are brewed with hard water. Many brewers also believe hitting certain mineral profiles with water can improve pale ales and IPAs.

PH

Of all the ways water can impact the overall outcome of beer, pH is probably the most important factor to control. In chemistry, pH is a measure of the acidity of a water-based solution. Pure water has a pH of 7, which is considered to be neutral. Solutions below 7 are considered to be acidic, while solutions above 7 are considered alkaline or basic.

To put things into perspective, lemon juice gets its sour taste from citric acid, which has a pH of 2.2. Milk has a neutral pH between 6 and 7, and ammonia is highly alkaline with a pH of 11 to 12.

The pH level is important in the mash, the boil, and fermentation. To put it plainly, brewing at optimal pH levels makes beer better. In fact, excellent beer requires perfect pH. Enzymes require a certain pH for efficient conversion of starch into sugar. Yeast requires a certain pH for efficient conversion of sugar into alcohols. The color of beer depends on the pH. Flavor, mouthfeel, head retention all depends on, you guessed it, pH!

Burtonizing Water

Why would brewers go through the trouble of adding minerals to water when soft water is perfect for brewing? Hard water can improve hop-centric beers like pale ales and IPAs. The English brewers in Burton-on-Trent were the first to discover this around 1822, when they started to brew versions of the increasingly popular pale ales of London. What they, and the rest of the brewing world, found was that the sulfate-rich hard water of Burton made pale ales taste cleaner, crisper, and downright hoppier. Nowadays, some brewers choose to mimic the hard water of Burton by adding calcium sulfates, mostly in the form of gypsum, to many styles of beer, including, but not limited to, pale ales, IPAs, German pilsners, stouts, porters, and saisons. In homage to the place of origin, it's often called Burtonizing the water.

Note: Outside of hardening brewing water, gypsum is a coagulant in tofu making, a primary ingredient in plaster, and used as a binder in fast-dry tennis court clay.

The main benefits of brewing within an optimal pH range:

Increased enzymatic activity in the mash

More zinc, an essential yeast nutrient, in the solution

Faster fermentation and greater attenuation of beer

Improved filterability

More rounded, fuller, and softer beer

Crisper, more fresh, beer that shows more character

More pleasant hop bitterness that doesn't linger

More stable and denser foam

A lighter color of beer

Improved haze stability

Reduced susceptibility to microbial spoilage

chapter eleven

EVALUATING BEER

If you've made it this far, you've learned about the various styles of beer, how beer is made, and the ingredients that go into it. Now it's time to drink—errrr—taste it. While tasting beer can certainly be as detailed and intense as tasting wine, in this book we're not preparing for an exam. That means we'll cover the basics of how to evaluate beer, but we'll also have some fun. Speaking of beer, is your glass empty? You're going to want to grab a beer for this section. Trust me.

Starting with Ideal Tasting Conditions

If you're out having a beer for fun, chances are you can't control the conditions. Poor lighting, food aromas, smoke, perfume, and even noise are a fact of life—and they all impede our ability to objectively taste and evaluate beer. However, if you intend to taste beer for educational rather than recreational purposes, I highly recommend controlling everything you can. Set yourself up in a proper tasting environment. Overall, think neutral—neutral aromas, neutral sounds, neutral lighting, and so on. Keep the focus on the beer. Below are some key things to keep in mind.

Time of day matters: When you taste beer can have a surprisingly big impact on your overall perception of it. Think of your nose as if it were powered by batteries: the more you use it, the less juice it has. As you go about your daily life, your nose is experiencing all sorts of sensations—fresh cut grass, car exhaust in traffic, your co-worker's Chinese takeout, your boyfriend's cologne, the sweaty gym, and so on. By the end of the day, your nose is drained from its eight-hour-long smell-a-thon. This is why midmorning is typically the best time of day to do a pro-style beer evaluation. Give your nose and tongue just enough time to wake up, but not enough time to exhaust it to the point of no return.

Don't ruin your palate: This might sound obvious, but *do not drink coffee or smoke cigarettes* right before you taste beer. It is, however, important to eat before tasting beer. Alcohol on an empty stomach can quickly impair your ability to properly evaluate beer, after all. Just avoid spicy and heavily seasoned foods, especially garlic. Opt for a nice, bland, oatmealy breakfast.

Neutralize yourself and the room: Avoid wearing perfume, cologne, lotion, lipstick/gloss, hairspray, body spray, and pretty much anything that smells like anything. Even neutral ChapStick is a no-no since oils can flatten the head of a beer. Fragrance-free shampoos, soaps, and deodorants are ideal, but really, as long as you didn't just jump out of the shower your normal products are likely just fine. As far as the room goes, you want to make it odor free, of course. You should also make sure it's not too noisy or crowded, and that it's well lit. As any test-taker knows, noise can quickly affect your concentration. And if you can't clearly see the beer, you're robbing yourself of key visual data.

Use tasting glassware: In some situations, using a plastic cup is unavoidable. However, if you're organizing a tasting in your own home, use clean glassware instead—and do not use the same glass for multiple beers unless you thoroughly clean it between pours. Proper glassware typically doesn't matter in this case, especially since you'll likely be pouring small quantities. (Speaking of which: If you plan to taste multiple beers, definitely limit yourself to small pours.) Personally, I find brandy snifters to be a nice choice for a tasting glass. You can easily swirl the beer around the glass, agitate it a bit, and get a good whiff of its aroma. However, if you are evaluating one beer in its entirety, pouring it into its recommended glassware will of course be the closest way to evaluate it under its own ideal serving conditions.

Cleanse your palate—heck, cleanse your nose: It's always smart to have a glass of water as well as some unsalted water crackers or white bread on hand. In multiple beer tastings, you'll need all the help you can get to neutralize and refocus your palate. Sometimes, when tasting and evaluating several beers in a short period of time, you'll find it's not just your mouth getting tired. The nose can get overwhelmed, rendering it desensitized and making it extremely hard to detect aromas. It might sound weird (or gross), but one of the best ways to bring your nose back to center is to smell yourself. Yep, put your nose on your arm, heck go for the armpit, and give yourself a few sniffs. If there is one smell that your nose knows best, it's you. It's like a palate cleanse, but for your nose.

Tasting Beer

There are basically two ways to conduct a group beer tasting: open tasting or blind tasting. In other words, you either know what the beer is ahead of time or you taste it blind with no prior knowledge. There are advantages to both methods. If you are tasting beer to train your palate on a particular style, it is helpful to know about the beer and the brewery before tasting it, but if you are tasting beer to test your palate and knowledge, then blind tasting is the way to go.

When tasting beer, beer judges primarily evaluate four key areas:

Appearance

Aroma

Flavor

Mouthfeel

APPEARANCE

You know the saying, "You eat with your eyes first"? Well, the same applies to beer. The first sip happens as soon as you look at it. It's no wonder whenever you see a beer commercial it features at least one shot of a freshly poured or pouring beer!

In addition to whetting your thirst, a beer's appearance can tell you a lot about it. The most obvious is color, which is the first clue to the style. Is it golden, orange, red, brown, or black? This will help you narrow down the beer to a few categories, and you'll likely be able to anticipate some of the aroma and taste by color alone.

Next, observe the beer's clarity. Is it hazy and cloudy, or brilliant and clear? Some styles are famous for their cloudy appearance, like wits, while others like lagers tend to be super brilliant. Many beer styles can go either way though depending on the preferences of the brewer. Haze can simply mean the beer is unfiltered, or it can be a sign the beer was made with a large amount of hops.

Last but not least, observe the finer details. Look at the head, head retention, and lacing. How effervescent does the beer appear to be? How much head was there when you first poured the beer? How quickly did it dissipate? As you drink the beer, does it leave behind a firm rim of lacing with every sip? Or does it appear flat? The answer can vary greatly with style. For example, a Belgian-style tripel may have a large, fluffy head that laces down the glass while a British-style bitter may have hardly any head at all due to its low carbonation.

AROMA

Now it's time to smell the beer. But wait! Before we take a sniff, let's talk briefly about smell vs. taste.

Technically speaking, your tongue can only detect five basic taste sensations: sweet, salty, bitter, sour, and umami. Everything else is smell. In fact, it is estimated that 75 to 90 percent of what we taste is actually smell. The sensation of flavor, as a whole, is actually a combination of taste and smell; both need to work in tandem.

It took me a while to learn this lesson. When tasting wine, I had a habit of saying "this smells sweet." I was told repeatedly that was an incorrect observation. Eventually, I did realize that while you taste sweet, you can't smell it. What you smell is actually fruit (cherry, raisin, fig, apple, etc.), caramel, toffee, brown sugar, and honey—things that make you think of a sweet taste. However, you don't smell the actual sweet.

When smelling a beer for the first time, take three separate sniffs before making an observation about it. First, stick your nose in the glass and inhale deeply, purging your nose of any other smells. Then, take two shorter sniffs. Before you even take that first sip, aroma can tell you a lot about a beer. Here are a few things to consider:

Are there fruity esters on the nose or is it clean? This will help you figure out if the beer is an ale or a lager. (Ales tend to have fruity esters where lagers have extremely clean, ester-less aromas.)

Is the aroma balanced more toward the malt or toward the hops?

What type of malt notes are you getting? Is the aroma biscuity, nutty, toasty, roasty, chocolaty, toffee, or coffee-like?

Is the hop presence strong or not? What hop notes do you detect? Do you smell spicy, earthy, floral noble hops or citrusy, pine-like American hops?

What other yeast character do you detect? Do you detect spicy phenols?

Are there undesirable aromas like DMS, skunk, or diacetyl present (see page 135)?

FLAVOR

Now, it's finally time to put the beer in your mouth. As with wine tasting, I find it is ideal to breathe in with your nose while taking a sip, in order to get the full sensory experience. Allow the beer to fully cover your tongue, lightly swirling it around your mouth, before swallowing it.

Yep, unlike with wine, in beer tasting you swallow. One reason I've been told is that there are important flavor receptors at the back of your throat and that swallowing is the only way to reach them. Granted, I've never done the research to prove this theory true, but in this particular instance, ignorance is bliss. Also, most beer tastings you'll do with friends are informal drinking occasions, so what's the point in spitting?

When it comes to taste, there are all sorts of elements to consider. There are the palate sensations as well as the flavors. Here are some things to consider:

Is the beer balanced toward the hops or the malt?

What kind of malt flavors do you detect—biscuit, toast, caramel, chocolate, rye, smoke, wheat, etc.?

What impression do you get from the hops? Are they super strong and resinous on your tongue or is there little to no hop presence? Do they leave your palate dry and tingly or are they subtle, earthy, and spicy?

What kind of yeast characteristics are you picking up? Is the beer fruity? Is it funky? Is it sour? Or is it just super clean?

Do you detect any undesirable flavors or flaws?

How did tasting the beer compare to what you expected when you had only seen and smelled the beer? What stayed the same? What changed?

MOUTHFEEL

Mouthfeel typically talks to the weight of the beer, the carbonation, alcohol presence, and the finish.

Is the body of the beer light, medium, or medium-high?

Is the beer well carbonated, or does it have low carbonation?

Does the beer finish dry, crisp, and clean, or does it have some residual sweetness? Is there a lingering bitterness on the finish?

Is the alcohol detectable? Is there an alcohol burn?

Which flavors linger the longest?

OVERALL IMPRESSION

After evaluating the appearance, aroma, flavor, and mouthfeel, it's time to give the beer an overall assessment. Did it fit the style guidelines? What were some positive attributes about the beer and what were some of the things you didn't like? How drinkable was the beer? And, most important: Did you like it?

Off-flavors: Stuff You Should (Almost) Never Taste

Have you ever taken a sip of beer and thought to yourself something just isn't right? Well, before you start questioning your palate, let's discuss the not-so-desirable flavors that can be present in beer. With more and more craft breweries opening every day, and with many of them producing beer as fast as they can, mistakes can happen. Fermentations can be a little too rushed. And of course, the brewery can only control the beer until it leaves the door. Bars and retail stores can certainly ruin a good beer with poor storage or serving conditions.

It is important to note that some off-flavors are acceptable or appropriate in certain styles. For example diacetyl, which has a buttery aroma, is usually a flaw. However, it can be both to style and pleasant in small amounts for some British beers. For the most part though, the following compounds and chemicals are considered flaws.

ACETALDEHYDE

Flavor/aroma: If you're smelling a green apple aroma from your beer, first double-check that someone didn't pour you a cider. If it is indeed beer, you've got yourself acetaldehyde off-flavors.

Cause: It's a by-product of fermentation. Various causes include premature removal of the wort/beer from the yeast, premature flocculation (the yeast quits early), and oxygen depletion.

Acceptable? Acetaldehyde is inappropriate for most styles, but low levels are acceptable for some American lagers (most famously, Budweiser).

ALCOHOLIC

Flavor/aroma: True, some big barleywines can warm you from the inside out, but that sensation is welcome. In a pale ale? Not so much. Most beer should never have an aggressively hot, warming sensation on the lips, tongue, and back of throat.

Cause: High levels of ethanol, sometimes referred to as fusel alcohols, typically come from a rushed or hot fermentation.

Acceptable? A moderate and pleasant amount is appropriate in higher alcohol styles like barleywines and bocks.

ASTRINGENT

Flavor/aroma: Tannic, mouth-drying beer is unpleasant. If you're trying to describe it, some say it's reminiscent of grape skins.

Cause: Over-milling the barley, excessive high-temperature sparge, high-sulfate water, bacteria, and excessive hopping can all be culprits.

Acceptable? Nope.

ISOVALERIC ACID

Flavor/aroma: Often simply referred to as cheesy, isovaleric acid is a rare off-flavor. It can also come across as sweat or must.

Cause: It's a compound released by old hops, so somebody should have thrown them out and bought fresh hops before they brewed.

Acceptable? Nope.

DIACETYL

Flavor/aroma: If you take a sip of beer and feel like you're at the movies, chances are you're sipping on one with some diacetyl. Diacetyl tastes so much like butter, the compound is actually used to flavor some prepackaged popcorns.

Cause: Diacetyl is a natural by-product of fermentation, but the yeast usually takes care of it before the beer ever makes it to the keg or bottle. It is present in beers that were prematurely racked, meaning pulled off the yeast before the fermentation was complete.

Acceptable? Low levels are appropriate in some styles including Scotch ales, English bitters, dry stouts, and Czech pilseners.

DIMETHYL SULFIDE (DMS)

Flavor/aroma: Cooked corn, stewed vegetables, and cabbage: If these aromas are noticeable in your beer, feel free to send it back.

Cause: The precursor S-methyl-methionine occurs naturally in the endosperm of the grain. It turns to DMS with heat and evaporates during the boil. If the DMS is not boiled off properly, it will remain in the wort and, ultimately, the final product.

Acceptable? Low concentrations of the cooked corn variety can be appropriate in light lagers and cream ales.

METALLIC

Flavor/aroma: Rusty coins and iron may not be familiar flavors, but just think of the last time you bit your lip. If you taste that metallic twang, similar to blood, you have yourself this off-flavor.

Cause: Metallic flavors can be extracted from metal brewing equipment, bottle caps, kegs, or from using water with high iron content.

Acceptable? Typically undesirable but very low levels can be tolerable.

OXIDATION, CARDBOARD (ALSO CALLED TRANS-2-NONENAL)

Flavor/aroma: Cardboard, wet paper, and stale bread are common descriptors for oxidation.

Cause: Exposure to oxygen and age are the two main culprits.

Acceptable? No.

OXIDATION, SHERRY-LIKE

Flavor/aroma: While the bad oxidation, the kind caused by unintentional oxygen pickup at some stage, tastes like cardboard, there is another kind of oxidation. When properly made and stored beer is cellared, it can take on sherry, vinous (wine-like), dried fruit, and leather notes thanks to a slower oxidation process.

Causes: Aging or cellaring high-alcohol beers is the main way beer develops these flavors.

Acceptable? This form of oxidation can be appropriate for aged strong beers like barleywines, strong Belgian ales, imperial stouts, and English old ales.

PHENOLIC

Flavor/aroma: Band-Aid, clove-like, medicinal, plastic—phenolic flavors can vary a bit, depending on the cause.

Cause: Some phenols are released by specific yeast strains at certain temperatures, while others occur from improper sanitation or chlorophenols in the brewing water.

Acceptable? Clove phenols are appropriate in many Belgian and wheat styles, but Band-Aid or plastic phenols are never to style and are considered a flaw.

SKUNKED/LIGHT–STRUCK

Flavor/aroma: This is the classic green-bottle beer off flavor: skunky with a touch of sulfur.

Cause: Light reacting with isomerized alpha acids—in other words, beer is exposed to light. Beer stored in clear or green bottles is the most susceptible to skunking. Technically minded folks refer to this flaw as Mercaptan.

Acceptable? No (and easily avoidable, too).

SOLVENT-LIKE

Flavor/aroma: Solvent-like off-flavors can come off similar to alcoholic ones, though they're typically a bit more offensive: think paint thinner or nail polish remover aroma with a burning sensation in the throat.

Cause: Phenols released at high fermentation temperatures can get solvent-like, and oxidation causes them, too. It's rare, but if a brewer lets wort or beer come into contact with plastic that isn't food grade, that can be a cause as well.

Acceptable? No.

SOUR/ACIDIC (INFECTION)

Flavor/aroma: Sour beers can be a beautiful thing (see page 88); however, unintentionally soured beer is rarely tasty. Most come across as tart but vinegar-like.

Cause: Wild yeast or acid-creating bacteria like lactobacillus, pediococcus, or acetobacter (bad bacteria) are the primary culprits. Unintentional infection with these microbes occurs due to poor sanitation practices.

Acceptable? Yes, but only when the brewer intends it. Sourness is appropriate in lambic styles, Flanders ales, Berliner weisse, gose, some barrel-aged beers, and on occasion, witbiers and saisons.

SULFUR

Flavor/aroma: While no off-flavors sound appealing, there's not much worse than a big whiff of sulfur. Think rotten eggs, struck match, garlic, or burnt rubber.

Cause: Bacterial contamination, wild yeast, and rapid temperature changes to fermenting wort can all cause sulfur production.

Acceptable? Not usually, but hydrogen sulfide can be a positive attribute in fresh German beer and Burton-on-Trent pale ales.

chapter twelve

RESPECTING BEER

In a perfect world, beer would always be served in the perfect glass at the perfect temperature. The beer would have been perfectly stored and the glass would be perfectly clean. Now, what if I told you that you could easily live in this perfect little world? This chapter will show you how.

One important note: there will always be circumstances that trump perfect drinking conditions. Sometimes you need a beer at the beach, in a canoe, or while hiking, biking, camping—*I think you know where I'm going with this*. Remember that, first and foremost, beer should be fun. Being a stickler about proper glassware can be a good thing, but no one likes a beer snob, or broken glass in the canoe for that matter.

Storing Beer

Once a beer leaves the hands of the brewer, it becomes extremely vulnerable. The more it changes hands, the greater the risk it will not be as fresh-tasting when it reaches you. As with most perishable products, packaged beer has three main enemies: light, heat, and oxygen—all of which will expedite the aging process of beer and all of which can completely ruin a beer.

Regardless of package type, beer should always be stored in cool, dark places. Kegs and cans are inherently protected from light, but they are not protected from heat. Since light, especially sunlight, can also be a source of heat, the darker the storage space the better.

Pale lagers and hoppier beer styles are most susceptible to light damage. When UV light hits the beer, it breaks up the chemical compounds in hops, releasing a chemical found in skunk spray. When this happens, these beers are often called light-struck or skunked. When it comes to preventing skunked beer, the bottle color is important. Clear glass is the worst, since it lets through absolutely everything. Blue and green are bad, too. Brown is the most protective color of glass; it blocks 98 percent of the light rays that skunk beer. Cans, kegs, ceramic bottles, and bottles in closed-case boxes offer the best protection from light.

If you want to train your palate to recognize the effects of light damage, one of the best ways to do so is to grab two green bottles of the same pilsner. Expose one of the green bottles to light. It only takes a few seconds, but leave it out for a few minutes for good measure. Put both in the refrigerator for a few hours, pop them open and taste them side-by-side. The difference should be very noticeable.

Freshness

The general rule of thumb is that when a beer is released from the brewery, it is ready to drink. Beer almost always tastes best when it is consumed fresh.

Lower alcohol beers and hop-forward styles are the most vulnerable to aging, which may seem odd considering that hops have preservative properties that assist with the shelf life and stability of beer. However, even though hops can help a beer last longer (when properly stored), hop flavor and aroma rapidly deteriorates over time—especially when hoppy beers are stored at room temperature. Low-alcohol beers are the most susceptible to harmful aging conditions. Light, heat, and oxygen will destroy lower alcohol beers (especially pale lagers) the quickest.

If you're ever ordering beer for a restaurant or bar, inspect the dates on the keg and cases of beer before receiving them. Most larger beer distributors rotate inventory and destroy old beer, which lowers the chance of being sold old beer. But, it's still important to check the dates upon delivery (just in case). After the beer is received, it's important to rotate the beer. Sell the oldest beer first, then restock with the next oldest and so on. Even if you're just picking up a beer at the store, it's important to check any dating on the package, especially for those hoppy beers.

Beer stays freshest and lasts longest when kept consistently refrigerated—or at least at a constant temperature. Extreme changes in temperature (like going from a refrigerator to a hot car to a refrigerator) are not good for beer. Even beer stored consistently at room temperature will last much longer than beer stored at varying degrees of temperature. The most optimal condition is constant refrigeration, though.

Since the majority of craft beer sold is not pasteurized, refrigerated draft beer is good for around 45 to 60 days (pasteurized beer can last about 90 to 120 days). Bottled beer can be good for up to six months if it's kept refrigerated and up to three months when its not. Again though, the fresher the better when it comes to hoppy or low-alcohol beers.

CELLARING BEER

Unlike wine, very few beers are brewed with the intention of being aged. The assumption is the other way around: Most beer leaves the brewery at the exact moment the brewery feels it is ready for the consumer. That means even barrel-aged beers, sour beers, and other beers that benefit from aging are often aged right inside the brewery before they ever reach the beer-drinking public.

However, many beers can change over time and develop desirable characteristics if aged at cellar temperatures. Can a beer get better over time? That is debatable from beer to beer and from person to person for the same beer. What's not debatable is that all beer changes over time, and that most beers will have some obvious changes in just a year or two. There are few beers that truly benefit from a decade or more of cellaring.

So what style of beer should you look for if you're inclined to collect and savor later? There are a few options. Most beers with high alcohol levels (above 8 percent) can change and often improve with age—the exception being double IPAs and imperial IPAs since hops don't age well. Imperial stouts and barleywines are perhaps the most popular styles of beer for aging. Both have a rich malt character that will develop ever-evolving flavor notes as they age.

Many bottle-conditioned Belgian-style beers are also great candidates for aging. In fact, bottle-conditioned beers were originally designed for cellaring. Since the yeast is still active in bottle-conditioned beers, it keeps working slowly and actually helps the flavors evolve. The yeast also slowly increases the carbonation level of the beer, which is why bottle-conditioned beers need to be stored and opened carefully. These beers should be stored upright. Whatever you do, don't agitate the yeast. If the bottle is accidentally shaken, give it a few hours to settle down before serving.

Examples of bottle-conditioned beers that can be cellared include many Trappist and Abbey ales—like St. Bernardus Abt 12, Orval, Westmalle Tripel, and Westvletern 12—many farmhouse ales (like Saison Dupont), and many sour beers and lambics (like Russian River Sanctification and Cantillon Classic Gueuze). Like fine wines, bottle-conditioned beers develop new flavors and aromas as they age.

BEER STYLES FIT FOR THE CELLAR

Baltic porters
Barleywines
Barrel-aged beers
Belgian tripels, dubbels, farmhouse beers
Doppelbocks and eisbocks
Imperial stouts
Sour beers (lambics, wood-aged, etc.)
Wee heavy/Scotch ales

UNFIT FOR CELLARING

Pale ales (browns, ambers, etc.)
Pilsners and most lagers
IPAs and double IPAs

The ideal time to age a beer depends on the beer itself. Often there's no clear recommendation, and the best thing to do is to buy multiple bottles of a beer you like and try them at regular intervals. This sort of experimentation can be taken pretty far. I have had some really old beers before—aged for more than ten or fifteen years. Some of them have been outstanding, some of them not so much. I would say five to ten years is a solid time window for most imperial styles. Some bottle-conditioned Belgian beers and some sour beers can develop even longer than that.

One of the best ways to observe the effects of cellaring on a beer is to drink what's called a vertical tasting of a certain brand of beer. A vertical refers to a lineup of the same beer brewed by the same brewery from different years. This may sound time-intensive and expensive—and it can be. However, it can easily be done with an affordable strong beer, such as Sierra Nevada's Bigfoot Barleywine. Also, some beer bottle shops have started cellaring beers for consumers. You may very well be able to find a four- to six-year vertical put together for you with only a minor upcharge for the convenience.

If you're fascinated by cellaring and think it might be for you, I recommend cataloguing the beers as you collect them and keeping a good set of notes. If the bottle doesn't have a packaging date on it, use a metallic marker to write the purchase date and or year on the bottle. Keep a cellar log with the name of the brewery, the brand, and the brew date or date of purchase, and the location of the beer (whether it's in a box, on a shelf, or in a refrigerator). There's nothing worse than turning a carefully planned cellar purchase into a mystery beer!

Pouring Beer

Serving beer, for the most part, is straightforward. Beer should be served cold, but not too cold, and in a clean glass.

The perfect pour isn't rocket science; it's just about controlling foam. When pouring from a bottle, tilt the glass at a 45-degree angle and pour down the side of the glass until the glass is about two-thirds full, then straighten the glass and slowly pour the rest of the beer into it. If it's a bottle-conditioned beer, you will need to pour it slower than usual and keep the glass tilted longer than usual. Bottle-conditioned beers tend to be more highly carbonated than normal beers, so you just need to keep the pour slow.

When it comes to pouring beer from a tap, the first thing to remember is to open the tap completely. Always pull the tap handle back *all the way* to allow the full flow of beer. Pouring from a partially opened faucet creates a foamy mess. Tilt the glass 45 degrees toward the tap but *do not* touch the glass to the tap (that is how bacteria spreads). Do not put the tap in the beer glass, either. Keep the glass tilted until it's about half full, then pour the beer straight down into the glass, filling it until there is one inch (two fingers' worth) of foam for the head. *Note:* the tap nozzle should never ever come into contact with the beer in the glass.

TEMPERATURE (BOTTLES)

Sadly, the marketing departments of large corporate breweries have brainwashed many people into thinking that beer needs to be served as cold as possible. While extremely cold beer can be refreshing, it numbs the tongue, preventing a great tasting experience as well as preventing the detectability of some aromas. Also, since beers that lack flavor and imagination don't necessarily benefit from warmer serving temperatures the same way as more complex beers, it's important that they are served as cold as possible. If there's not much to taste, it might as well be refreshing, right?

Craft beer, on the other hand, should not be served ice cold. It also shouldn't be served at room temperature or too warm. The sweet spot for most beers is somewhere between 38 and 59 degrees Fahrenheit. On average, beer should be poured a few degrees cooler than the optimal serving temperature so that the beer can slowly warm up to the desired drinking temperature while you're drinking it. What is the optimal serving temperature? It varies a bit by style and the intensity of the beer:

Cold: Lighter styles of beer are best served cold, between 39 and 45 degrees Fahrenheit. Beers in this group include the kölsch, helles, pilsner, Berliner weisse, Belgian wit, black lagers, lighter American wheat Beers, lighter summer seasonal beers, and lambics.

Cool: Most medium-bodied, medium-alcohol beers should be served cool, but not too cold, somewhere between 45 and 50 degrees Fahrenheit. This includes pale ales, amber ales, browns, blondes, golden ales, hefeweizens, stouts, porters, dunkels, dark wheat beers, tripels, dark sour ales, amber lagers, and bocks. When in doubt, serve beer in this temperature range. It can always warm up to cellar temp.

Cellar: Fuller bodied beers with higher levels of alcohol and complex malt and hop flavors should be served at cellar temperatures—typically between 54 and 57 degrees Fahrenheit. Cask-conditioned beers should also be served at cellar temperatures. Beers that should be served at cellar temps include India pale ales, imperial/double IPAs, other imperial styles, dark Abbey beers, dubbels, barleywines, Baltic porters, bocks and doppelbocks, bitters, premium bitters, old ales, bière de gardes, and Belgian strong ales.

TEMPERATURE (DRAFT)

When it comes to serving temperatures, draft beer is totally a different beast. Most American draft beer dispensing systems have been standardized to store and pour beer at a constant 38 degrees Fahrenheit. This means that all the beer in the draft system, regardless of style, will dispense at the same super-cold temperature.

For obvious reasons, this poses a challenge for any restaurant or bar wishing to pour its beers at optimal serving temperatures. It is increasingly common for bars to work with a draft technician or buy a customized draft system with temperature control. However, if you find yourself at a bar where all draft beer is served on the cold side, you do have some options.

You can order your beer in a bottle instead, of course. If it arrives too cold, there's no harm letting it warm up tableside for a couple of minutes before you pour it in a glass. You can stick to a pilsner or other light beer on draft, since it will likely be fairly close to the temperature you want. Or you can see if the bar has any thinner glassware, such as tulips or snifters. The thin glassware will let you order a beer on the cold side and warm it up quickly with the ambient temperature, or the warmth of your hands.

Glassware

Oh, glassware, where do we begin? Some experts can get pretty snobbish about glassware, arguing all the reasons why every single beer needs to be partnered with its most perfect glass. While those opinions aren't entirely without merit, I do think that the glassware argument tends to get a little more pretentious than it needs to be.

Let's start at the beginning: What's the advantage of a glass over drinking straight from the bottle or the can? In a word: aroma. Canned beers in particular are awesome for many reasons. They are lighter to carry and can be smashed after consumption, which makes them ideal for "carry in, carry out" adventures like hiking, camping, rafting, and so on. But the tough part about cans is that, although they look cool to drink from, they prevent you from being able to smell the beer, which means you will never fully taste what's inside.

One of my first epiphanies regarding glassware happened with a double IPA in a can. I cracked it open, ready to enjoy what the rest of the world was bragging out. I took a sip, straight from the can. And all I tasted was bitter. Not a good hoppy bitterness but a really bad, off-putting bitterness. My mouth was not happy. I was not happy. And I was confused. What was the big deal about this beer?

Then I poured the can into a glass and gave the beer a big whiff. There it was—the citrus, the pine, and the grapefruit pith from the hops. I took a sip and instantly the beer was better. It was brighter. It was no longer one-dimensional. It had real character. But I would never have known this if I hadn't poured it into a glass. This makes sense since so much of what we taste comes from what we smell.

Ray Daniels, from the Certified Cicerone program, created a great exercise that does an even better job of proving how important your nose is to the overall tasting experience. He places a bunch of red jelly beans into a bag with instructions to plug your nose; then he has you put the jelly bean in your mouth, chew for ten seconds, and then open your mouth.

Appearance is a lot, but it isn't everything. Red dye No. 40 isn't exactly a spoiler; it still could be cherry, fruit punch, raspberry, cinnamon, or something else. When you plug your nose, your tongue is the only thing doing the work. A random red jelly bean on the tongue tastes like sugar—and that's about it.

When I tried this out, most people made the assumption that the jelly bean was flavored like cherry. But when they unplugged their nose: bam, cinnamon in their face. I was right there with those tasters and that test blew my mind. Cinnamon is an extremely potent flavor, but, without the nose, my tongue only tasted sugar.

Pouring a beer into a glass, first and foremost, lets you savor the full jelly bean, as it were. The aroma will open up in a big way. However, you also get loads of other sensory data. You get to see its color, which tells you a bit about the malt blend. You also get to observe a beer's clarity and carbonation. Is it filtered (clear), is it hazy, does the head linger or dissipate, are there ribbons of foam left on the glass with each sip? Without decanting a beer into a glass, you would never know.

When it comes to special glassware for different types of beer, I'll be the first to admit that it can enhance the experience. It will not dramatically change the beer, however. At the end of the day, a bad beer is going to taste bad regardless of the shape or size of the glassware, and a good beer is always going to taste good. Can a glass make a good beer taste better? Yes, it can.

Let me explain with an example. Years ago, I was a competitive swimmer. My best event was the shortest event. If you aren't familiar with the idiosyncrasies and oddities of the swimming world, I apologize for this story now. Swimmers—especially sprinters—typically stop shaving their legs toward the end of the season, before the championship meet. On race day, they shave down—arms, legs, heads (for the men), you name it. Why? Swimming is an extremely mental sport. The act of shaving was supposed to make our bodies more streamlined and faster through the water. Most people who shaved down for a swim meet ended up dropping time. But whether or not shaving actually makes you faster is debatable to say the least.

Yet when you go from not shaving your legs for weeks, to diving into a pool with freshly shaved, super smooth legs, you feel faster. It's a great sensation. But lack of leg hair has no impact on your muscle strength, it has no impact on your technique, and it has nothing to do with your training. It's a mental thing. Glassware is the same. It won't change the recipe of the beer and it won't go back in time and affect how the beer was brewed. What glassware will do, however, is enhance your perception of and experience with the beer.

TYPES OF GLASSWARE

There are zillions of types of beer glasses out there and more are being developed each day. Some experts and beer snobs argue that the regular old shaker pint glass is the worst glass on the planet. I get it, and for the most part, I agree with them. But you know what? A well-cleaned shaker pint glass is still far better than no glass at all.

While I have an entire cupboard full of beer glassware in all sorts of shapes and sizes, nine times out of ten I drink beer out of my favorite crystal wine glasses. The experts might tell me it isn't the most optimal vessel. But you know what? I freaking love the thin, long stem; the lightness of the glass; and how pretty a freshly poured beer looks in it. So for me, it is guaranteed to enhance the experience, and that's what matters.

The same is probably true for you. Whatever glass you like best is going to be the best glass for most of the beer you drink. It's quite simple when you think about it. If your brain thinks that a beer tastes best in the glass that you love the most, then the beer is going to taste best. We're emotional beings, not robots.

Still, it is important to note that the shape and size of a beer glass can be extremely important. Since people have put a lot of thought into this and arrived at some generally accepted standards, let's take a look at the five main types.

PINT GLASS (SHAKER AND NONIC)

Also called a tumbler, the shaker pint is the most common glass used in the United States for beer, soda, and even water. They are typically 16-ounce glasses with a conical shape (a cone that tapers in diameter from the bottom to the top).

However, the nonic pint glass, also known as the English pub glass, is the preferred pint glass for many craft beer fans and brewers. These glasses bulge out at the top. According to the experts, the design of the glass helps to improve grip, reduce chipping, and add strength. These glasses typically hold 20 ounces of beer (no wonder people love them!).

Most English and American-style ales under 8 percent alcohol are served in pint glasses. Lighter Belgian styles and lagers can also be served in this type of glass.

PILSNER GLASS

The average pilsner glass is smaller than the pint glass and only holds about 12 ounces of beer. They are tall, slender, and slightly tapered—a shape that best displays a pilsner's brilliant clarity and golden color. For the most part, pilsner glasses are used for pale lagers, including, of course, pilsners. However, it's not uncommon for people to serve bottled beer in them, as most bottled beer comes in a 12-ounce serving.

TULIP GLASS

Originally designed for Belgian beers, the tulip is a great vessel for many aromatic and flavorful styles. It is suitable for IPAs, stouts, some barrel-aged beers, and sours. The tulip glass is characterized by its "tulip" shape. It has a large bulb at the bottom and the sides of the glass taper in and then taper out at the top to form a wide lip. Between you and me, I think the glass resembles the body of a voluptuous woman more than it looks like a tulip. These glasses typically hold around 13 ounces of beer, but larger versions are available.

Almost any style can be served in a tulip glass, but the styles that should almost always be served in a tulip include most Belgian beers, saisons, sour beers, lambics, Scotch ales, and bière de gardes.

THE SNIFTER

Primarily used for brandy, cognac, and some whiskeys, snifters are short-stemmed glasses that have a wide-bowled bottom and a relatively narrow top. This design is especially good for beers with high levels of alcohol, typically above 8 percent ABV. The rounded bottom allows the glass to be cupped by the hands, which helps to warm up the beer. The narrow top helps to trap the aromas in the glass.

The snifter is an ideal glass for big, bold, and brazen beers like barleywines, imperial stouts, barrel-aged beers, and some double IPAs.

WEIZEN GLASS

Similar in shape to the pilsner glass, Weizen glasses were designed to accommodate the larger heads produced by wheat beers. This glass tends to be taller than a pint glass and comes in a range of sizes from 12 to 20 ounces. Obviously, the ideal beers for this glass are German wheat beers.

"Beer-clean" glassware

Although the shape of glassware is worth thinking about, the cleanliness of the glass you use is more important. Residual grease or oil from hands, lip products, or food residue are all gross. Even in small amounts, residue can kill carbonation, which impacts the appearance and the aroma of beer. Leftover soaps and suds can also kill carbonation, as well as leave the beer tasting soapy or "off."

When you're ordering a beer from a bar or restaurant, one of the easiest ways to tell if a glass is clean is to look at the head. When you receive your beer, does it have a strong two-finger head on it? How quickly does the head disappear? If the beer comes to you with little to no head and the head disappears almost instantly, there is a good chance that the glass was not properly cleaned.

Another sign of a really clean glass is lacing—those ribbons of foam that form rings around the glass with each sip. No lacing, like no head, is a sign of a dirty or poorly washed glass. Conversely, lots of lacing is a sign of a clean glass and that the bar has done well getting their glasses in shape.

How do you make sure a glass is clean when you are the one pouring the beer—either behind the bar or at home? There are three standard tests that will help you determine whether or not your current glass-cleaning system is efficient or not.

TESTING FOR A "BEER-CLEAN" GLASS

1. The Sheeting Test: If you wash your own car, you might be familiar with the concept of sheeting. Take the freshly cleaned glass and dip it into water. If the glass is clean, the water will cascade evenly down the sides of the glass—like a sheet of water. If the glass is dirty, water will break up into droplets on the inside surface.

2. Salt Test: First, wet the inside of the glass. Then sprinkle salt all over the interior. If it is clean, salt will adhere evenly to the clean surface. If it is dirty or greasy, the salt will not adhere to those parts of the glass.

3. Lacing Test: This is the more risky test as you could end up wasting beer—or drinking beer from a dirty glass. Pour beer into the glass. If it is clean, the beer will leave rings of foam around the inside of the glass after each sip, forming a lacing pattern. If not properly cleaned, foam will adhere in a random pattern, or may not adhere at all. It is important to note that some lower carbonation styles—like cask ales, high-gravity beers, and sours—leave little to no lacing. This is OK, so don't panic.

CLEANING GLASSWARE (AT HOME)

There is some debate about whether or not the average home dishwasher can properly clean glassware. We've all seen the commercials—some detergents and dish soaps leave a white film and spots on glassware while some claim to leave glasses sparkling. Next time you run your dishwasher, subject a newly cleaned glass to one of the three "beer clean" glass tests. If it fails the test, try switching your detergent. If it fails again, it could be the dishwasher.

Lucky for me, I haven't had a dishwasher since I left my parent's house for college. The only choice I've had is manual dishwashing. And I've learned a lot of lessons over the years:

The Magical Powers of Vinegar

My mother is one of those tree-hugging hippies who is against the consumption of artificial products and synthetic chemicals. She is the reason I know about the powers of vinegar. Several times a week, she would go around the house spraying down all the glass surfaces with a white vinegar solution and then wipe them clean. The house smelled horrible, but everything sparkled.

I eventually learned that vinegar is also a great tool for cleaning dull and cloudy glassware. The cloudiness and spots are typically due to hard water deposits. Vinegar helps to dissolve these hard water spots.

The simplest method is to fill a deep pot or dish with hot water and 2 cups of white vinegar. Allow the glasses to soak for a bit. You can also give them a good scrub while soaking. Pull them from the water, give them a good rinse in hot water and let them air dry. You can also add vinegar to your dishwasher before you run it.

1. If you are cleaning glasses at the same time you are cleaning food dishes, clean the glasses first. If there is grease or oil on your other dishes, there is a good chance it will transfer to the glasses. Make life easy on yourself.

2. Spend a little extra time scrubbing the rims of the glassware. That's where the majority of the grease residue will be.

3. If you can, dedicate a sponge to glassware. This will help ensure that food grease and oils don't transfer from other dishes.

4. Rinse your glassware in the hottest water you can tolerate. Use gloves to protect your hands.

5. Air-dry your glasses on a rack—not a towel or rubber pad. Clean the rack and the tray underneath regularly to prevent transferring food residue or bacteria to the glassware.

6. Do not use a towel to dry your glasses; it will leave lint on them. The exception is a microfiber glass cloth, which is used in many restaurants to shine wine glasses. These work great on beer glasses as well, of course.

7. Do not chill your glasses in the freezer. The frost on the glass picks up all sorts of flavors from the freezer, which in turn imparts those flavors into the beer. Frozen glassware can also create foaming problems during pouring. Frozen glassware: just don't do it.

As for dish soap, I don't really have a brand preference. In general, use ones that have the least amount of chemicals in them—the ones that are best for the environment.

SECTION
three

HAVING FUN WITH BEER

Pairing Beer with Food, Cooking with Beer, Beer Mixology

chapter thirteen

PAIRING BEER WITH FOOD

Nothing in this world beats an amazing beer and food pairing—at least not outside of the bedroom! Some experts argue that there is a true science to food pairings, not unlike gastronomy or mixology. According to the experts, becoming an expert yourself will take years and years, if not a lifetime, of experience. You'll have to discipline and train both your mind and your palate.

But don't let that intimidate you. Designing food pairings is actually not that hard—especially when it comes to beer. Also, with beer it's a lot cheaper to "gamble" on a new pairing than with most wines. Worse case scenario: the pairing sucks, the dish makes the beer taste horrible, the beer makes the dish taste horrible. Solution? End the pairing like an amicable divorce. Eat and drink the two separately, enjoying each for what it is on its own. No need to waste either of them. You learned that they are better apart than they are together.

Granted, coming up with food pairings is actually quite challenging. Not only do you have to understand the entire spectrum of beer styles, you also need a solid foundation and understanding of food, including the ingredients, various culinary methods, historical traditions, seasonality, and so on.

I've had beer pairings that have completely blown my mind—pairings that leave you speechless, as if you traveled into a different dimension in time. Gravity no longer exists and the only thing that is real is you, the beer, and the food. However, I've also been to my fair share of beer dinners where the beer and the food pairings have been a little bit off. And, at the end of the day, it really didn't matter. I was drinking good beer and eating good food with friends. Ultimately, endorphins kick in, and everything feels and tastes good. Those neurotransmitters just about always override taste receptors—full tummy, happy buzz, happy brain, and happy body.

The Three Beverage and Food Pairing Experiences

First and foremost, successful pairings come about only when you enjoy both of the partners, the food and the beverage, individually. If you hate bacon (wait, does anyone hate bacon?!), you are probably still going to hate it regardless of the beer with which it's paired. If you loathe hoppy beers, no amount of fried salty goodness is going to make you love hops. If you already don't like an aspect of the pairing—a food ingredient or the beer—then you won't like the pairing. It's that simple.

Once you have beer and food that you like, you'll usually find yourself in one of three different types of pairing scenarios: mismatched pairings, middle of the road pairings, and pairing epiphanies.

1. Mismatched pairings: Both the flavors of the beverage and the food are lost, if not destroyed. This is rare, but if you want to experience it, try eating hot wings with a really tannic red wine or high-octane imperial stout. It's not pretty.

2. Middle of the road pairings: Either the beverage or the food is the star, while the other plays a supporting role that is often overshadowed. For example, think of really powerful beers, like imperial IPAs, paired with delicate foods, like fresh seafood. Conceptually, some aspects of the pairing might work, but one side dominates. This is probably the most common scenario when pairing, and oftentimes, giving beer the advantage is actually OK.

Why would we want to give beer the advantage? The real question is, why not? Most of the time, beer plays a supporting role to food. Beer helps bring out flavors in the dish, making the food taste more intense and brighter. Beer is also a palate cleanser. Its bubbles like a little scrub brush on the tongue, lifting the lipids off and preparing it for the next bite. If you're planning a beer dinner, or other beer pairing event, flipping the script and putting the focus on the beer will almost always be the more novel approach. As long as the food complements the beer, your friends will be suitably impressed.

3. Pairing epiphanies: Some rare pairings enhance and heighten each other to a level of euphoria. These pairings drive you to take another bite, and then another sip; you never want the experience to end. These are the moments when you realize that you may never be able to eat that dish without that beer ever again.

4. Cheese! OK, I know I said there are three main types of pairings, but we have to talk about the exception to all exceptions. There is no such thing as a bad beer and cheese pairing. I don't know if anyone has actually said this before, so I should probably say it again, just to make sure that I get attributed with the quote: *There is no such thing as a bad beer and cheese pairing.*

Some may try to argue that cheese, like beer, is extremely complex and deserves to be paired with great care and respect. I understand that, which is why we will discuss specifics of cheese pairings in its own section (see page 174).

However, my point is this: whereas some beer styles are arguably better matches for certain types of cheese, all cheese goes with beer and all beer goes with cheese. I have never eaten a piece of cheese with a sip of beer and spit it back out in disgust. Perfect pairing or not, try eating any type of cheese with any style of beer and your mouth will be completely and utterly happy (if not, I'm happy to take that beer and cheese off your hands).

Getting Started

There are a few different schools of thought when it comes to pairing food with beer. My method is a hybrid based on various styles that I've learned over the years. In fact, I guess I should start with a not-so-guilty confession: Everything I learned about beer pairings, I learned from working with wine. Although the two beverages are extremely different, the science behind pairing food with them is quite similar.

I used to have a really backward way of figuring out beer pairings. I would start with the dish and then come up with a wine that I thought would pair best with it. I would ask myself why I came up with that wine pairing. And then, I would apply that same method of thinking to choosing a beer. Not exactly the easiest or most logical path to take. Ultimately, I was able to eliminate the wine step from my pairing routine and start thinking about the beer as its own entity (which is why this book isn't called *The Wine Wench's Guide to Beer*).

It's important to keep in mind that everyone is different—and that is okay. If anything, we all need to accept that we all have different palates and not everyone enjoys the same thing. That goes for experts and those who are certified tasters as well. Just because someone is an expert in something doesn't mean you have to like what he or she recommends or that you're wrong if you disagree.

WEIGHT AND INTENSITY

Constructing a beer and food pairing doesn't have to be extremely complicated. The most important thing to keep in mind is the balance of weight and intensity between the food and the beer. Balancing both weight and intensity ensures that neither of the two partners overshadows the other, a situation that is more common than not.

WEIGHT

In almost every situation, the weight of the beer should match the weight of the dish. This doesn't mean you need to put your portions on a scale! When it comes to beer, weight is typically related to body. Beer can be described as light, medium, full-bodied, or somewhere in between one of those options. Dishes can also be light, medium, or heavy, which is often thought of in terms of richness. Lighter dishes should be matched with lighter-bodied beers, while richer dishes need fuller-bodied beers.

INTENSITY

The intensity of a dish or beer is directly related to its flavor. Flavors can range from extremely delicate to tremendously powerful. If a super powerful beer is paired with a really delicate dish, it will overpower it. And vice versa. Intensity, like weight, should almost always be in balance. Delicate with delicate, intense with intense, and middle of the road with middle of the road.

WEIGHT AND INTENSITY TOGETHER

If you were to combine weight and intensity, you would essentially have four categories most food and beverages can fall under. These are:

Heavy and intense
Beer examples: barleywine, imperial stout, wee heavy, IPA
Food examples: red meat, blue cheese, bacon, smoked salmon

Heavy and delicate
Beer examples: Belgian tripel, bière de garde, bocks
Food examples: butter sauces, oysters, pork, brie

Light and intense
Beer examples: black lager, Berliner weisse, pale ale
Food examples: spicy peppers, white fish, grapefruit

Light and delicate
Beer examples: pilsner, Belgian wit, kölsch
Food examples: veggies, eggs, goat cheese, salads, shrimp

Why isn't there an option for medium? There are dishes and beer styles that aren't exactly heavy, but aren't really light, or that aren't particularly intense, but aren't really delicate either. Matching these up can be near impossible. As you get less extreme and closer to medium, the subjectivity of taste derails any consensus.

Two Approaches to Pairings

Now that we've considered weight and intensity, let's take a look at how to use that information to create pairings. There are essentially two options: You can either choose to pair a dish with a beverage that shares a lot of flavor characteristics, flavor intensity, and weight in common, or you can chose to do the opposite. I refer to the two methods as "like with like" and "opposites attract." Each method will result in entirely different experiences. Try a couple of ideas from each and see what style you enjoy most before continuing exploration.

LIKE WITH LIKE

At the most basic level, like with like starts with the five tastes: sweet with sweet, sour with sour, bitter with bitter, salty with salty, and umami with umami. Obviously, flavor comparison goes deeper than that, but it's a good place to start. Pair sweeter dishes and desserts with sweeter beers, pair bitter foods with hoppy beers, pair acidic foods with sour beers, and so on.

EXAMPLES

Pairings that come to mind along these lines include stouts with chocolate and coffee desserts, Belgian dubbels with dried fruits like figs and raisins, smoked beers with grilled or smoked meats and fish, Scotch ales with honey glazed pork, and saisons with mushrooms. Of course, you don't have to think about the beer in terms of what style it is; just consider what flavor and aroma is dominant.

Beer Flavor	Complementary Food Flavor
Bread (malt, yeast)	Bread, biscuits, pie crust
Brown sugar, graham cracker (malt)	Brown sugar, graham cracker
Caramel, toffee (malt)	Caramel, toffee, sugar cookies
Citrus (hops, yeast, adjuncts)	Citrus, orange, grapefruit, lemon
Charred, roasted (malt)	Grilled meats, coffee
Chocolate, coffee (malts, adjuncts)	Chocolate, coffee, espresso
Banana (yeast)	Banana, melon
Earthy (yeast, malt, hops)	Mushrooms, beans, earthy cheese
Floral (hops, yeast, adjuncts)	Lavender, rose, hibiscus
Herbal (hops, adjuncts)	Basil, thyme, sage
Honey (malt, adjuncts)	Honey, agave nectar
Molasses (malt, adjuncts)	Molasses, burnt caramel
Nutty (malts)	Nuts, seeds, coconut
Pine/Resin (hops)	Kale, arugula, artichoke
Stone Fruit (yeast, adjuncts)	Figs, raisins, apricots
Toast (malt)	Toast, nuts
Tropical (hops, yeast)	Pineapple, mango, papaya

CREATING COMPLEMENTARY PAIRINGS

When creating complementary pairings, I start with the basic flavor first—is the beer sweet, bitter, sour, or earthy? (I like to use earthy instead of umami because beer is rarely savory.) Then I ask, why? For example, why is the beer sweet? Is it because of the malts? Is it because of the yeast? It is because there is a lot of alcohol in it? Then I pick out the specific flavors: Is the beer toffee sweet, caramel sweet, dried fruit sweet, fresh fruit sweet, honey sweet, or molasses sweet? Then I figure out which foods share those flavor characteristics and I work to find a perfect pairing.

Here are some examples:

Beer flavor: Sweet and fruity

Reason: Residual sugar (caramelized malts), yeast (fruity esters), fruit or sugar additions

Example styles: Wee heavy, doppelbock, barleywine, Belgian dubbel, imperial stout, Belgian tripel, fruit lambics

Complementary pairings: Sweet barbecue sauces, roasted meats, braised meats, pork, fruit salads and desserts, roasted duck, fruit jams and sauces, cookies, caramel desserts

Example pairings: Belgian dubbel with roasted duck and fig jam, Scotch ale with pulled pork, Belgian tripel with bananas foster, kriek (cherry lambic) with cherry pie

Beer flavor: Bitter

Reason: Hops (pine, resin, citrus, grapefruit) or dark malt (astringent, coffee-like)

Example styles: Pale ales, bitters, IPAs, pilsners, dry stouts

Complementary pairings: Bitter and earthy greens (arugula, kale, chard), artichokes, olives, blue cheese, unsweetened cocoa, coffee, walnuts

Example pairings: Pale ale with an arugula-topped pizza, English bitter with collard greens, IPA with blue cheese-stuffed olives, dry stout with dark chocolate

Beer flavor: Sour

Reason: Wild yeast (tart, yogurt-like, funky, acidic)

Example styles: Berliner weisse, Flanders red and brown, lambics

Complementary pairings: Vinaigrettes and vinegar or citrus-based sauces, pickled veggies, fruit desserts, lemon-pepper chicken, ceviche, kimchi, goat cheese

Example pairings: Flemish red with balsamic-glazed chicken or veggies, gueuze with goat cheese-stuffed apricots, Berliner weisse with halibut ceviche, fruit lambics with fruit tarts

Beer flavor: Earthy

Reason: Dark roasted malt (chocolate, coffee, burnt bread), wild yeast (funky)

Example styles: Stouts, porters, black IPAs, black lagers (extremely subtle)

Complementary pairings: Grilled foods, red meats, chocolate and coffee desserts, mushrooms, smoked meat (bacon, ribs, turkey), potatoes

Example pairings: Dry stout with coffee-rubbed New York strip steak, black lager with grilled portobello mushrooms, black IPA with a black and blue burger, chocolate stout with tiramisu

OPPOSITES ATTRACT

Developing contrasting pairings is arguably the more exciting, yet risky, approach. It involves choosing opposing elements from the beer and the dish and matching them to create a whole new flavor and sensation on the tongue.

A great example of a classic contrast that just clicks is anything salty with most styles of beer. In addition to making you thirsty, there's a reason peanuts and pretzels are classic bar snacks. Sweet, sour, and bitter—notes often found in beer—all help to balance salty foods. Salt also helps to mellow and smooth out sweetness, tartness, and bitterness.

Sweet and sour is another common contrast. Classic sweet and sour combos include many fruit desserts, vinaigrettes, pineapple and ham, and many Asian dishes. In some circumstances, a beer can be both sweet and sour. Sweet and bitter are also frequently found together: milk chocolate, coffee with sugar, and tea with honey. What follows are my four favorite food and beer contrasts.

SALTY FOODS WITH HOPPY BEERS

Hops love salt—and vice versa. I'll never forget the moment I first figured this out. My boss and I had just delivered two kegs of our IPA to a local sushi restaurant and decided to sit down and have some lunch. Naturally, we ordered a round of our IPA (you know, for quality control). We were then given a small bowl of miso soup—a really salty and savory broth-based soup made of fermented soybeans.

I took a big spoonful of soup and then a sip of beer, and then stopped. *Wowza!* I never thought that something so simple could be so eye opening. The bitterness in the beer was extremely refreshing and helped to balance out the saltiness in the soup. And the salt smoothed over the bitterness in the beer, which allowed the hop flavor to shine through. Because the salt had diminished the beer's bitterness, I was able to taste all sorts of interesting hop flavors: grapefruit, lemon, pine, and fresh cut grass. The flavor of the beer brightened with each bite of soup.

This same principle applies for cheese, chips, pretzels, salted nuts, and many fried foods. They are all amazing pairings for hoppy beers.

SPICY (HOT) FOODS WITH HOPPY BEERS

It's no secret that I am obsessed with chicken wings. For me, the hotter the better. My pairing of choice is an American IPA—wait, hold that. Make that a West Coast–style IPA with lots of bright citrus and pine flavors, a strong bitter bite, and little to no caramel malt flavor. Then I take a bite of a steaming, deep fried, super juicy, lightly crunchy wing smothered in a thick, spicy hot, buttery sauce and wash it down with that delicious beer, and repeat.

Although hops can be pretty abrasive and bitter, they also have a powerful cooling effect when paired with spicy food. The bitterness in the beer helps to calm the heat from the food, while the heat tends to neutralize the bitterness in the beer. Keep in mind, however, that there are some extreme levels of heat that even the hoppiest of beers cannot cool. In these circumstances, I recommend having a few glasses of water on hand (to prevent the chugging of the beer).

If you take one thing away from this, know that it is *very important* that you avoid high alcohol beers with hot spicy foods. Alcohol intensifies heat and typically makes the pairing painful. Tannins can also have this effect, so I also recommend staying away from overly dry, roasted malt beers as well.

SWEET FOODS WITH ROASTY (DRY, BITTER) BEERS

The bitterness in beer typically comes from one of two sources: the alpha acids in hops or tannins in roasted malts. Roasty, dry bitter beers that have pronounced dark chocolate and espresso notes are a great contrast for sweet, rich, and caramelized desserts and dishes. Caramel desserts and fruit pies are perfect with dry, roasty porters and stouts.

My guilty (like super guilty) dessert pleasure is a really rich cheesecake topped with brandied cherries. That thick, creamy, and sweet cheesecake partnered with boozy, tart, and rich cherries sounds like a perfect pairing in its own. But what if I told you that I could take that pairing to the next level?

Oh yes, a deep, dark, and roasty imperial stout can cut through the thickness and the sweetness of the cheesecake while adding deep flavors of chocolate and coffee. In the mouth you get bitter chocolate and roasty coffee beer, rich and fatty cheesecake, sweet and tart cherries—does that not sound amazing? Make that a bourbon barrel-aged stout where you get to throw in oak, caramel, and vanilla notes and *bam, wham, thank you ma'am*.

FATTY FOODS WITH ALL BEER

Another way to create a contrasting pairing is through texture. The carbonation in beer acts as a palate cleanser; the tiny little CO_2 bubbles scrub the tongue free of all lingering lipids and sugars from food.

Here is my system for tasting fatty foods with beer: First, take a sip of the beer. Reflect on its flavors and the sensations it leaves on your tongue. Next, take a bite of food and notice how it feels and tastes in your mouth. Then take a sip of beer and note how the food and beer play with each other in your mouth. Then take another sip or two of beer to cleanse the tongue and then another bite of food. And so on and so forth.

Fried foods are the king of the fatty foods, and it's really hard to go wrong with the beer pairing. Sour beers bring a pleasant, palate-cleansing tartness, while hoppy and roasty beers bring a palate-cleansing dryness. Sweeter beers balance out salty richness. Win, win, win.

Putting It All Together

Food is rarely served at its most basic, where one ingredient is prepared with a very simple method. Instead, you'll find most food is served in the form of a dish that includes two or more ingredients, and most dishes employ cooking or baking techniques that alter the chemistry and flavors in the dish.

In short, food is multi-dimensional. Most meals and even snacks combine several flavors, textures, and tastes sensations. A chip might seem simple, but it's not a single note. A chip is made of potato, oil, salt, and a combination of other seasonings and flavors. Meat is rarely ever boiled without seasoning. It is usually marinated with a tenderizer and cooked in a variety of ways that enhance and intensify the flavor of the meat. And it is rarely served alone. Even if it's not part of a more complex dish, it will come with sides to make it a meal.

Soups, salads, sandwiches, tacos, pizza, stew, and the list goes on. These foods are multifaceted, which means there are multiple ways to approach a food and beer pairing. You can focus purely on a complementary pairing or you can complement and contrast a dish at the same time. The sky really is the limit.

Something that most of my mentors recommend, and I agree with, is to try two noticeably different beer options with each dish. This not only gives you two opportunities to find an ah-ha pairing moment, it also shows just how dynamic and flexible beer pairings can be.

MATCH MADE IN HEAVEN

Before we move on, I have to mention that there are some foods that should always be paired with beer. The only exception allowed is if you are eating them somewhere where beer cannot be legally consumed. Most bars, pubs, and breweries have at least one, if not a wide variety of these foods on their menu for a reason.

FOODS THAT SHOULD *ALWAYS* BE PAIRED WITH BEER:

Bacon	Fried things:	Fish and chips
Burgers	Calamari	Garlic (anything)
Cheese	Cheese	Mussels and clams (steamed in beer)
Chicken wings	Chicken	Nachos
Chili	Olives	Pickles
	Onion rings	Pizza
	Potatoes	Sandwiches
		Sausage
		Tacos

Designing a Perfect Pairing

The only question to ask before you start making that menu is, should you start with the beer or start with the dish? Let's look at both options.

Starting with the beer: Starting with the beer is probably the more adventurous and creative route. It is the most proactive approach to pairing. It also provides pairing insurance—after all, you are designing the dish specifically for the beer, not just trying to pick the most optimal beer after the fact. This means you can really play with the dish. You have the chance to incorporate certain flavors into the dish that you know work well with the beer. You can even choose to add subtle spices and herbs that complement the beer and some that contrast it.

Starting with the dish: Starting with the dish is the more reactive pairing menu. Essentially, the dish already exists and you are trying to find the best match for it. Start by picking out the strongest, most dominate flavors in the dish. Then decide whether or not you want to complement or contrast those flavors. Keep in mind that you still want to pick styles of beer that match the dish in both weight and intensity.

Let's look at a couple examples:

BEER FIRST

The beer: Barleywine

The dish: Dried black mission figs stuffed with blue cheese and wrapped with prosciutto

Suggested beers: Avery Hog Heaven, Dogfish Head Old School Barleywine, Sierra Nevada Bigfoot, Stone Old Guardian Barley Wine, Flying Dog Horn Dog Barley Wine, Anchor Steam Old Foghorn

Why the pairing works: Barleywine is one of the most potent beers styles out there. Not only is it big, bold, and boozy, it is also extremely rich, malty, and bitter. It is sticky sweet, which makes it a great match for dried fruits. It is bitter and pungent, which makes it a great match for strong cheeses and salty and fatty foods. The verdict: dried fruit stuffed with pungent cheese and wrapped in cured meat.

And that brings us to the love affair between the barleywine and blue cheese. Blue cheese loves barleywine. Barleywine loves blue cheese. They want to make babies. This I can promise you. But the question is, why?

Blue cheese is one of the most pungent styles of cheese, period. This is a result of using cultures of the mold Penicillium in its production. It takes quite some time to acquire a taste for the style, needless to say. The most well-known, readily available versions of bleu cheese include roquefort, gorgonzola, and stilton.

Since the flavor of the blue cheese is so strong, it needs an equally strong beer to match it. Anything weaker will be overwhelmed. High-gravity styles with large malt and hops bills tend to accompany blue cheese well. Excellent pairing styles include stouts, IPAs, double IPAs, Belgian strong ales, and barleywines.

One of my favorite ways to serve blue cheese is to stuff it into dried figs (fresh figs when in season), and then wrap the figs with prosciutto. There is a lot of balance in this dish. The figs bring flavors of concentrated fruit and sweetness. The prosciutto adds a richness from fat, a bit of smoke, and saltiness. The sweetness in the figs helps to mellow the pungency of the blue cheese, while the fat and saltiness of the prosciutto complements the fat and salt in the cheese. Each little bite-sized morsel just bursts with intense flavor.

The figs complement the caramelized sweet flavors in the barleywine, while the alcohol and intense flavors of the barleywine help to mellow the salty fat in the prosciutto and the pungency of the blue cheese—and vice versa. Both the dish and the beer have a lot of complex layers of flavor. Both are extremely strong, powerful beasts. Both are beautiful on their own, and together they are magical.

DISH FIRST

The dish: Poke is a raw fish "salad" served as an appetizer in Hawaiian cuisine. It is similar in concept to Japanese sashimi and tuna tartar.

The beer: West Coast IPA

Suggested beers: Port Brewing Wipeout IPA, Green Flash West Coast IPA, Russian River Blind Pig, Bear Republic Racer 5, Kern River Brewing Just Outstanding IPA

The pairing, Why it works: Poke is made up of raw ahi tuna, soy sauce, sesame oil, and chili pepper. The dish is prepared using all raw ingredients, with a focus on fresh, simple flavors. So although it is a richer dish, the flavors and overall experience is fresh, which means it needs an equally light and refreshing beer pairing.

High fat foods, such as omega-3–rich tuna, require highly carbonated beers (moderate to low in alcohol). The carbonation helps to remove the rich layer of lipids that tends to coat the tongue when consuming high-fat ingredients.

There are two reasons I chose the West Coast IPA to pair with this dish: (1) IPAs love salt. Salt intensifies the citrus notes in hops, really bringing out their bright, floral character. The soy sauce, salt, and seaweed in the dish help to intensify the hop flavors in the beer. (2) IPAs are a perfect match for dishes that possess heat from spice. The refreshing nature of hops allows them to serve as a natural cooling agent. The IPA helps to cool the burn from the chile peppers and jalapeños (especially fresh) in this recipe.

Overall, both components of this paring are highly flavorful, fresh, and bright. Neither completely dominates the palate, and both help to enhance the flavor of the other in some way shape or form, making it an ideal pairing.

The recipe: Although the exact recipe varies with region, modern poke typically consists of cubed ahi (yellowfin tuna) sashimi marinated with sea salt, a small amount of soy sauce, inamona (roasted crushed candlenut), sesame oil, limu seaweed, and chopped chile pepper. Variations on the basic recipe might include addition of avocado, roe, or chopped toasted macadamia nuts. It all depends on preference and access to ingredients.

Beer vs. Wine

Regardless of what some wine snobs might say, beer has always had a place on the dining table. The most pretentious of wine drinkers will tell you that beer is a blue-collar beverage that could never possibly hold a light to wine, especially when it comes to food pairings. Good thing we aren't in that camp. But let's just say, for one second, we wanted to be a little bit arrogant and self-entitled. If this were the case, then we would say that these so-called wine snobs are full of crap.

Wine's main advantage over beer is that it underwent an industry revolution first. The alcohol industry was completely annihilated by Prohibition. Rye, bourbon, wine, beer—it didn't matter. The production of alcohol in all its forms came to a screeching halt. Everyone struggled to rebuild; however, the wine industry got back on its feet first.

But today craft beer has evolved to become more than just a product made from malt, hops, water, and yeast. Finding inspiration from both the wine world and culinary arts, brewers are continuously pushing the boundaries of craft beer by incorporating techniques and skills learned from winemakers, distillers, bread makers, and chefs into the brewing process. Unique ingredients, the utilization of unique yeast strains, blending, and barrel-aging are just some examples of the latest trends in the craft brewing industry.

Craft beer is not trying to replace or become wine, despite some claims. Critics need to differentiate between inspiration and imitation. Craft beer is a completely separate entity from wine, successfully paving its own course. Yet the complexities and nuances in beer surpass those in wine, in many respects, and I truly believe it is a better pairing for most food.

BEER'S ADVANTAGES

It all starts with carbonation. When it comes to food pairings, beer possesses a key component that wine almost completely lacks: *carbonation*. Richer, more flavorful foods such as cheese, butter, and meats, leave a layer of lipids on the tongue. The carbonation in beer helps to break apart the lipids, cleansing and preparing the palate for the next bite or next sip of beer. With the exception of champagne, wine lacks the carbonation needed to scrub the tongue clean.

Next, unlike wine, a lot of foods and beer actually share ingredients in common. Many animals that we eat (save for seafood) are fed a grass or grain diet, and many of them are fed barley, which is the main ingredient, by weight, in beer. Even if you don't believe you can taste the influence of grain in meat or in cheese, there are all the other cereal grain-based foods like pasta, bread, biscuits, pizza dough, and so on.

Also, many brewers incorporate other herbs, fruits, and food ingredients into their recipes. The ability to brew with adjuncts only increases beer's advantage over wine in the food-pairing realm. Since some beers actually feature ingredients like chocolate, berries, and spice, the diversity of flavor and direct parallels to food surpass that of wine (which is limited to the flavors and aromas that grapes can create on their own).

Real Life Palate Fatigue

I never, and I mean never, go to the actual movie theater. So when I finally get the opportunity, I like to go big. Now, we are all adults here. And I think some of us can admit that movies are just a little bit more fun when booze is involved. In some places, adult beverages are available for purchase in movie theaters. This is not always the case, however.

Back in the day, when I called Napa my home, my movie theater beverage of choice was wine. One time, I brought a bottle of chilled Marlborough sauvignon blanc (white) and a half a bottle of chianti reserva (red) to split with a friend. Not one to insult the fine beverages with improper glassware, I brought along two handy dandy plastic wine cups specifically designed for fashionably drinking wine on the go.

Although not a fan of corn and corn products (thank you, Michael Pollan), I am oddly obsessed with popcorn. Maybe that's because popcorn is just a vessel for eating butter—and this girl loves her some butter. And when it comes to popped corn, nothing quite beats the uber greasy, super salty crunch of movie theater popcorn lathered up with extra butter.

After buying the largest tub of crunchy grease, we grabbed some seats in our theater and I poured my friend and I a glass of the crisp, highly acidic sauvignon blanc. The wine was sharp, clean, and boasted intense notes of grapefruit and

PALATE FATIGUE

Now, one advantage that wine has over most beer styles is acidity. Acid can be a solid palate cleanser, but only to a point. It can also work against you: Acidity, when combined with bitter tannins, creates astringency—the drying and sometimes puckering sensation experienced in the mouth after tasting most red wine. Astringency can be difficult to clear from the mouth, especially after repeated exposure. (Sour beers can have this effect as well.)

Furthermore, the sugars, tannins, and alcohol in wine all coat the tongue and sides of the mouth, making it increasingly difficult to taste things as the night goes on. Once the tongue is overwhelmed and desensitized, food becomes bland and it can be hard to detect specific nuances and flavors. This point of tongue desensitization is often referred to as palate fatigue or palate exhaustion.

grass. As the movie went on, we chowed down hardcore on popcorn, stopping every few minutes to wash it down with some wine. About halfway through the film, the bottle of white was kicked and I poured us both the red. More popcorn, more wine, lots of laughing in between.

While leaving the theater, my friend turned to me and said, "Hey, wait! I didn't get to try any of the red wine."

I burst into hysterical laughter. "Yes, you did," I said. "I poured it for you twice." "You did?"

"Yes. Scouts honor."

In the dark of the theater, it was virtually impossible to see what we were drinking. However, the two styles of wine sit on opposite sides of the spectrum: New World white wine fermented in stainless steel tanks boasting intense citrus flavors vs. Old World red wine fermented in oak boasting rich, earthy dark fruit flavors. The kicker? My friend has been working in the beverage industry for more than a decade. He has a discerning palate, but for some reason he couldn't taste the difference between white and red wine.

The culprit? Butter.

It is so high in lipids that it coats the tongue with a layer of fat and oils, making it difficult to taste. Unfortunately, the fructose in wine is not a good palate cleanser. In fact, it just adds a layer of sugar on the lipids, further coating the tongue and affecting taste.

This brings us to the conclusion that once again beer would have been a more ideal pairing for the rich, salty, buttery popcorn. But what style, you ask? Ah, great question. In this situation, I would opt for an IPA (most likely a West Coast IPA) with bright citrus, high-alpha hops. The salt brings out the hops, while the carbonation in the beer helps to break up the lipids, cleansing the palate. Bada bing, bada boom.

Beer can also lead to palate fatigue, but not as quickly as wine. After all, alcohol in both wine and beer is a major factor in palate fatigue. It's a mind-altering drug that lowers inhibitions and impairs motor skills, brain functions, and can impede your ability to smell and taste things. However, beer typically does not pack as much alcohol as wine, ounce for ounce. (Hops can also cause palate fatigue: The high alpha acids in many Pacific Northwest hop varietals can be extremely astringent and palate-wreckingly bitter.)

Whether you're pairing with wine or beer, remember that longer dinners and larger servings mean that people will start to get tipsy (if not drunk) and the tongue can only handle so many flavors and so many dishes until it is forced to wave the white flag in surrender. Alcohol can also lead to dehydration, which only accelerates palate fatigue. So when you're planning a beer dinner, make sure to serve plenty of water to the guests and keep the beer pour sizes reasonable. Leaving enough space between courses to allow for a palate rest is also a good idea.

Seven Craft Beer Counter-Pairings for Classic Wine Pairings

Sadly, many people have been trained to think that certain foods belong only with certain beverages. This is especially the case with fancy and expensive food. After all, if the food is so expensive and fancy, shouldn't you pair it with something just as expensive and fancy? You know, like wine? That's what the pompous wine experts would like you to think.

Well, folks, I'm not here to put down wine (well, not too much). The seven classic wine pairings that follow are amazing, but it is important to note that craft beer can be just as extraordinary with these rich foods, if not better. Please keep in mind that these are recommendations based on my palate and experiences, which changes from person to person.

CAVIAR

Classic wine pairing: Champagne

Craft beer alternative: American IPA

Commercial examples: Caviar is made from roe, fully ripe fish eggs. Although the most expensive roe comes from wild sturgeon in the Caspian and Black seas, many cultures around the world eat roe from all sorts of fish. Caviar is very salty, but also very delicate. Some would argue that, since it tends to be expensive, caviar deserves to be partnered with the most exquisite and elegant sparkling wines in the world. I don't think that is an entirely fair approach.

Here is my most basic and simplest description of caviar: It tastes and feels like you are eating little tiny bubbles of salty seawater. The texture is typically silky, sometimes butter-like. It should taste fresh, shouldn't be overly fishy, and is typically served on toast or as a garnish on other foods (roe is a common topping for sushi).

As I've mentioned already, I'm a huge fan of really salty foods with hoppy styles like American IPAs. Caviar is no exception, regardless of how expensive it is. The bitterness in hops is a great neutralizer for salty foods and helps to reduce any fishiness. The salt actually works with the hops to bring out more of the citrus, pine, and tropical notes in the hops. The carbonation makes an excellent palate cleaner, preparing your tongue for the next bite.

Want to go outside the box? Try a gose, a tart and sour wheat beer brewed with salt. The salt from the beer will complement the salt in the caviar, while the tartness will contrast it.

FOIE GRAS

Classic wine pairing: Sauternes

Craft beer alternative: Barleywine, preferably aged

Commercial examples: Sierra Nevada Bigfoot, Bell's Third Coast Old Ale, Stone Old Guardian Barley Wine, Rogue Old Crustacean, Avery Hog Heaven

Why it works: Le sigh. I can already hear the groans on this one. Some of you, like me, might choose to ignore the morality issues and indulge in the deliciously decadent stuff. However, I'm sure a few of you readers take an adamant stand against it. (If so, feel free to skip right ahead.)

Why do I love foie gras? In a word, well, two, it's *meat butter*. By definition, it's a product made from the liver of a goose or duck that has been purposefully fattened, typically through a force-feeding—hence the controversy. French law (specifically French rural code L654-27-1) states that, "Foie gras belongs to the protected cultural and gastronomical heritage of France."

But many US cities and states have banned the production and sale of foie gras because of its controversial production methods.

Despite all that, the little French girl inside of me loves foie gras. I can also see why wine experts usually reach for a sauternes, a richly sweet, heavier bodied white wine with notable acidity. It works because both the foie gras and the wine are heavy and both have super intense flavors. When looking for a beer alternative, it is important to choose a style that can match the richness of the foie gras as well as its intense flavor.

Barleywines, on the other hand, are rich and boozy with intense caramel and roasted malt flavors and aromas. I think you'll find that the rich dark caramel, toffee, and molasses flavors in a barleywine pair perfectly with the rich fattiness of the foie gras. The buttery saltiness of the foie gras helps to bring out any underlying citrusy hop profile in the beer. The carbonation, even if light, rinses the palate, leaving a dry and bitter finish, prepping the tongue for more foie gras.

Want to go outside the box? Try a Flemish red ale, a sweet and tart, almost vinegar-like sour beer. The tartness in the beer will counter the rich fattiness of the foie gras.

OYSTERS

Classic wine pairing: Chablis

Craft beer alternative: Dry stout or oyster stout

Commercial examples: 21st Amendment Marooned on Hog Island, Flying Dog Pearl Necklace, Upright Brewing Oyster Stout

Why it works: The dry stout is by far the most popular and time-tested pairing for oysters. A stout brewed with oysters only enhances this euphoric experience. The first known account of an oyster stout

dates back to 1929 in New Zealand. Although not as common as most styles, the oyster stout has seen a mini-revival in the past decade or so, especially in coastal breweries. Some breweries brew with only the shells, while others opt to brew with the entire oyster, shell and all. Oyster stouts are typically dark, roasty, and dry, with a mild brininess or slight gaminess. Can't find an oyster stout? Grab a dry stout for an equally great pairing.

A beer industry colleague of mine once told me an interesting tale about oysters and beer. I'm not entirely certain its true, but it is a story that I love to share: He was out to eat with a cocktail-loving friend of his. They ordered a dozen oysters. My friend ordered a dry stout, his friend a martini. The martini guy argued incessantly that his martini was by far the better pairing. In an effort to prove his friend wrong, my friend poured a splash of his beer onto one of the oysters. He then poured a splash of his friend's martini on a different oyster. The oyster with the beer instantly got plumper, while the oyster with the martini shriveled up. "See that?" he said. "Oysters prefer beer!"

Want to go outside the box? Try an American IPA with an oyster dressed with hot sauce or a jalapeño-based mignonette. The hops will help to cool the burn, and the dryness of the beer will cleanse the palate for another shot of oyster.

LOBSTER

Classic wine pairing: Chardonnay

Craft beer alternative: Belgian tripel

Commercial examples: Westmalle Tripel, Chimay Tripel, Victory Golden Monkey, Ommegang Tripel Perfection, New Belgium Tripel

Why it works: Lobster is sweet and fatty, yet delicate, which means it deserves an equally powerful, yet subtle partner. Most wine-pairing experts lean quickly toward chardonnay, which can range from crisp, dry, and tart (unoaked) to creamy, buttery, and full-bodied.

Full-bodied, dry, and fruity with hints of citrus and spice—it sounds like the Belgian tripel is an excellent alternative to the chardonnay. It has enough body, acidity, and creamy flavor to hold up to the luxurious nature of lobster, but is soft enough that it will not overwhelm it. Belgian tripels also tend to be extremely carbonated, which helps them cut through the rich butter sauces that tend to accompany lobster.

Want to go outside the box? Try a Berliner weisse, a creamy, lemon-sour wheat beer. Lemons are a classic pairing with shellfish and the lemony flavor in a Berliner weisse is no exception. Plus, this style tends to have a rounder, almost yogurt-like mouthfeel (from the use of lactobacillus) that helps it hold up to richer dishes and butter sauces.

DUCK

Classic wine pairing: Pinot noir

Craft beer alternative: Belgian dubbel

Commercial examples: Ommegang Abbey Ale, Allagash Dubbel Ale, Goose Island Pere Jacques, Sierra Nevada Ovila Abbey Dubbel, Lost Abbey Lost and Found

Why it works: More often than not, duck is prepared and served with fruit sauces or glazes, especially those made from dried stone fruits (figs, plums), dark berries, and cherries. Pinot noirs (especially those from Burgundy) can be very earthy with bright and complex dark cherry flavors. The Belgian dubbel has delightful dried cherry, fig, and plum flavors and aromatics that pair very well with duck. Regardless of how the duck is prepared, the dubbel has layers of flavor to complement the richness of duck.

Since duck is so rich and fatty, it should be paired with a fuller-bodied beer that has enough carbonation in it to help cleanse the palate. The Belgian dubbel does all this and more. Aged dubbels will have even deeper and more complex dried fruit characteristics to them, so bust open the cellar when the duck hits the table.

Want to go outside the box? Try a Belgian witbier, a lighter wheat beer brewed with orange peel and coriander. Another common preparation of duck is duck à l'orange —aka duck with an orange glaze. The dried orange peel in a witbier is a great match for the orange flavors in the glaze.

STEAK

Classic wine pairing: Cabernet sauvignon

Craft beer alternative: Russian imperial stout

Commercial examples: North Coast Old Rasputin, Oskar Blues Ten FIDY, Stone Russian Imperial Stout, Brooklyn Black Chocolate Stout, Bell's Expedition Stout

Why it works: The flavor of steak depends on the cut, but for the most part, steak is rich, bold, and fatty. This is why steak is often paired with the most powerful and tannic red wines—typically, cabernet sauvignon (or syrah for grilled steak). However, red meats, especially beef, pair really well with roasted malts. Just think of that meat grilled or pan-roasted with a hint of char. Like the seeds and skins in grapes used to make red wine, roasted malts have tannins in the husks, which adds a substantial amount of bitterness and astringency to imperial stouts. The sweetness and high alcohol in the beer makes it strong enough to stand up to the most powerful of steaks, especially those with cream, butter, or sweet bourbon sauces and rich side dishes like mashed potatoes. Take the dish to the next level with a bourbon barrel-aged stout.

Want to go outside the box? Try a barleywine with a steak garnished with gorgonzola cream sauce or blue cheese butter. This pairing is extremely bold and powerful from both ends: fatty, rich steak; pungent, super-sharp cheese; bitter and caramel-sweet beer. Total flavor overload.

LAMB

Classic wine pairing: Bordeaux

Craft beer alternative: Robust porter or smoked porter

Commercial examples: Anchor Porter, Bell's Porter, Great Lakes Edmund Fitzgerald Porter, Alaskan Smoked Porter, Stone Smoked Porter, Yazoo Sue

Why it works: Often described as gamey, lamb is an acquired taste for many people. Its rich and earthy flavors demand an equally robust and rustic pairing—which is why lamb is typically paired with big, rich, and earthy red wines from Bordeaux. The dark roasty and lightly burnt malt flavors in a porter heighten the earthiness and gaminess of the lamb, while its dry, roasty finish and moderate carbonation cut through the fat, acting as a perfect palate cleanser. When it comes to grilled lamb dishes, the smoke and char flavors in smoked porters really make the pairing pop.

Want to go outside the box? Try a saison, a Belgian-style farmhouse ale that is often spiced with flowers and herbs. Not only do saisons pair well with just about any food under the sun, the saison's earthiness and funk is a great match for the gaminess in many meats, like lamb.

PAIRING BEER WITH CHEESE

You can't really go wrong when eating cheese with beer. In fact, I think beer pairs better with cheese than wine ever could. (See page 157 for my reasons why.) However, some styles of beer do work better than others with certain types of cheeses.

When thinking about these pairings, I like to start with the cheese. This might be because I know far less about cheese than beer, which means it's easier for me to choose the beer once I understand the cheese; but you can just as easily start with the beer.

There are hundreds of types of cheeses, which can make categorizing them very hard. Cheese is often classified by the type of milk used, the method of making it, the aging process, flavor characteristics, the region of origin—or a combination of some or all of those factors. On the pages that follow, we'll keep things on the simple and practical side when it comes to classification.

FRESH CHEESE

About: Fresh cheeses are the least processed of the cheeses. They are not aged and are typically spreadable, though some can be crumbly.

Common examples:

Burrata (mozzarella and cream): Buttery, milky, rich, creamy

Chèvre (fresh goat's milk cheese): Mild, milky, tangy, creamy, soft, spreadable

Feta (sheep or goat milk): Tangy, salty, dry, crumbly

Halloumi: Mild flavor, does not melt, can be grilled

Mascarpone: Slightly sweet flavor, buttery, creamy, spreadable

Mozzarella: Mild, milky flavor, sliceable, melts really well

Ricotta: Slightly sweet, milky flavor, creamy, spreadable

Pairing with beer: These are the lightest of the cheeses, in flavor and in weight. They tend to pair best with light- to medium-bodied beers with lower levels of alcohol and lower IBUs. These cheeses also play well with wheat, sour, and fruit beers.

Recommended styles: Belgian wit, Berliner weisse, English bitter, fruit beers, gose, lambics, kölsch, pilsners

SOFT-RIPENED CHEESE

About: Also called bloomy rind cheeses, soft-ripened cheeses have a thin, white, sometimes edible rind that ripens the cheese from the outside in. These cheeses are typically soft and very creamy and are quite good baked.

Common examples:

Brie: Earthy, mushroom-like flavor, rich, creamy, more pungent with age

Camembert: Almost identical to brie

Humboldt Fog (goat's milk): Creamy, light, mildly tart, made by Cypress Grove

Pairing with beer: Berries and cherries are a traditional pairing for soft-ripened cheeses, making fruits beers—especially lambics—an ideal pairing. The fruit flavors blend with the cheese while the carbonation cleanses the palate for the next bite of these rich cheeses. Sweeter, nutty styles can also provide a good complement.

Recommended styles: Fruit beers and lambics, kriek, nut brown ales, Scottish ales

SEMI-SOFT CHEESE (NO RINDS)

About: Semi-soft cheeses are broken up into two categories: no rinds and washed rinds. The rindless semi-soft cheeses tend to be milder, if not bordering on bland, in flavor. They are easily sliced, cubed, or shredded, making them ideal toppings for sandwiches, tacos, pizza, etc. They are often blended with each other or made with herbs, garlic, and peppers.

Common examples:

Havarti: Danish table cheese, buttery, sweet, often flavored with dill and cranberry

Monterey jack: California cheese, melts really well, often made with peppers

Muenster: American cheese, can be bland or sharp, smooth, melts well

Provolone: Like mozzarella, but firmer and more flavorful, melts well

Pairing with beer: Since these cheeses tend to be used more as toppings for things than eaten alone, the entire preparation must be considered. Pale ales are some of the most versatile styles of beer around. They are excellent with sandwiches and pizza, both of which are usually topped with these cheeses.

Recommended styles: Pale ales, pale lagers, American amber ale

WASHED RIND CHEESE

About: Washed rind cheeses are bathed in a saltwater brine and occasionally with the addition of wine, brandy, spirits, or Abbey ales. This method allows the important cheese-aging bacteria—*Brevibacterium linens*—to be present on the rind, while inhibiting the growth of bad bacteria or mold. Washed rind cheeses tend to be some of the most pungent and stinky out there. But once you get beyond the smelliness, they can taste slightly fruity, sweet, and earthy.

Common examples:

Limburger: Extremely strong, stinky, salty German cheese

Epoisse: Pungent flavor, strong smelling, extremely creamy texture

Pairing with beer: Because this family of cheeses is so pungent, they require stronger beers with equally intense flavors. Since historically many of these cheeses were made by monks, they pair very well, by nature, with strong Abbey and Trappist-style beers. And because they are so funky and weird, they are also a good match for the funkier, barnyard-like farmhouse ales and spontaneously fermented beers.

Recommended styles: Belgian Trappist and Abbey strong ales, Belgian strong dark ale and Belgian quad, doppelbock, Bière de Mars, gueuze

SEMI-HARD CHEESE

About: As you might assume, these cheeses tend to be firmer than all the aforementioned cheeses. They are often crumbly and many of them are great melting cheeses. Because they are so balanced, semi-hard cheeses tend to be among the most popular. Key flavors include nutty, earthy, sharp, slightly salty, buttery, and fruity. Many of these cheeses are aged, which hardens the cheese and concentrates and intensifies its flavors.

Common examples:

Cheddar: Nutty, slightly salty, sharp, naturally acidic, firm

Edam: Very mild flavor, slightly salty, nutty, smooth texture

Gouda (young): Mild flavor, buttery, semi-sweet, creamy, often smoked

Swiss: Creamy, buttery, slightly sweet, ideal for melting

Pairing with beer: Since this family of cheeses tends to be the most balanced, they should be paired with styles of beer that are equally balanced. Roasted and caramel malts work really well with the nuttiness of these cheeses, and the light saltiness in the cheese helps to bring out the citrus flavors in hops.

Recommended styles: Black lager, brown ale, dry stout, dunkel, IPA, pale ale, Oktoberfest

BLUE-VEINED CHEESE

About: Blue-veined cheese is made with the mold *Penicillium roqueforti*, which turns a bluish green when exposed to oxygen. They tend to be sharp, salty, and intensely pungent.

Common examples:

Gorgonzola: Earthy flavors, typically softer, creamier, and subtler than other blues

Roquefort: Intensely sharp, tangy, salty, notable taste of butyric acid, name is protected by the AOC

Stilton: Pungent, creamy, salty, and more intense than most blue cheeses, name is protected by the European Commission

Pairing with beer: These extremely powerful cheeses require equally powerful beers—think big, bold, and brazen; super hoppy; or super malty.

Recommended styles: Barleywine, chocolate stout , double IPA, wee heavy, imperial stout

AGED HARD CHEESE

About: This catchall category of cheese includes types of cheeses that are matured and cured in a controlled environment, like a cave or a cellar. Different cheeses are aged for different specific periods of time; it can vary from weeks to months to even years. Members of the aged cheese group have been cured in a cave or cellar for at least six months. These cheeses tend to be sharp, nutty, and hard or firm in texture.

Interesting fact: The lactose in milk is broken down during the aging process. The longer the aging, the less lactose that remains in the final product. Many aged cheeses are actually tolerable, if not completely harmless, for those that are lactose-intolerant.

Common examples:

Aged asiago: Sharp, rich flavor, salty, often used for grating

Aged cheddar: Strong sharp flavor, nutty, salty crystals

Aged gruyere: Distinctively nutty, salty crystals, smooth texture

Parmesan: Extra hard, granular cheese, salty, typically used for grating

Pairing with beer: These tend to be the saltiest of the cheeses, making them a fantastic match for hop-forward beer styles like pale ales and IPAs. The nuttiness of this family also makes them a great match for roasty brown ales, bocks, milds, and Scotch ales.

Recommended styles: Bitter, bocks, brown ale, IPA mild, pale ale, Scotch ale

PAIRING BEER WITH TACOS

When it comes to pairing tacos with craft beer, there are two major aspects of the dish that I take into consideration: the type of protein (and how it's cooked) and the toppings, sauces, and garnishes used.

Some people might argue that the vessel in which the taco is served—hard corn shell, soft corn tortilla, flour tortilla, fried tortillas, and so on—also plays an important role in the overall pairing experience. This may be true, but I still think the best rule of thumb is to choose the shell you like best and focus on pairing your beer with the ingredients inside. Shells are subtle compared to the fillings.

Below are some of the most popular and well-known types of tacos, typical toppings that come with them, and general beer pairing recommendations for each preparation.

TACOS DE ASADOR: GRILLED FILLINGS

Meat is cooked using dry heat methods, typically by grilling on a hot comal.

Common variations: Carne asada (grilled steak), chorizo (Mexican sausage), pollo asada (grilled chicken), or tripita (grilled tripe).

Common toppings: Chopped onion and cilantro, guacamole

Recommended beer pairing: Black lager (schwarzbier), porter, black IPA

TACOS DE CAZO: FRIED FILLINGS

Meat is slow-cooked in a simmering pot of lard and made crispy on a hot comal.

Common variations: Carnitas (slow-cooked pork shoulder), suadero (brisket)

Common toppings: Chopped onion and cilantro

Recommended beer pairing: Vienna lager, American amber ale

TACOS AL PASTOR: SPIT-ROASTED FILLINGS

Meat is marinated in a mix of dried chiles and spices, roasted on vertical rotisserie (spit), and served thinly sliced.

Common variations: Pork (traditional Mexican), lamb (Middle Eastern)

Common toppings: Chopped onion and cilantro, pineapple, lime, hot salsa

Recommended beer pairing: Pilsner, saison, American pale ale

TACOS DE PESCADO: FISH TACOS

Fish is typically seasoned and grilled or battered and fried.

Common variations: White fish, such as mahimahi, tilapia, and halibut; camarones (shrimp); ahi tuna; lobster

Common toppings: Fresh avocado, flavored mayos, fruit salsas, slaw

Recommended beer pairing: Pilsner, American IPA, Belgian wit

VEGETARIAN TACOS (YES, EVEN VEGETARIANS EAT TACOS)

These tacos normally consist of black or pinto beans and a mix of grilled or roasted veggies.

Common variations: Portabella, butternut squash, meat substitutes like seitan and tofu

Common toppings: Cheese, avocado, roasted corn, slaw, salsa

Recommended beer pairing: Porter (grilled veggies, mushrooms, black beans), spiced beer or Belgian wit (butternut squash), Munich helles (avocado, cheese, spicy salsa)

PAIRING BEER WITH PIZZA

Pizza is perhaps the most classic pairing with beer. Rarely will one find a brewpub without pizza on the menu or a pizzeria without beer on the menu. Italian wine lovers can fight me on this, but beer is and will always be a perfect match for the cheesy, saucy, bready goodness that is pizza.

Although pizza is typically viewed as being a heavy and somewhat fatty dish, its base ingredients (dough, tomato sauce, and mozzarella cheese) are relatively light in flavor. That means the average pizza pairs really well with beers that have little to no roasted malts and a notable hop presence. When in doubt, pale ales and lagers almost always pair great with pizza.

When it comes to the perfect pairing of pizza and beer, my rule of thumb is to pair styles of beer with the sauce and the toppings. Tomato sauce tends to be acidic, which makes it a good match for beer styles that have a hint of caramel sweetness, like ambers. White and cream sauces tend to be richer and can stand up to styles with roasted malts. Pesto sauces tend to match up really nicely with pale ales and lagers that have a bright herbal and citrus hop presence.

There are a few beer styles I almost always avoid pairing with pizza. These include most imperial and high-alcohol styles, which will inevitably overpower the pizza; most stouts, because roasted malts do not work well with the acidity in tomato-based sauces; and sour beers, because they increase the acidity in tomato-based sauces in an unpleasant way.

Outside of the type of sauce used on the pizza, it is also important to take the other toppings into consideration. The sky is really the limit when creating a pizza, but below are some of the most common toppings and the beers styles I recommend for pairing.

CLASSIC TOPPINGS

Tomato, mozzarella, parmesan, and basil

Recommended styles: Pale ale, pilsner, amber ale, helles lager

---

SPICY TOPPINGS

Spanish chorizo, pickled jalapeño peppers, pepperoni, Italian sausage, pepperoncini peppers

Avoid: High-alcohol beer like barleywines and imperial stouts

---

Recommended styles: American pale ale or IPA, saison, pilsner

---

SMOKED, GRILLED, AND ROASTED TOPPINGS

Bacon, dry cured salami, roasted piquillo peppers, barbecued chicken, chipotle peppers, caramelized onions

Recommended styles:
Smoked beers (porter or lagers), IPA (especially black), amber ales

MILD AND EARTHY TOPPINGS

Artichoke hearts, goat cheese, mushrooms, onions, green peppers, spinach

Recommended styles:
Saison, porter (with white sauce), pilsner, pale ales

PUNGENT AND STRONG TOPPINGS AND CHEESES

Feta, blue cheese, anchovies

Recommended styles:
American IPAs, stouts, Belgian strong ales

chapter fourteen

COOKING WITH BEER

I love to cook. I love beer. So of course I love to cook with beer. Chances are if you're reading this chapter, you'll love cooking with beer, too.

An easy way to start is with any recipe that requires some sort of liquid (water, wine, broth, stock, and so on). Most recipes can be prepared easily with beer as a substitute. Soups, stews, and especially chilis are all ideal recipes for introducing beer into the cooking process.

Of course, there are several other ways to incorporate beer into recipes. Beer flavors can be infused into marinades, sauces, glazes, braising liquids, and in the baking process. Some chefs skip the beer all together, opting to infuse food with beer ingredients like hops, wort, or malted barley instead. Mmmmm, malted barley. OK, let's get going!

The Basics

Did you know not all beers can be cooked? It's true, and it means if you aren't used to cooking with beer it's probably best that you test the beer you want to cook with first just to make sure it will cook down in a desirable fashion.

The best way to test the ability of a beer to successfully cook down and reduce is to cook it over low to medium heat in a saucepan on the stove. Taste the beer as it cooks down—does it taste good or are less than desirable flavors being produced? Naturally, things like sugar and acid can be added to reductions to change the taste. But first and foremost, you need to decide if the beer tastes good, or even decent, when cooked on its own.

So what makes a beer cook-able? Generally speaking, beers with higher malt content reduce the best. Residual sugars in the beer caramelize as the beer cooks down and, if enough water is evaporated off and some sugar is added, malty beers can reduce down into some amazing syrups and glazes.

Styles with a significant amount of caramel malts, like ESBs, Belgian dubbels, and Scottish ales, work really well with a variety of foods, especially pork, duck, dried fruits, and nuts. These beers can cook down to a syrup that is comparable to caramel, so these beers also make excellent glazes. Dubbels can get fruitier when reduced with sugar.

Roasted malt beers, like stouts and porters, typically work best with dark meats, like steak and lamb, chocolate dishes, and mushroom sauces. Roasted malt is extremely complementary to browned meat, coffee, chocolate, and earthy foods. However, roasted malt is typically too strong and overwhelming for more delicate foods like shellfish, chicken, and vegetables. (When reduced down all the way, these beers resemble chocolate and coffee syrups.)

Wheat beers, pale Belgian styles, and pale lagers make excellent cooking partners for the lighter meats like chicken, seafood and shellfish, veggies, and fruit desserts. They are also the preferred styles for beer batters. They reduce to honey-like syrups (especially the Belgian beers).

Hoppy beers are typically the hardest styles to work with in the kitchen. The bitterness in the hops tends to concentrate as the beer reduces, making for a really bitter sauce. These beers are typically reserved for marinades and dressings. They can also be used for beer batters and, on occasion, they may be used in super spicy recipes.

In some circumstances, the beer isn't cooked. Instead, it's used as a marinade or in dressings. But first, let's discuss the various cooking-with-beer techniques.

BOILING AND POACHING WITH BEER

Some grains and starches, such as rice and couscous, absorb all of the liquid in which they are cooked. This means that they also absorb all of the flavors in the liquid that you use when cooking them. It is common practice in restaurants to cook certain things in stock and broth to add more flavors. Cooking starches with beer is another opportunity to infuse unique flavors into a recipe.

Barley is one of the tastiest grains to cook in beer. That should come as no surprise. Since most beer is made from barley, they complement each other well. I almost always avoid strongly hopped, aggressively bitter beer styles for this method of beer infusion. Ales with strong caramel and roasted malt character typically work best.

Vegetables, eggs, and some meat can also be poached in beer. This process usually doesn't impart as much beer flavor as boiling does, but it still adds a notable zest.

BRAISING WITH BEER

Braising is essentially a two-step process. First, the meat (or vegetable) is pan-seared, which browns the surface and enhances flavor. Then a braising liquid of some sort is added to the pot, covering two-thirds of the meat or vegetable. The dish is covered and cooked at a very low simmer until it becomes extremely tender. A lot of the time, the braising liquid is turned into a sauce or gravy to be served with the dish.

If you're braising with beer, dark beers like porters and stouts typically work best. Dark Belgian ales and stronger Scotch ales can also impart great flavor, but try to avoid overly bitter beers and IPAs, as the bitterness will only become more concentrated as the braising liquid cooks down.

BAKING WITH BEER

When it comes to baking, the same rules apply as for other techniques. You can almost always replace one or more of the liquids with beer. The key, though, is to decarbonize the beer before mixing it. For fruitier recipes I like to use Belgian beers, wheat beers, and fruit beers. For chocolate-based recipes, chocolate stouts are amazing but can be substituted with regular stouts or porters.

BEER MARINADES

The alpha acids and tannins in beer are excellent for tenderizing meats. Marinating meat in beer for at least an hour before cooking or grilling can take the meal to the next level. Most marinades typically contain three main ingredients: a type of acid for tenderizing, a form of oil to seal the meat surface from the air, and then a blend of herbs and spices for flavor.

A simple yet great beer marinade is beer, lemon juice, extra virgin olive oil, garlic, fresh ground pepper, and salt. For darker meats like beef and game, opt for a darker beer marinade. For pork and other sweeter meats, go for an amber or Scotch ale. For duck, choose a Belgian dubbel or quad. For chicken, try a pilsner or pale ale. For white fishes, use a Belgian wit or blonde, and for salmon, be rebellious with an IPA.

BEER GLAZES AND SAUCES

These are recipes where beer is cooked down with other ingredients into a thick sauce or paste that is either applied to the meat or veggie products consistently during cooking or tossed with it at the end. When it comes to glazes, beers with caramel and roasted malts and very low bitterness levels work best. But when it comes to sauces, the sky is the limit. Just about any beer style can be modified and balanced with the addition of sugars, acids, spices, and herbs. Keep in mind that some sauces, like a beer hollandaise, won't be cooked. This is actually beneficial for the beer as it helps to keep all of its flavors chemically intact.

Now that we've covered the basic techniques for incorporating beer into food recipes, it's time to explore some of these techniques with recipes.

ONION SOUP

Recipe by Brewery Ommegang | www.ommegang.com | Serves 8–10

This recipe highlights the use of beer as a fresh flavor addition as opposed to using it more like a wine for deglazing and reducing. Caramelizing the onions heightens the malty undertones of these rich darker beers. Also, the caramel notes will bring out the Belgian candi sugar that is used in the brewing of these styles.

Ingredients

4 stems fresh thyme, including leaves

4 stems fresh parsley, including leaves

2 bay leaves

4 oz. butter

6 lb. small yellow onions, sliced thin

1 tbsp. brown sugar

6 c. beef stock

12 oz. Brewery Ommegang's Abbey Ale, Three Philosophers, or other Belgian or Belgian-style dubbel or quadruple

Salt and pepper

Baguette or similar white bread, sliced ½-inch thick and toasted

2 c. grated Gruyère cheesee

Instructions

Prepare a bouquet garni by placing thyme, parsley, and bay leaves in a square of cheesecloth. Tie into a bundle with butcher's twine and set aside. In a stockpot, melt butter over medium-low heat. Add onions and cook on low for 30 minutes, stirring occasionally. As the onions soften and start to caramelize, add sugar and stir. Continue to cook the onions until they reach a very dark brown color; this is where all of your flavor will come from. Add ½ cup of beef stock every few minutes five times, and then add the remainder of the stock, the bouquet garni, and the beer. Let simmer for 30 minutes, then add salt and pepper to taste. Remove the bouquet garni. Heat the oven to 450 degrees Fahrenheit or turn on the broiler to high. Place toast on a baking sheet, and sprinkle slices with equal amounts of cheese, then season with salt and pepper. Place in the oven or under the broiler until the cheese is melted. Serve soup in a bowl with a slice of Gruyère-topped toast.

WISCONSIN BEER CHEESE SOUP

Recipe by Lucy Saunders, author of *Dinner in the Beer Garden* | www.beercook.com | Makes 2 ½ quarts (6–8 bowls)

My friend Lucy Saunders has written five cookbooks, most recently *Dinner in the Beer Garden*. Lucy also lives in Wisconsin, where making beer cheese soup is part of the state's DNA. This is an easy recipe to make ahead, but just be sure to warm gently over very low heat, as the lactose in the cheese can scorch.

Ingredients

1 c. finely diced carrots

1 c. finely diced onion

1 c. finely diced celery

⅓ c. butter

5 garlic cloves, peeled and minced

½ c. all-purpose flour

2 c. vegetable broth

12 oz. red ale or bock, at room temperature

1 tsp. dijon mustard

1 tsp. dry mustard

1 tsp. Worcestershire sauce

1 tsp. hot sauce, or to taste

Salt and black pepper

1 c. cream

2 c. half-and-half

½ c. crumbled gorgonzola, room temperature

8 oz. cream cheese, room temperature, cut into 1-inch cubes

4 c. shredded sharp cheddar, room temperature

Garnish: diced red bell pepper, minced scallions (green onions), or popcorn

Instructions

In a 1-gallon stockpot, simmer carrots, onions, and celery in butter for 10 minutes. Add garlic, and cook additional minute. Add flour, a bit at a time and stir constantly. Cook roux for a few minutes. Stir in broth, beer, mustards, Worcestershire sauce, hot sauce, salt, and pepper. Bring to a simmer and simmer 10 minutes.

Turn heat to low and whisk in cream, half-and-half, and gorgonzola, stirring until melted, then add cream cheese one cube at a time, whisking until smooth after each addition. Remove from heat, and whisk in grated cheddar cheese, ¼ cup at a time, stirring constantly. Garnish each bowl as desired.

To make ahead, prepare the soup base following the above instructions, but do not add the grated cheddar. Refrigerate. When ready to serve, reheat the soup to a simmer, and add the grated cheddar just before serving.

TEXAS-STYLE BEER CHILI

Recipe by the Beer Wench | Serves 6–8

The secret to a great chili is making it the day before you want to serve it. This allows the flavors to really mesh. But who are we kidding? I've never met a person that can resist eating the chili as soon as it's done. So make sure to make a lot of it so you can save some for the next day.

This recipe calls for an imperial stout, which might sound crazy, but I assure you it works. The dark, malty richness of the beer helps to make a thicker, richer, and deeper-flavored chili. Can't find an imperial stout (or don't wish to waste one)? Opt for a smoked porter or chocolate stout.

Since I'm not a fan of beans, this chili is legume-less (hence, "Texas-style"). But feel free to modify the recipe if you're a bean lover.

Ingredients

Olive oil

2 lb. steak or stew meat, cut into bite-sized cubes

½ lb. ground beef

12 oz. chorizo sausage (ground)

1 large yellow onion, coarsely chopped

5 cloves of garlic, minced

3 jalapeños, sliced with seeds

¼ c. chili powder

2 tbsp. cumin

1 tsp. cayenne pepper

2 chipotle peppers in adobo sauce, minced

2 tbsp. adobo sauce (from can of chipotle peppers)

12 oz. imperial stout

1 28 oz. can whole tomatoes, drained

1 14 oz. can crushed tomatoes

1 4 oz. can tomato paste

Salt and pepper

Instructions

Heat oil in a sauté pan over medium heat. Brown the steak or stew meat in batches. Remove meat and add ground beef, chorizo, and onion to the pan and brown, breaking up the meat as its cooks. Option 1: Put all the ingredients in a large soup or stockpot. Bring to a boil, reduce heat, and simmer for 2 hours. Stir occasionally, breaking up tomatoes. Option 2: Put all the ingredients in a slow cooker and cook on low heat for 6–8 hours or on high heat for 3–4 hours. Stir to break up tomatoes. Serve in a bowl with diced avocado, cheddar cheese, and a side of beer cornbread (see recipe on page 191).

STOUT BEEF STEW

Recipe by the Sierra Nevada Brewing Company | www.sierranevada.com | Serves 6–8

Since beer is a natural meat tenderizer, stews make an excellent canvas for cooking with beer. Stouts and porters add an amazing depth and flavor to beef stews that would not exist otherwise. The flavors of the roasted malt concentrate as the stew cooks down and the chocolate, espresso-like notes of the beer actually come through in the final dish. You would be crazy to make stew without beer—just my two cents.

From Sierra Nevada: Searing the beef helps add depth to a dish that already turns corner after corner of new flavor. The specialty malt of our stout seeps into the myriad ingredients for robust spoonfuls with dashes of roasted sweetness. The list of ingredients looks long, but the recipe is really easy. After the initial prep steps, all you have to do is sit back and let your oven work its magic.

Ingredients

½ c. flour

1 ½ tsp. salt

3 lb. beef chuck, trimmed and cut into 1 ½-inch pieces

¼ c. vegetable oil

1 tsp. dried thyme

1 tsp. dried oregano

1 tsp. dried rosemary

½ tsp. pepper

2 bay leaves

8 cloves garlic, whole

1 c. stout

1 ½ c. beef broth

1 lb. carrots, peeled and cut into 1-inch pieces

4 stalks celery, cut into 1-inch pieces

1 lb. button mushrooms, washed and cut in half

2 red peppers, cut into 1-inch pieces

12 oz. fresh or frozen peas

Instructions

Preheat your oven to 350 degrees Fahrenheit. Mix the flour and salt in a large bowl. Toss the meat in the mixture, coating it well. Shake off excess flour and salt.

Pour the vegetable oil in a 5-quart, ovenproof pot and place over medium heat. Add half of the beef, brown well, and set aside on a plate. Repeat browning with remaining beef. (Browning in two steps ensures even exposure of all meat to heat.)

Return all of the meat to the pot and add the thyme, oregano, rosemary, pepper, bay leaves, and garlic, stirring over medium heat for 1 minute. Add the stout and broth to the pot, pouring the remaining stout in a glass to enjoy on the side. Bring the medley to a boil briefly, then cover the pot and place it in your oven for 90 minutes.

Remove the pot from your oven. Add the carrots, celery, mushrooms, red peppers, and peas, cover the pot once more, and return it to your oven for an additional 45 minutes or until the meat and vegetables are tender. Adjust seasoning with additional salt and pepper.

BEER CORNBREAD

Recipe by the Beer Wench

Baking recipes are some of the easiest to incorporate beer into, as most of them require liquid ingredients such as milk or water. Some or all of the liquid in the recipe can be substituted with beer. Here is my tried-and-true cornbread recipe, but feel free to use cornbread mix from the box, substituting the milk or water with beer and adding a few diced jalapeños into the mix.

Ingredients

1 c. flour

1 c. yellow cornmeal

¼ c. granulated sugar

4 tsp. baking powder

½ tsp. salt

½ c. milk

1 egg, beaten

½ c. beer (pale ale, lager, or pilsner work best)

½ c. fresh corn, cut from the cob

Diced jalapeño, optional

Instructions

Preheat oven to 350 degrees Fahrenheit. Grease a 9-by-13-inch baking pan. Combine flour, cornmeal, sugar, baking powder, and salt in a large bowl and stir until well blended. In a separate bowl, combine the milk, egg, and beer, and whisk until blended. Pour the wet mix over the dry mix and stir until most of the lumps are dissolved. Don't overmix. Add the corn and jalapeños (if using). Pour the batter into the prepared pan, and smooth the top. Bake for 30 to 35 minutes, or until a toothpick comes out clean. Cool and cut into large squares.

LOOSE LEAF ALE BANANA BREAD

Recipe by Odell Brewing | www.odellbrewing.com

Beer shares flavor and characteristics in common with bread that water and milk don't (unless you're drinking weird milk with barley and yeast). So think about replacing one or the other with beer in a quick bread and muffin recipe. This recipe from Odell does just that. It calls for their light and citrusy Session Ale, which adds a bit of citrus zest that wouldn't otherwise be present.

Ingredients

2 c. sugar

1 c. butter, softened

4 ripe bananas, mashed

4 eggs, beaten

2 ½ c. flour

1 tsp. salt

2 tsp. baking soda

¾ c. Loose Leaf (a kölsch, pilsner, or lightly hopped Session Ale will also work)

Instructions

Preheat oven to 360 degrees Fahrenheit and grease 2 loaf pans. Mix sugar and butter. Add bananas and eggs. Sift flour, salt, and baking soda. Blend flour mix with banana mix. Add Loose Leaf. Do not overmix. Bake bread for 55 minutes, or until a toothpick comes out clean. Turn out immediately. Enjoy!

SNOW WIT WAFFLES

Recipe by the Sierra Nevada Brewing Company | www.sierranevada.com | Serves 2–3 (makes about 6 waffles)

I'm a huge fan of whisking pale Belgian-style ales into pancake and waffle batters. These styles tend to impart a pleasant fruitiness and spice, as well as a bit of fluffiness, into the recipe. Complete this recipe by making a syrup and butter out of the same beer, and you will never eat brunch at a restaurant ever again.

From Sierra Nevada: Snow Wit's Belgian yeast offers a nutmeg-like spice that latches onto and enlivens the maple, and discerning diners might catch a hint of hop character from the beer's seven-variety lineup.

WAFFLES

2 c. flour

3 tsp. baking powder

2 tbsp. sugar

½ tsp. salt

½ c. Snow Wit

3 eggs, separated into yolks and whites

1 c. milk

7 tbsp. butter, melted

Instructions

In a large bowl, mix the flour, baking powder, sugar, and salt. In a smaller bowl, mix the Snow Wit, egg yolks, milk, and melted butter. In another large bowl, with an electric mixer or whisk (how fierce are your forearms?), whip the egg whites to stiff peaks. Mix the Snow Wit–spiked wet ingredients into the dry ingredients, *then* fold in the egg whites. Proceed to cook your waffles according to the manufacturer's directions for your waffle iron. Serve with Snow Wit Syrup and pecan butter. Now get to stackin' these beauties or share them with friends and family.

SYRUP

1 ½ c. Snow Wit   1 c. maple syrup

Instructions

Combine the Snow Wit and maple syrup in a skillet over medium heat, reducing the mixture to 1 cup over the course of about 20 minutes.

PECAN BUTTER

¼ c. Snow Wit syrup   ½ lb. butter   1 c. pecans, chopped

Instructions

Mix the syrup, butter, and pecans until smooth.

PUB PRETZEL

Recipe by Deschutes Brewery | www.deschutesbrewery.com | Serves 16

The love affair between beer and pretzels predates that of peanut butter and jelly, fish and chips, and pretty much any classical pairing out there. Pretzels, both soft and hard, have been a staple of pubs and beer festivals for centuries. The recipe makes a lot of pretzels. Feel free to freeze them (after baking) and defrost and warm them up, as you want to eat them. Or make them for a party.

Ingredients

1 oz. yeast	1 tbsp. salt	2 lb. 4 oz. high-gluten flour
2 tbsp. sugar	1 egg	3 tbsp. baking soda
2 ½ c. Deschutes Inversion IPA	2 tbsp. butter, softened	

Instructions

Combine yeast, sugar, and beer until proofed. Mix in salt, butter, and flour with a dough hook in your mixer. Place the dough in an oiled container and let it double in size (about an hour). Cut into 16 equal pieces. Roll into balls, cover with plastic, and let sit until relaxed. Roll each ball into a rope about 4 feet long, twist into pretzel shape, and place on a tray in the fridge or freezer. Bring a large pot of water to boil and add the baking soda. When pretzels have risen a little but are fairly firm, boil them for 1 minute each, then place them on an oiled baking sheet. Whisk an egg in a bowl and brush the egg onto the pretzels, then salt them. Bake at 400 degrees Fahrenheit for about 20 minutes. Cool and serve with cheese dip and your favorite Deschutes beer.

BLACK BEER BREAD

Recipe by Dr. Rebecca Routson (my sister) | Makes 1 loaf

This recipe was extremely difficult for my sister to develop because, unlike the other members of my family, she does not drink beer. But that didn't stop her from wanting to bake bread with it!

Rebecca's goal was to make a bread that was rich, soft, dense, with notes of coffee and chocolate but little to no hop bitterness. I recommended that she use a black lager or schwarzbier and, after testing out the recipe a few times and sweetening it up with molasses, she was able to create this super-dense and super-yummy black beer bread. Not too shabby for a non-beer drinker, if I do say so myself.

Ingredients

12 oz. bottle of a black lager	2 tbsp. dry milk powder	3 tbsp. unsweetened cocoa powder
⅓ c. molasses (dark)	2 c. bread flour	1 tsp. salt
1 ½ tsp. instant coffee (Rebecca used espresso)	1 c. whole wheat flour	2 tbsp. butter, softened
	1 c. rye flour	2 tsp. bread machine yeast

Instructions

Place the ingredients into a bread maker in the order they are listed. Put the bread maker on the dough cycle. When the dough cycle has ended, knead the dough and shape it in a ball. Allow it to rise for 40 minutes. Preheat the oven to 350 degrees Fahrenheit. Bake bread for 35 minutes or until it sounds hollow when tapped. When it is done, take it out of the oven to cool. Enjoy immediately, slathered in butter. Yum!

CLASSIC BEER BATTER MAHIMAHI (OR TOFU) TACOS WITH ZESTY COLESLAW

Recipe by the Beer Wench

Beer batter is seriously one of the easiest things to make and it is virtually impossible to screw up. But beware: Once you start making your own beer batter at home, you will get addicted to battering and frying *everything*. My favorite things to fry are pickles, fish, onion rings, and mushrooms, but you can literally use this thing on anything you want.

When it comes to beer pairings, this recipe can go several ways, which is what makes it so exciting. My top three choices include pilsner (a classic pairing for tacos), Belgian wit, and American IPA.

FRUIT SALSA

1 c. fresh tomatoes, diced	1 cup red onion, diced	1 clove garlic, minced
1 c. pineapple, diced	1 serrano chile pepper, minced	¼ c. cilantro, roughly chopped
		Juice of 1 lime

ZESTY COLESLAW

1 tbsp. lemon juice	1 tsp. lemon zest	¼ c. mayonnaise	1 c. shredded cabbage

CLASSIC BEER BATTER

¾ c. beer (pilsner or Belgian wit)	¾ c. flour	¾ tsp. salt

MAHIMAHI (OR TOFU) TACOS

Canola oil for frying	Classic Beer Batter	Zesty Coleslaw
1 lb. mahimahi (or tofu), cut into 1-inch strips	Soft corn tortillas	Fruit Salsa

Instructions

For the salsa, mix the tomatoes, pineapple, red onion, serrano chile, garlic, cilantro, and lime juice together in a medium-size bowl until blended; set aside.

For the coleslaw, mix the lemon juice and zest with mayonnaise in a medium-size bowl. Add the cabbage and toss until evenly coated. Set aside.

For the beer batter, combine the beer, flour, and salt in a medium-size bowl until smooth. To thicken, add more flour. To thin out, add more beer. Feel free to flavor with cayenne pepper for an added kick.

Heat the canola oil in a tall pot over medium-high heat. Add the mahimahi or tofu to the beer batter and coat thoroughly. Slowly add the battered fish to the oil and fry for 3–6 minutes. Remove from the oil and drain on a paper towel. Sprinkle with sea salt.

Assemble the tacos by adding the fish to the tortillas first, followed by the slaw, and then the fruit salsa.

BEER MUSTARD WITH BLACK BUTTE PORTER

Recipe by Deschutes Brewery | www.deschutesbrewery.com

Some people use white wine and some even use pickle juice in mustard—but really? Beer mustard trumps all other mustards and, once you make this original recipe from Deschutes, you will never eat non-beer mustard ever again. Personally, I love dark beer mustards, but feel free to experiment with all sorts of styles until you find your own signature blend.

Ingredients

½ c. dry mustard

2 tbsp. granulated sugar

2 tbsp. malt vinegar

⅛ c. honey

2 tbsp. lemon juice

¾ c. mayonnaise

¼ c. Black Butte Porter

Instructions

Mix the dry mustard and sugar together in a bowl. Add the vinegar, honey, and lemon juice to the dry ingredients and mix together until it forms a thick paste. Add the mayonnaise and mix thoroughly. Finally, gently stir in the Black Butte Porter. Serve as a soft pretzel dip or as a sandwich spread. It's all good!

BEER VINAIGRETTE

Recipe by Jon Wojtowicz, Short's Brewing Company Head Beer Liberatorm | www.shortsbrewing.com

From Jon: Soft Parade is our rye ale brewed with pureed strawberries, blueberries, raspberries, and blackberries. If you're not able to find our beer, this recipe turns out well with most fruit beers but especially those brewed with berries. A framboise (sour raspberry lambic) or kriek (sour cherry lambic) would be ideal. The goal is to make a salad dressing with a nice pop: it has tart, bold, and sweet flavors to splash on your favorite mix of greens.

Ingredients

2 tbsp. sugar

1 tsp. garlic powder

½ tsp. dry mustard

1 tsp. onion powder

¼ tsp. white pepper

6 tbsp. Short's Soft Parade, or any similar fruit-infused beer

3 tbsp. apple cider vinegar

3 tbsp. white vinegar

1 ½ tbsp. all-purpose cherry juice concentrate

1 c. extra-virgin olive oil

Instructions

Combine the sugar, garlic powder, dry mustard, onion powder, and white pepper in a mixing bowl. Whisk in the beer, cider vinegar, white vinegar, and cherry juice concentrate until blended. Slowly whisk in the olive oil to emulsify the vinaigrette.

Salad recommendation

This vinaigrette recipe pairs wonderfully with the traditional Michigan Salad. To make the salad, place greens, goat cheese, dried cherries, and pecans into a large salad bowl. Toss to combine.

Note: The vinaigrette also pairs well with grilled chicken.

HOPPYUM IPA BARBECUE WING SAUCE

Recipe by Shane Morre, executive chef at Foothills Brewing | www.foothillsbrewing.com | Yields 2 ½ quarts

As you already know by now, I love wings paired with an IPA. So, of course, I was excited to see a recipe from Foothills Brewing in North Carolina that integrates the IPA right into the wing sauce.

From Shane: The sauce base here is essentially a tangy barbecue sauce. The Hoppyum IPA adds a nice hoppiness and bittering quality that brings the flavors full circle. You can make this sauce in advance of wing day and refrigerate it for up to two weeks.

Ingredients

5 c. ketchup

¾ c. water

1 ¼ c. vinegar

¾ c. brown sugar

¾ c. granulated sugar

1 tbsp. lemon juice

2 tbsp. Worcestershire sauce

½ oz. black pepper

½ oz. onion powder

½ oz. dry mustard

1 small shallot, diced

½ c. red wine vinegar

8 oz. Hoppyum IPA
   (or other American IPA)

Instructions

Place all ingredients except the beer in a large pot and simmer for 20 minutes. After 20 minutes add the IPA and cook for an additional 5 minutes.

Note: Wing sauce recipe yields enough sauce for 5 lb. of wings.

IPA Barbecued Beer Wings—Three Ways

1. Fried Wings: Drop the wings in a fryer (in batches of 6–10) for 8–10 minutes, depending on size. They will float to the top when finished (check the internal temperature for minimum 165 degrees Fahrenheit and make sure the probe is not hitting the bone). Drain the wings and toss with Hoppyum IPA Barbecue Wing sauce.

2. Oven-Roasted Wings: Rub the wings with salt and pepper and let sit overnight in the refrigerator. Place seasoned wings on a baking sheet, and bake for 35 minutes or until done. Check the internal temperature for minimum 165 degrees Fahrenheit, and make sure that the temperature probe is not touching the bone. Take the wings off the baking sheet and toss with Hoppyum IPA Barbecue Wing Sauce.

3. Smoked Wings: Rub the wings with salt and pepper and let sit overnight in the refrigerator. Place the wings on a rack in a smoker. Smoke approximately 2 hours over hickory chips. When finished, check the internal temperature for a minimum 165 degrees Fahrenheit. When done, toss the wings in Hoppyum IPA Barbecue Wing Sauce.

BEER MOLE

Recipe by Erin Jimcosky, editor in chief, *CRAFT by Under My Host* | www.craftbyundermyhost.com

From Erin: Mole can be intimidating to make, but you really shouldn't let it get the better of you. The varied blend of fruit, nuts, spices, and chile is so delicious and versatile you'll appreciate having it in your arsenal. What sets this mole apart is the addition of pilsner, which carries flavors well while enriching them, and gives the liquid base a good structure without taking over. If you can find El Mole Ocho from New Holland, you should definitely give it a try in this recipe. It will take things to a whole different place.

Ingredients

10 dried ancho chiles (remove the seeds if you don't want it spicy)

3 tbsp. canola oil

2 onions, diced

1 ½ tsp. sea salt

2 tbsp. sesame seeds

¼ c. cumin seeds

1 tsp. peppercorns

5 whole cloves

1 tsp. anise seed

3 tbsp. tomato paste

24 oz. pilsner (or New Holland's El Mole Ocho)

½ c. dried cherries

¾ c. walnuts, chopped

5 oz. dark chocolate, chopped

Instructions

In a well-ventilated area*, toast the chiles on a skillet or grill until they have a bit of color on all sides. Set aside.

Warm the oil in a medium-sized pot over medium-low heat and caramelize the onions with the salt. When the onions are golden brown, stir in the sesame seeds, cumin seeds, peppercorns, cloves, and anise seeds, and allow to toast for a minute before stirring in the tomato paste. After another minute, stir in the beer, cherries, walnuts, and chiles, and simmer for 15 to 20 minutes. Stir in the chocolate. Carefully transfer the mixture to a blender and puree until smooth.

*This is important if you don't want to choke on capsicum fumes.

BEER MOLE BABY BACK RIBS

Recipe by Erin Jimcosky, editor in chief, *CRAFT by Under My Host* | www.craftbyundermyhost.com

Ingredients

1 rack baby back ribs   2 c. prepared mole sauce   Sea salt

Instructions

Remove the thin membrane from the back of the ribs. Sprinkle the ribs with salt and coat with ½ cup mole. Allow to rest for a minimum of 1 hour.

Heat the coals in a grill according to the manufacturer's instructions and cook the ribs over indirect heat for about 2 ½ hours at around 300 degrees Fahrenheit. Baste every 15 minutes or so with the remaining mole. The ribs are done when the meat begins to pull away from the bone.

BEER MOLE CHILI

Recipe by Erin Jimcosky, editor in chief, *CRAFT by Under My Host* | www.craftbyundermyhost.com

Ingredients

Oil for searing

4 chicken thighs

Salt and pepper

1 onion, diced

4 oz. tomato paste

5 c. red beans, cooked

1 recipe mole sauce

1 12-oz. bottle pilsner

Sesame seeds

Fresh cilantro, to garnish

Instructions

Season the chicken thighs with salt and pepper. Heat a large pan over medium-high heat and add a little oil. Sear chicken on both sides until brown but not cooked through. Remove from the pan and set aside. Lower the heat and add in the onion. Cook until soft, then stir in the tomato paste. Add the seared chicken, beans, mole, and beer to the pot and simmer for 60 minutes or so.

When the chicken is tender, remove it and allow to cool. When cooled, shred the chicken and add it back to the pot, stirring to distribute. Serve topped with sesame seeds and a sprinkling of cilantro.

PALE ALE JALAPEÑO CHEESE DIP

Recipe by Deschutes Brewery | www.deschutesbrewery.com

When beer and cheese are combined, the love child they create is not just amazing, it's out of this world. If you've never melted down beer and cheese—in a dip, soup, or even mac and cheese recipe—you are definitely missing out. Have no fear, Deschutes has created this tried-and-true recipe for a beer-infused cheese dip with a kick. It's perfect for a late-night snack or party appetizer.

Ingredients

1 tbsp. butter

⅓ c. yellow onion, finely chopped

2 jalapeño peppers, finely chopped

1 small can diced green chiles

2 cloves fresh garlic, finely chopped

1 tsp. ground cumin

1 tsp. fresh oregano, chopped

Salt and pepper

6 oz. Mirror Pond Pale Ale

1 lb. cream cheese

½ lb. shredded monterey jack cheese

1 c. fresh spinach, cooked, drained, and chopped

Instructions

In a saucepan over medium heat, sauté onion, jalapeños, green chiles, and garlic in butter until translucent but not browned. Season with cumin, oregano, and a pinch of salt and pepper. Add beer and cream cheese, and bring to a low simmer until cream cheese is melted. Add the monterey jack and spinach and stir until fully incorporated. Serve with tortilla chips, pita chips, or a crusty baguette.

ABBEY ALE BRAISED PORK SHANKS

Recipe by Brewery Ommegang | www.ommegang.com | Serves 4

The list of ingredients might seem daunting, but the technique for this recipe is really quite simple. First the ingredients must be seared—or browned. Then beer is added to create the braising liquid in which the meat will cook for several hours until it is fall-off-the-bone tender. If you aren't familiar with braising meats in beer already, prepare yourself for the inevitable addiction.

Since the meat and veggies undergo a Maillard reaction (see page 112) when they're browned, that makes them an obvious pairing for any beer style that uses caramel or crystal malts (which also undergo a Maillard reaction while they're being made). Pork tends to be a sweeter meat as well, which is just another argument in favor of using beers with a high-caramel malt content. For example, the featured beer: Ommegang Abbey Ale.

While this dish pairs perfectly with a Belgian-style dubbel, it can also pair with a Belgian quadruple, a malty stout, an American brown ale, an eisbock, a malt-balanced old ale, a Munich dunkel, a Strong Scotch Ale, a Scottish 80 Shilling, a Baltic porter, or a Belgian dark strong.

Ingredients

1 c. dried porcini mushrooms	4 pork shanks	3 sprigs thyme
2 c. dried figs	½ c. olive oil	3 bay leaves
3 12-oz. bottles Abbey ale or other Belgian or Belgian-style dubbel	1 lb. onions, small dice	3 sprigs parsley stems
	2 cloves garlic, chopped	1 star anise
2 c. flour	½ lb. carrots, small dice	3 tbsp. tomato paste
Salt and pepper	½ lb. celery stalks, small dice	1 qt. beef stock

Instructions

Bring the porcini mushrooms, dried figs, and Abbey ale to a boil. Remove from heat, cover, and let steep until Abbey ale mixture reaches room temperature. Preheat the oven to 325 degrees Fahrenheit. Strain the mushrooms and figs, saving all of the liquid. Pass the liquid through a cheesecloth or fine strainer to remove all dirt and grit. Cut the figs in quarters and put them in the fridge. Heat a large braising pan over medium-high heat. Season the flour with salt and pepper. Season the shanks with salt and pepper. Dredge the shanks in flour. Add olive oil to the pan and sear the shanks until they have a nice color. Remove the shanks from the pan and set aside.

Pour off half of the oil, and in the same pan, add the onions and sauté until translucent. Add the chopped garlic, carrots, celery, thyme, bay leaves, parsley stems, and star anise and cook until vegetables are just barely soft. Stir in the tomato paste. Cook the mixture down a little, then deglaze the pan with the strained liquid. Add the beef stock and bring to a boil. Lay down a single layer of cheesecloth across the vegetables and braising liquid. Place the shanks and figs on top of the cheesecloth to separate them from the vegetables.

Cover the pan with a lid or foil and put in the oven and braise until the meat is tender and just about to come off the bone, about 2 ½ hours. When the pork is done, remove the shanks and figs by lifting out the cheesecloth and placing on a clean pan. Make the sauce by pureeing some of the braising vegetables. Season to taste with salt and pepper. Serve with mashed potatoes (IPA garlic flavored?) or roasted root vegetables and maybe a gremolata (minced garlic, lemon zest, and parsley).

SAMUEL ADAMS BOSTON LAGER
MARINATED SIRLOIN

Recipe by the Boston Beer Company | www.samueladams.com

As we've already discussed, beer contains enzymes that help break down tough fibers in meat, making meat more tender and flavorful. Since the malt flavors in Boston Lager are subtle and soft, they do not impart a strong beer flavor into the dish. This allows the flavor of the meat to shine through.

Ingredients

1 c. Samuel Adams Boston Lager

2 c. canola oil

3 cloves roasted garlic

2 tbsp. dijon mustard

1 tbsp. Coleman's mustard

2 tbsp. chili powder

1 tbsp. cayenne pepper

1 tbsp. paprika

1 tbsp. butcher black pepper

14-oz. steaks, trimmed

Instructions

Mix Boston Lager, oil, garlic, mustards, chili powder, cayenne, paprika, and black pepper together and marinate steaks in the mixture for 4 hours. Grill the steaks over medium heat approximately 5 minutes on each side until medium rare. Slice the steak crosswise against the grain.

CERVEZA CARNITAS

Recipe by Tatiana Peavy, founder of Sigil of the Goat and A Strong Fuggly Brew |
www.sigilofthegoat.com and www.fugglybrew.com

If you're entertaining a large group of people, the last thing you want is to be stuck in the kitchen filling beef Wellingtons or fussing with mini quiches. Carnitas have been a favorite party food for ages because they feed a good-sized group of people for a moderately low price, and they're not as challenging as you may think.

In this recipe, the beer is essentially used as a braising liquid and tenderizer for the pork butt. The richer the beer, the better the recipe. If you are partial to malty beers, consider the malt profile. Caramel malts only enhance the sweetness of the pork while roasted malts add a nice smokiness to the recipe. As long as you put beer in this recipe, no matter what style, it's going to be awesome.

Ingredients

Boston butt or pork shoulder

Kosher salt

2 bay leaves

1 ancho pepper (or one jalapeño)

½ a habanero (personal preference based on heat)

2 oranges, halved

2 tbsp. cumin

1 tsp. red pepper flakes

1 yellow onion, quartered

2 crushed cloves of garlic

Growler of beer (For this one I used Anderson Valley's Crema Cerveza; however, I have also used Organic Bison Chocolate Stout and Rogue Hazelnut Brown Ale and had fantastic flavor harmonies.)

Lard (optional based upon the leanness of the pork)

2 pieces Mexican chocolate

Instructions

The night before: Cover your Boston butt in kosher salt and wrap tightly in plastic wrap and refrigerate.

When you're ready to cook, slice the pork (1-inch slices for crispy, 3-inch for crispy with a tender center). In a deep pot (cast iron is preferable since it retains flavors and heat well), place meat slices along bottom then add bay leaves, peppers, oranges, cumin, garlic, and onion, adding enough beer to barely submerge the meat (all the liquid needs to be boiled off to have the rendered fat for frying), turn on medium-high heat, cover and cook for about 1 ½ to 2 hours. Be sure to turn meat over every 20 minutes or so, keeping an eye on liquid levels. Be careful not to leave the cover off too long (evaporation happens faster than you think).

Once the juices have been evaporated and you see a clear liquid at the bottom producing large, lazy bubbles (this is the rendered lard from the pork), turn down the heat. I like to take out the onion and orange at this part so it doesn't fry and char during the next part. Cover and cook for 30 minutes.

If there is less than an inch of the rendered pork fat on the bottom of the pan, add a couple of tablespoons of lard. (I never said this was a diet food!) Increase the heat and let it boil furiously, uncovered, until meat starts to darken. Add two segments of chocolate and mix briskly until the chocolate is melted and the meat is crispy and falling apart. Turn off the heat and remove the meat from the pan, and now you have your beautiful carnitas!

I like my carnitas served with my roasted green salsa and a bright jicama salad.

SALSA

2 lb. tomatillos

1 jalapeño

2 cloves garlic

1 large avocado

Salt

During the last 30 minutes of cooking, start roasting tomatillos and jalapeño by charring the skin over an open flame, until blistered. Place tomatillos, jalapeno, and garlic in a food processor with the avocado and pulse to desired chunkiness. Add salt to taste.

JICAMA SALAD

1 jicama root

2 oranges, peeled

1 cucumber

1 red onion

Salt

Chili powder

A few Key limes

Chop up the jicama, oranges, cucumber, and red onion. Place in a medium-size bowl, and add salt, chili powder, and lime juice to taste. Serve with tortillas and your favorite cerveza. Salud!

SUMMER ALE–INFUSED LOBSTER ROLL WITH SUMMER ALE "SLAW"

Recipes by the Boston Beer Company | www.samueladams.com | Serves 4

This is one of those awesome, yet rare, circumstances where beer is added to the recipe raw and it stays raw—by that I mean it's not cooked. Instead, in this recipe beer acts as more of a flavorful binder. It helps to reduce the thickness of the dressing and adds a very pleasant wheat and hop flavor that is not cooked out (as is the case with many recipes featuring beer).

LOBSTER ROLL

Ingredients

½ c. mayonnaise

2 tbsp. cream cheese

¼ c. Samuel Adams
   Summer Ale

16 oz. lobster meat (cooked)

¼ c. chopped celery

¼ c. chopped carrots

¼ c. diced green apples

4 tsp. tarragon

2 tbsp. lemon juice

4 artisanal rolls

8 shaved scallions

Instructions

Mix mayonnaise, cream cheese, and Samuel Adams Summer Ale together in a mixing bowl. Add cooked lobster meat, celery, carrots, apples, tarragon, and lemon juice in a mixing bowl and stir until combined. .Place one quarter of the lobster meat mixture into each roll. Top with shaved scallions to taste.

"SLAW"

Ingredients

4 tbsp. Samuel Adams
   Summer Ale

1 tsp. lemon zest

1 pinch grains of paradise

2 tbsp. olive oil

1 tbsp. white balsamic vinegar

1 tsp. salt

1 c. shredded purple cabbage

1 c. shredded green cabbage

Instructions

Combine Samuel Adams Summer Ale, lemon zest, grains of paradise, olive oil, balsamic vinegar, and salt in a mixing bowl. Mix in cabbage. Serve on a plate next to the lobster roll.

MOULES À LA BIÈRE

Recipe by the Beer Wench

I'm not going to lie: making beer steamed mussels is ridiculously easy, fast, and you can manipulate the recipe in a million ways to change the flavor of the broth. When it comes to styles of beer, I prefer to use pale-colored styles like pilsners, pale ales, Belgian wits, and golden ales. Caramelized and roasted malts are rarely a great match for shellfish (the obvious exception being stouts and oysters).

My favorite recipe is slightly adapted from Julia Child's *Mastering the Art of French Cooking*. She called her recipe Moules à la Marinière—aka mussels in a sauce of white wine. I call my version Moules à la Bière. The recipe calls for a Saison—a Belgian or French-style farmhouse ale. These beers have beautiful spice and fruit flavors that meld really well with the butter and herbs.

Ingredients

2–3 lb. scrubbed, soaked mussels

2 c. Saison (farmhouse ale)

½ c. minced shallots or green onions

8 parsley sprigs

1 bay leaf

1 tsp. thyme

1 tsp. pepper

6 tbsp. butter

½ c. roughly chopped parsley (garnish)

¼ c. raw bacon, diced (optional)

Instructions

If you've never seen a mussel before, this might sound weird but the first thing you need to do is "de-beard" the mussels. Most of the time, when you buy mussels, they come with a little bit of hair that sticks out of the shell when it's closed. Gently tug at the hair to remove it from the mussel.

If you chose to prepare this recipe with bacon, sauté the bacon in the pot first, until cooked, then proceed. Add the Saison, shallots, parsley springs, bay leaf, thyme, pepper, and butter to a large, deep sauté pan or pot. Bring to a boil and simmer for two minutes.

Add the mussels to the pan. Cover tightly and boil quickly over high heat. Every few seconds or so, grab the pot, hold the lid tightly, and toss the mussels up and down. Do this several times to make sure that the mussels rotate around the pot and cook evenly. After about 5 minutes, the shells will swing open and the mussels are done.

Scoop the mussels into bowls, first discarding any that did not open. Then ladle the liquid over the mussels, sprinkle with the parsley, and serve with crusty French bread and butter.

THAI-INFUSED BEER-STEAMED MUSSELS

Recipe by the Beer Wench

This is one of my all-time favorite ways to prepare mussels. Keep in mind, though, that I'm kind of a heat freak. Feel free to modify the amount of garlic, ginger, and Thai red curry in the recipe to make the dish mellower or more intense!

Ingredients

2 tbsp. peanut oil

2 tbsp. fresh ginger, minced

4 garlic cloves, sliced

2 red Thai chiles, thinly sliced

1 stalk of lemongrass, crushed

1 can unsweetened coconut milk

3 tbsp. fish sauce

2 tbsp. sugar

2 tbsp. soy sauce

2 c. Belgian wit or Belgian-style white ale

2–3 tbsp. Thai red curry paste (use less if you are a wimp)

2–3 lb. mussels, debearded and scrubbed

¼ c. chopped cilantro

Instructions

In a deep pan or pot, heat the peanut oil and sauté the ginger, garlic, chiles, and lemongrass for about a minute. Add the coconut milk, fish sauce, sugar, soy sauce, beer, and Thai red curry paste. Bring to a boil and simmer for about 3 to 4 minutes, stirring frequently to incorporate the Thai paste into the broth. Taste the broth and add more spice if desired. Add mussels to the pot and cover. Steam for 5 minutes until the mussels are open and cooked. Serve in bowls with Thai beer broth and crusty bread and garnished with cilantro.

CHOCOLATE STOUT BAKED MAC AND CHEESE

Recipe by the Beer Wench | Serves 4–6, but feel free to double it for a larger group.

Not to toot my own horn (too much), but this is one of the best recipes I've ever invented. It calls for five types of cheese, including gorgonzola, which is one of my favorite cheeses to pair with stouts.

Ingredients

2 c. dry elbow pasta

½ c. butter

¼ c. flour

¼ c. chocolate stout (or dry stout)

1 c. half-and-half

¼ lb. brie

8 oz. cream cheese

¾ c. crumbled gorgonzola cheese

1 ¼ c. shredded cheddar cheese

¾ c. grated parmesan cheese, divided

Salt and pepper

½ c. panko or bread crumbs

Instructions

Heat the oven to 350 degrees Fahrenheit. Boil pasta in salted water until al dente, strain, and put aside. In a medium-size, heavy-bottom pot, melt the butter over medium heat. Whisk in the flour to form a light roux. Slowly whisk in the beer and half-and-half. Add the brie and cream cheese to the sauce, stirring until the cheeses are melted and incorporated. Stir in the gorgonzola, cheddar, and half the parmesan. Stir until the cheese sauce is blended, then add the pasta. Taste and adjust the seasonings as desired with salt and pepper.

Pour the mixture into a greased baking dish and top with remaining parmesan cheese and panko crumbs. Bake until the sauce is bubbly and the toppings are crispy, roughly 30 minutes.

BEER RISOTTO

Recipe by Chef Christopher Hanson | Twitter: @Ilovefoie

From Christopher: Risotto is a northern Italian dish. The rice is cooked in a pot, and the creamy texture is achieved by constantly stirring and slowly adding in stock. To make beer risotto you simply use beer to deglaze instead of wine. I find lagers or pilsners without spices work the best, such as Speakeasy Metropolis, or if I want a little more flavor, Rogue's Dirtoir also works well. Big hoppy beers end up bitter and funky after cooking, so avoid them in this recipe.

Ingredients

3 tbsp. canola or rice oil

1 shallot, diced

2 c. arborio rice

1 bottle lager

6 c. stock

¼ c. butter

¼ c. cream (optional)

⅛ c. parmesan cheese, grated

Seasonal veggies, cooked

Spring: peas and carrots

Summer: spinach and tomato

Fall: butternut squash and kale

Winter: mushrooms

Instructions

In a medium-size pot, add the oil and heat on medium heat. Once the oil is hot, add the shallot and cook until just translucent. Add in the arborio rice and stir constantly so you don't burn the rice. Your goal here is to brown the rice just a bit. Once the rice has a little color, deglaze with about three-quarters of a bottle of beer; the rest is for you.

Let the beer reduce to a thick consistency while stirring at least twice a minute. Once the beer has reduced, add in ½ cup stock, stir, and reduce until thickened. Repeat this process until the rice is al dente. The constant stirring and slow addition of stock is the secret to a creamy risotto. To finish, add in butter, cream, and seasonal vegetables. Stir and reduce until thick again. Now it's ready to plate; garnish with parmesan. Open a few more beers and enjoy.

DOUBLE IPA BRAISED BEANS WITH SALSA VERDE

Recipes by Sophia Del Gigante, author of the blog NY Foodgasm | www.ny-foodgasm.blogspot.com

From Sophia: When it comes to cooking with beer recipes, there aren't many that are meatless—let alone vegan. But I like a challenge. What I came up with is one badass vegan recipe with imperial IPA. Braising the beans in imperial IPA brings some of the hoppiness to the beans, infusing them with that fresh grassy flavor and kicks up the green of the salsa verde to the next level. Serve this recipe with yellow rice and plantains for a satisfying meal that will please even the most carnivorous of friends.

Oh, and I recommend pairing this dish with a fruity wheat beer or a chili-infused IPA. With the fruit wheat beer, you'll get a sweet and spicy effect. With the chile-infused IPA you want to bring out more of the heat and the hoppiness of the meal.

BEER-BRAISED BEANS

Ingredients

1 tbsp. extra-virgin olive oil

½ onion, diced

1 can pinto beans, rinsed and drained

1 can white beans, rinsed and drained

2 cloves garlic, smashed

1 ½ c. double IPA (I like Stone Ruination)

Instructions

Preheat the oven to 350 degrees Fahrenheit. Drizzle olive oil into a cast-iron skillet on medium heat, and let it heat up for about a minute. Add the onion, and cook until caramelized, about 5 minutes. Add the beans and garlic and sauté for roughly 5–8 minutes until the beans get slightly browned and start to crack open. Add the beer and let simmer for about a minute, then transfer the skillet into the oven and cook for 25 minutes.

SALSA VERDE

Ingredients

14 tomatillos (small, ripe, and unhusked)

3 large cloves of garlic

1 ½ large green frying peppers

1 large serrano chile pepper

½ large Vidalia onion, sliced into rings (for easy grilling)

Juice of ½ lime

1 tablespoon extra-virgin olive oil

Salt and pepper

Instructions

Heat a grill on medium-high flame. Toss the tomatillos, garlic, frying peppers, serrano, and onion on the grill, and grill for about 10 minutes on each side. Carefully husk the tomatillos and remove singed skin from the peppers. For a more mild salsa, also remove the seeds from the serrano chiles. Pulse all grilled vegetables in a food processor, then add lime juice, olive oil, and salt and pepper to taste. Mix into the beer-braised beans or serve on top.

YELLOW RICE

Ingredients

2 c. brown rice   4 c. vegetable broth   1 tbsp. turmeric

Instructions

In a medium saucepan on medium heat, add bown rice, broth, and turmeric. Let cook at medium heat until most of the liquid has evaporated (about 15–20 minutes). Cover the pan and place on low for another 10 minutes; be sure to check on it. When it's done leave it covered to keep flavor in.

GRILLED PLANTAINS

Ingredients

2 large ripe plantains   2 tbsp. coconut oil   1 tbsp. vegan sugar   Juice of ½ lime

Instructions

In a small bowl, melt the coconut oil in the microwave for about 20 seconds. Add in the sugar and lime juice and whisk until dissolved. Cut the plantains in half lengthwise and again horizontally; brush on coconut oil mixture, and grill on medium-high heat 1 minute on each side. *Be careful* when flipping them and brushing on that mixture, as it makes the grill flame up.

BLACKOUT STOUT CHOCOLATE CUPCAKES

Recipe by Great Lakes Brewing Company | www.greatlakesbrewing.com |
Makes about 24 cupcakes or two 8-inch rounds

Because most baked goods require a liquid of sorts, whether it is milk or water or something else, they are some of the easiest recipes to infuse with beer, especially those with roasted malts (porters and stouts). The dark chocolate and espresso flavors in stouts make them a slam-dunk match for any chocolate dessert. And the richer (bigger and alcoholic) the stout, the richer the end product.

Ingredients

1 ½ c. Great Lakes Brewing Company Blackout Stout (or other imperial stout)

¾ c. cocoa powder

2 ½ c. brown sugar, packed

4 eggs

1 c. canola oil

2 tsp. vanilla extract

2 tbsp. coffee extract (or strong brewed coffee)

1 ½ c. sour cream (or plain Greek yogurt)

2 ¼ c. all-purpose flour

2 tsp. baking soda

1 tsp. salt

Instructions

Preheat oven to 350 degrees Fahrenheit. In a medium bowl, whisk together the Blackout Stout and cocoa powder and set aside. In the bowl of a mixer, combine the brown sugar, eggs, vanilla and coffee extract, and oil. Mix on medium speed until well-incorporated, about 2 minutes. Add the sour cream. Mix on medium speed until no lumps of sour cream remain, about 1 minute.

In a separate bowl, sift together the flour, baking soda, and salt. Add dry ingredients to the sugar mixture and turn mixer on low speed. While mixing, slowly add the Blackout Stout and cocoa mixture. Increase speed to medium-low and mix until just combined, about 1 minute.

Fill cupcake liners about three-quarters full and bake for around 16–18 minutes, or until a toothpick comes out clean. Or, line two 8-inch cake pans with parchment paper, fill three-quarters full, and bake for 22–24 minutes, or until toothpick comes out clean. Top with buttercream frosting or a frosting of your choice and enjoy!

Note: This recipe can easily be made vegan. Just substitute the sour cream for a nondairy yogurt and you're good to go.

MOODY TONGUE COLD-PRESSED WATERMELON CHEESECAKE

Recipe by Jared Rouben, Brewmaster at Moody Tongue Brewing Company | www.moodytongue.com

From Jared: At Moody Tongue, we see brewing and baking as one and the same. Both crafts use time, temperature, and meticulous measurements to create flavors that people crave. In this dish, the baking and beer come together. We soak the blueberries and raspberries in the wit and use the beer as an ingredient while baking. This ultimately helps with pairing as this is a great example of "bridging"—when a beer is paired with a dish in which the beer was used as an ingredient. In the cheesecake, the beer changes the dish's color to a light rose and adds a subtle watermelon flavor, with sweetness that naturally complements that of the cheesecake.

CRUST

Ingredients

2 c. finely ground
   graham cracker crumbs

½ tsp. ground cinnamon

½ tsp. brown sugar

1 stick unsalted butter, melted

Nonstick cooking spray

Instructions

Combine the crust ingredients in a bowl with a fork until evenly moistened. Lightly coat the bottom and sides of an 8-inch springform pan with a nonstick cooking spray. Pour the crumbs into the pan and, using the bottom of your nearest beer glass, press the crumbs down into the base and approximately 1-inch up the sides of the pan. Refrigerate this pan for 5 minutes.

RASPBERRY BLUEBERRY TOPPING

Ingredients

1 pint blueberries

1 pint raspberries

2 tbsp. sugar

1 pint Moody Tongue Cold-Pressed Korean Watermelon Wit (if beer is unavailable, substitute with your favorite Belgian beer brewed with fruit)

Instructions

In a small saucepan, add the blueberries, raspberries, sugar, and beer and simmer over medium heat for 5 minutes or until the fruit begins to break down. Leave to cool before spreading on the cheesecake.

CHEESECAKE FILLING

Ingredients

1 lb. cream cheese, softened

3 eggs

1 c. sugar

1 pint of Moody Tongue Cold-Pressed
Korean Watermelon Wit (or favorite
Belgian beer brewed with fruit)

Zest of 1 lemon

1 dash vanilla extract

Raspberry Blueberry Topping

Instructions

Preheat the oven to 325 degrees Fahrenheit. Beat the cream cheese on low speed for 1 minute in the bowl of an electric mixer until smooth. Then add the eggs (one at a time) and continue to beat slowly until the mixture is combined. Gradually add sugar and beat until creamy for 1 to 2 minutes.

Then add your beer, lemon zest, and vanilla to the mixture while intermittently scraping down the sides of the bowl and the beaters. The batter should be well mixed but not overbeaten. Pour the filling into the crust-lined pan and use a spatula to ensure the top is smooth.

Set the cheesecake pan on a large piece of aluminum foil and fold the foil up the sides of the pan. Place the cake pan in a large roasting pan. Pour boiling water into the roasting pan until the water is halfway up the sides of the cheesecake pan. (Note that the foil will keep the water from seeping into the cheesecake.) Bake for 45 minutes.

The cheesecake should still jiggle. Let it cool in the pan for 30 minutes. Chill in the refrigerator, loosely covered, for at least 3 hours. Loosen the cheesecake from the sides of the pan by running a thin metal spatula around the inside rim. Unmold and transfer to a cake plate. Using a spatula, spread a layer of the Raspberry Blueberry Topping over the surface.

STRAWBERRY LEMONADE BEER POUND CAKE

Recipe by Jackie Dodd, the Beeroness | www.thebeeroness.com | Makes 2 loaves

Citrusy, bready, and super smooth—wheat beers are a perfect match for fruit desserts, breads, and cakes. This recipe actually calls for the same beer in three different parts: the cake, the moist cake infuser, and the icing. Infusing the beer into three stages of the process strengthens the beer flavor in the end result.

CAKE

Ingredients

1 c. butter	1 tsp. vanilla extract	⅓ c. fresh lemon juice
2 ½ c. sugar	1 c. cake flour	¾ c. wheat beer
6 eggs	2 c. all-purpose flour	1 c. chopped fresh strawberries
¼ c. canola oil	2 ½ tsp. baking powder	
½ c. full-fat sour cream	½ tsp. salt	

SECRET MOIST CAKE INFUSER

Ingredients

¼ c. white sugar	2 tbsp. very hot water (or beer)	2 tbsp. lemon juice

ICING

Ingredients

4 c. powdered sugar	3 tbsp. lemon juice	¼ c. beer (or lemon juice)

Instructions

Preheat oven to 350 degrees Fahrenheit. To make the cake, in a bowl of a stand mixer, beat the butter and sugar until well combined. While the mixer is running, add the eggs, one at a time, scraping the bottom of the bowl between additions. Add the canola oil, sour cream, and vanilla extract, and beat until well combined.

In a medium bowl, sift together both kinds of flour, baking powder, and salt. In a small bowl, mix the beer and lemon juice. Alternating between the dry ingredients and the beer, slowly add both to the mixture, a little at a time until all ingredients are just combined. Add the strawberries, and stir until incorporated.

Grease and flour two large (1 ½-quart) loaf pans. Divide batter evenly between pans.

Bake until golden brown and the top springs back when lightly touched, about 26–28 minutes. Remove from the oven and allow to cool for 10 minutes.

To make the cake infusion, in a small bowl, stir together the hot water and sugar until the sugar has dissolved. If the sugar doesn't dissolve, microwave for 20 seconds. Stir in the lemon juice. Poke a dozen small holes in each loaf with a long wooden skewer. Drizzle the warm lemon simple syrup over both loaves (you can also brush on with a pastry brush). Allow to sit in the pans until cooled, about 2 hours. Remove the cake from the pans and refrigerate.

For the icing, stir together the powdered sugar, lemon juice, and beer. Pour over cakes, and chill until ready to serve.

BEERAMISU GELATO

Recipe by Celeste and Zach Blau, co-owners of the Sweet Spot | www.thesweetspotcleveland.com

When you're making ice cream with beer, a little goes a long way. Too much beer quickly dilutes ice cream and takes away from its creaminess. All sorts of beer styles can be use, but the chocolate and espresso notes in stouts and some porters make them two of the best styles to use in beer-infused ice cream. A dessert known for its coffee flavors, tiramisu plays well with those flavors and is a perfect inspiration for the base flavor of this ice cream.

This recipe is for 1 pint of gelato, which can be prepared in a home ice-cream making machine. For a larger batch, double or triple this recipe.

Ingredients

1 c. whole milk

⅓ c. whipping or heavy cream

¼ c. plus 2 tbsp. sugar

1 ½ tbsp. nonfat dry milk

1 tbsp. mascarpone

1 tbsp. plus 2 tbsp. porter or stout, divided

½ tbsp. instant coffee

⅛ tsp. cornstarch

⅛ tsp. guar gum

5 lady finger cookies

Instructions

Mix the milk, cream, sugar, dry milk, mascarpone, 1 tbsp. beer, instant coffee, cornstarch, and guar gum together in a bowl. Freeze the mixture in an ice cream or gelato machine, following factory instructions. While the gelato is freezing, crumble five lady finger cookies and mix with 2 tbsp. porter or stout. Stir into the gelato when transferring the finished gelato from the freezing canister to a permanent container. Freeze until ready to eat.

CHOCOLATE BEER MOUSSE WITH BACON SPOON

Recipe by Jennie Y. Chen, Ph.D., founder of MisoHungry | www.misohungrynow.com

Chocolate and malt is a classic flavor combination for American childhood, or it least it used to be. Whether or not you grew up with it, you can still revel in the flavor combination that was once the staple of brightly colored vinyl booths in diners across the country with this recipe.

From Jennie: In my testing, I used a local beer (512 Pecan Porter). However, it is not necessary to use a specific beer. Any stout or porter will do, and even a brown ale is a fine stand-in. This recipe as is produces a mildly sweet mousse. You can adjust the sugar and chocolate levels to your own taste. It will still have the essence of chocolate malt. In addition to the base recipe, I've included a list of garnishes and accompanying liquors that can dress this dessert to the nines. The bacon spoon is included as part of the garnish, but if you ask any carnivore, it is not to be left out.

Ingredients

2 ½ c. chilled heavy cream, divided

5 large egg yolks

3 tbsp. sugar

Salt

1 ½ c. porter or stout

7 oz. fine-quality bittersweet or dark chocolate, chopped

Equipment

Double boiler   Instant-read thermometer   2 large bowls   Electric mixer

Instructions

Heat ¾ cup cream in a 1-quart heavy saucepan until hot. Whisk together yolks, sugar, and a pinch of salt in a metal bowl until combined well, then add hot cream in a slow stream, whisking until combined. Add slowly so that the eggs do not curdle from the hot cream. Transfer the mixture back to the saucepan and cook over moderately low heat, stirring constantly, until it registers 160 degrees Fahrenheit on the thermometer. It is extremely important to reach at least 160 degrees or the custard may not set. Pour the custard through a fine-mesh sieve into a bowl.

Melt the chocolate in a double boiler or a metal bowl set over a pan of simmering water (or in a glass bowl in a microwave at 50 percent power 3 to 5 minutes), stirring frequently. Whisk the custard into the chocolate until smooth, then cool. Once it is smooth, whisk in the beer. The beer may start to fizz, but just keep whisking. Allow to cool to at least room temperature.

Whisk the remaining 1 ¼ cups of cream in a bowl with an electric mixer until it just holds stiff peaks. Fold the whipped cream into the cooled chocolate mixture. If it is not cool, the whipped cream may cease to be whipped. I do it by pouring the cooled chocolate mixture into the bowl of whipped cream. This process will be time consuming, but do not stir. You must fold, fold, fold, or else you'll lose the air that is in the mousse. Make sure that you incorporate the liquid at the very bottom of the bowl into the whipped cream, or you will end up with mousse on top and liquid chocolate beer on bottom.

If you would like to portion out the mousse prior to serving, spoon or pipe mousse into eight 6-ounce stemmed glasses or ramekins and chill, covered, at least 6 hours. The mousse will stay edible for about 10 days refrigerated. If it gets to room temperature, it may start to lose its shape, but once refrigerated, it should stiffen up again.

Presentation and garnish

Mousse can be served in individual cups (clear plastic or glass makes for a pretty presentation). You can do this before or after the chill time. For the following spirits, you can drizzle, spritz, or rinse the glass. Rinse is to coat the inside of the glass, though you can coat just the rim as well.

The goal isn't to drink or necessarily taste the spirit. The goal is to have the aroma of the spirit enhance the chocolate mousse experience. For the appropriate garnishes, you can rim the cups with the spirit and dip it into the garnish. This would work particularly well with chocolate shavings, coco nibs, or toasted fine coconut.

Raspberries + Chambord

Toasted coconut + coconut rum

Bacon + bourbon

Oatmeal cookies or
  biscotti + whiskey

Spicy chocolate shavings +
  Ancho Reyes

Coco nibs + Kahlua

Mint sprig or peppermint
  chips + Absinthe

Maple bourbon pecan or any
  other candied nut + pecan
  praline liqueur

Luxardo cherries + Luxardo

Smoked salt + Mezcal

Chocolate chip cookies + tequila

Banana chips + crème de banana

Note: For the bacon spoon, cook 2 pounds of maple or plain bacon until crisp. Do not get peppered or spicy bacon unless you are going for the ancho chile combination.

chapter fifteen

BEER MIXOLOGY

Some purists in the beer industry have referred to beer mixology as the bastardization of beer, arguing that mixing beer into cocktails degrades its integrity. After all, beer is already a perfectly crafted cocktail of hops, barley, yeast, and water. Why would anyone even want to destroy such a perfect balance, a product the brewer intended to be consumed as is, by integrating it into cocktail recipes?

Beer mixology is not an attempt to make beer better or to alter and change the quality and flavor of that particular beer. Nor is it an attempt to fix anything wrong with the cocktails already out there. Both beer and cocktails can and should continue to exist independently as their perfect selves. Rather, beer mixology is about introducing a new ingredient, one that is complex and flavorful, to add a new dimension to cocktail culture.

Opening Your Mind to Beer Cocktails

Before we delve into the mixology itself, let's briefly stop to think about some of the primary benefits of the beer cocktail for the nonbeer drinker: It gets even those who may not know what craft beer is to try something new. It's a way for the beer industry to cross-pollinate with the spirits industry. It is a means for educating a new segment of the population about the intricacies of craft beer. Cocktail drinkers may be surprised that beer these days has flavors and textures unmatched by any other ingredient used in cocktails. How else would a Hop Gimlet get the signature aroma of pine and citrus? How else could a BBQ Bloody Mary achieve those unique roasted notes?

Which brings us to our next point: the artistry and science involved in creating beer cocktails. You see, crafting a perfect cocktail requires much more skill than most realize. To claim the title of mixologist demands respect, akin to that of executive chef, master distiller, or brewmaster. Mixologists, like chefs, distillers, and brewers, are dedicated to producing the most well-crafted and enjoyable products possible. In the scope of beer cocktails, brewers and distillers are the farmers; they produce high-quality ingredients to serve as the base and inspiration for the mixologists.

So the next time you come across a critic, skeptic, hater, or naysayer of beer mixology, ask her to think really hard about why she is so quick to reject the concept. Remind her that classically trained chefs got their panties in a twist when molecular gastronomy first emerged. Or, even further back, some chefs stubbornly clung to fine dining styles as they were obliterated by completely new concepts like eating local.

At the very least, remind them of this quote from Aristotle: "It is the mark of an educated mind to be able to entertain a thought without accepting it."

Getting Started

Although mixing cocktails with beer is not exactly a new idea, many mixologists and bartenders are still hesitant to experiment with beer as an ingredient. I attribute part of this problem to lack of resources on the subject; most traditional cocktail books and classes train people how to manipulate spirits with the use of bitters, syrups, juice, herbs, spices, and even other spirits. Virtually none of them talk about using craft beer.

But perhaps the real issue is not the lack of talent, but the lack of achievable education. Expecting a mixologist to know everything about beer would be like expecting a beer expert to know everything about wine. Not all alcohol is created equal, and it is extremely hard to be an expert at them all. This is why it is crucial for beer experts and professional mixologists to work together in crafting beer cocktails.

Beer professionals and mixologists have already created a wide variety of cocktails, and there are essentially two camps—those with spirits and those without. I like to call the spiritless category "beer blends." These spiritless beer cocktails are typically easy to make, often requiring only two or three ingredients. Beer cocktails with booze are typically more complicated because they require the same caress and balance of flavors that normal cocktails demand.

BEER BLENDS (THE SPIRITLESS COCKTAILS)

This category of beer cocktails is made either by blending beer with other beer, or by mixing beer with cider, juice, soda, or spices. The most popular beer blends are the Black and Tan (typically Guinness and pale ale), the Snakebite (beer and cider), the Shandy (beer and lemonade), and the Michelada (beer and tomato juice), but there are also lots of other fun concoctions that you can make!

The Black and Tan

Black and Tan was first used in reference to a breed of beagles (black and tan coon-hounds) used as hunting dogs in Ireland. The term was also used to refer to a regiment of British soldiers recruited to serve in Ireland after World War I. As a drink, the Black and Tan tradition varies from person to person, depending on experience, culture, or preference. Almost everyone agrees the "Black" part of this drink has been Guinness. The "Tan" part is usually the greatest source of debate.

Contrary to popular belief, Black and Tan is not a drink commonly consumed in Ireland. (There is some debate as to whether or not it is appropriate to order a Black and Tan in Dublin.) The style is believed to have actually originated in British pubs. This is why many consider the classic Black and Tan combination to be Bass Pale Ale and Guinness.

Ingredients
Pale beer
Dark beer
Spoon
Pint glass

Instructions

Pour the pale beer extremely slowly down the side of the glass and try to get as little head as possible. Fill it halfway and stop. Take the spoon and flip it so that the back of the spoon is facing up. Hold the spoon over the glass, touching the edge to the glass. Very slowly, pour the Guinness (or other dry stout) over the back of the spoon. It should cascade slowly off the spoon onto the side of the glass. And if all goes according to plan, you will have a perfect half-and-half beer. But, have no fear: If you mess it up, it's still going to taste the same once you take that first sip. It just won't look as impressive.

SNAZZ IT UP

No one said the Black and Tan has to be the only layered mix. As long as you keep the pour super slow, you can layer most beers on top of each other. The exception is higher alcohol beers, which tend to be heavier. But, as long as the heavy beer is on the bottom, you are good to go.

THE SHANDY

Originally called a Shandygaff, the Shandy has been around in Europe for several centuries. Originating in England, the Shandy is popular in Germany and Austria, where it is known as a Radler. The original Shandy recipe is a mixture of beer and lemonade, but the term now represents a category of drinks consisting of beer mixed with citrus-flavored soda, carbonated lemonade, ginger beer, ginger ale, or cider.

Another popular Shandy recipe is cider blended with beer, which is also known as a Snakebite. The original Snakebite called for lager and dry cider, but many variations have emerged featuring blends of all sorts of beer styles and types of ciders. The Snakebite is usually served in a pint glass with no ice and is typically layered so that the beer floats on top of the cider, similar to that of a Black and Tan.

No matter what mixer you choose, these drinks are supposed to be refreshing and enjoyed during the warmer spring and summer months.

BLACKBERRY LEMONADE SHANDY

A typical Shandy mixes lemonade and beer in a 50/50 proportion; however, I like to prepare this particular Shandy more like a cocktail. The base of the recipe is a concentrated blend of lemon juice, agave nectar, and muddled blackberries—one of my favorite berries. The mix is shaken and double strained over ice to remove any seeds, then topped off with a crisp pilsner.

Ingredients

4 large blackberries

1 oz. agave nectar

2 oz. fresh-squeezed lemon juice

8 oz. pilsner

Instructions

Muddle the blackberries with the agave nectar in the bottom of a cocktail shaker. Add the lemon juice and shake vigorously with ice for 5 seconds. Double strain the mixture into a glass over ice and top off with the beer.

MULLED BEER

Most people are familiar with mulled wine and cider but mulled beer? Yes, mulled beer is far from being a modern-day concept. Its origins date back to the sixteenth century. Refrigeration as we know it didn't exist back then, and most beverages (including beer) were consumed at room, cellar, or sometimes even warmer temperatures.

As with wine and cider, making mulled beer is simple and the flavor combinations are endless. Personally, I prefer to use dark, spiced, or Belgian beers for the base. Hoppy beers tend to get bitter when warmed and reduced, which isn't ideal for this type of drink. Recommended styles include pumpkin beers, Christmas beers, spiced porters, and Belgian dubbels.

I prefer to mull beer with a combination of fresh and dried ingredients, which both brightens and deepens the flavor. Note that I used whole spices rather than powdered, but in a pinch, powdered can be substituted. Just be mindful of how much you add (start small because you can always add more later). If it tastes too heavily spiced when you finish mulling, you can also dilute the mixture with more beer.

THE WENCH'S MULLED BEER

Being the boozehound that I am, I sometimes like to spike my mulled beer with a splash of bourbon—a step that can be omitted but brings a certain *je ne sais quoi* to this warm (and warming!) holiday beverage.

Ingredients

1 12 oz. bottle of pumpkin, Christmas, or Belgian dark ale

4–5 slices of fresh ginger

2 whole cinnamon sticks, set aside one for garnish

1 tsp. dried cloves

1 tsp. dried coriander

1 tsp. whole black peppercorns

Peel of 1 orange, with one long strip reserved for garnish

1 tbsp. raw honey or agave nectar

½ oz. bourbon (optional)

Instructions

Add the beer, ginger, cinnamon, cloves, coriander, peppercorns, and orange peel (except for garnish) to a medium saucepan. Warm over low heat for 30 minutes, just below a simmer. Do not boil. After 30 minutes, add the honey or agave. Taste for sweetness and add more if desired. Remove from heat, strain into a mug or a heavy, stemmed glass (so you don't burn yourself holding it). Add the bourbon (or spiced rum) and garnish with the orange peel. Serve warm with gingerbread cookies, a slice of pumpkin pie, or a piece of coffee cake.

THE MICHELADA

The Michelada is a Mexican Shandy often made with pale lager, lime juice, hot sauce, soy sauce, Worcestershire sauce, and peppers. It is typically served in a chilled, salt-rimmed glass.

For a twist on the traditional recipe, I like to substitute the Worcestershire and soy sauces with Bragg Liquid Aminos (which is slightly healthier). For an extra spicy-tart flavor, add pepperoncini juice.

THE BEST MICHELADA EVER

Ingredients

1 oz. lime juice, lime wedges reserved

4 dashes Bragg Liquid Aminos

2 dashes of your favorite hot sauce (I like Tapatío)

¼ oz. pepperoncini juice (optional)

Sea salt

Cayenne pepper

12 oz. bottle pilsner

Instructions

In a shaker, mix the lime juice, Bragg Liquid Aminos, hot sauce, and pepperoncini juice. Set aside. Mix the sea salt and cayenne pepper in equal parts in a shallow dish. Rub the rim of a tall Collins glass with a squeezed lime wedge. Dip the rim of the glass in the salt mixture. Fill the glass with ice. Pour in the lime mixture and top off with the pilsner. Garnish with a lime wedge.

BLACK VELVET

The Black Velvet was originally created to mourn the death of Prince Albert—no, not the one in a can. It is a blend of dark beer and champagne prepared similar to a Black and Tan. First the champagne is poured and then the dark beer is layered on top.

When making this cocktail, I recommended using Brut Cava, a Spanish sparkling wine that is much cheaper than champagne and just as good for a mixed drink. Although the original version is interesting, I prefer to make my champagne and beer cocktails with fruit lambics. It's kind of like a mimosa—but better. I call it a Red Velvet.

RED VELVET

Ingredients

3 oz. brut rosé sparkling wine (such as cava)

2 oz. fruit lambic (such as kriek)

Small spoon

Luxardo maraschino cherry

Instructions

Pour the sparkling wine slowly into the flute glass. Wait for all the bubbles to settle. Just as if you were making a Black and Tan (see page 227), touch the spoon to the edge of the glass and pour the lambic slowly on the back side of the spoon to layer it on top of the sparkling wine. Garnish with a Luxardo maraschino cherry, because they are the best.

Best Michelada Ever

Red Velvet

Bittered Beermosa

THE BEERMOSA

You're probably familiar with the mimosa, aka champagne and orange juice. It's not a bad way to drink with your brunch, but let's get a little creative with it, shall we? Now, not all beer styles can be used in a beermosa. Stout and OJ? Gross. But a wheat beer and orange juice, that's what I'm talking about.

This is one beer blend where I don't recommend going fifty-fifty on each beverage. Orange juice tends to be really sweet and can overpower the beer quickly.

BITTERED BEERMOSA

Ingredients

2 oz. orange juice

4 oz. Belgian wit (or other wheat beer)

Dash of bitters

Instructions

Pour the orange juice into a champagne flute, then top it with beer (it will mix naturally). Add a few dashes of bitters for an extra complexity.

Beer Cocktails (with Spirits)

Although many people categorize beer blends as beer cocktails, I prefer to define beer cocktails as a class of alcoholic beverages that contain beer and at least one spirit. Tackling the beer cocktail concept can be intimidating because it requires knowledge and skill in two areas of expertise, beer and cocktails.

The easiest way to construct a new beer cocktail is to use existing cocktail recipes as a base. Pick one that you're familiar with, and that you like. Then try to replace an ingredient (or two) with beer. Recipes with soda and tonic are the easiest to manipulate because of the carbonation. For example, turn a mojito into a brewjito or take a crack at mixing a beer fizz (gin fizz with beer).

However, there is the unconventional winging-it route, arguably the hardest way to design a beer cocktail. This is when the mixologist or bartender creates a beer cocktail entirely from scratch. The reason this is so hard is that not only are there dozens of styles of beer and many types of spirits, there are literally hundreds, if not thousands, of brands of each, many with their own nuances and defining characteristics.

When it comes to building a new beer cocktail, there are three approaches I like to take: I lead with the spirit, I lead with the beer, or I lead with a particular flavor profile (fruity, spicy, citrusy, savory, and so on). Although the combinations are virtually endless, I have found that, through some trial and error, some spirits pair best with certain styles of beer. This is usually because they share flavor characteristics in common or complement each other in some way.

The one exception is vodka, a spirit specifically designed to be flavorless. The only thing vodka really imparts in a cocktail is alcohol. It doesn't really add to the flavor and, if anything, it actually dilutes the drink. Now, the exception to that exception is vodka infusions, and I'm not referring to artificially flavored vodkas. A lot of bartenders have created interesting and unique vodka infusions, like hop vodka, which partner well with some beers.

Other options include reducing some styles of beer down to a syrup and using that instead of simple syrup, agave nectar, or other sugar sources. Or you can try using malt syrups or hop bitters as another way to infuse beer flavors into a cocktail with or without using beer itself.

BEER AND SPIRITS SYNERGY

Here is a breakdown of the most common mainstream spirits and the styles of beer that I personally think work well with them. Please keep in mind that there is a huge spectrum of spirits, distilled wines, cordials, and liqueurs. Also, understand that this list is a guideline for creating beer cocktails, not a set of pairing rules.

Bourbon: The toasted oak, vanilla, maple, toffee, nutty flavors in bourbon are a great match for the flavors of really malty beer, especially those with a lot of roasted malt character. Bourbon works really well with stouts, barleywines, and some dark Belgian styles. Some breweries also age beer in bourbon barrels. Any beer style that is suitable for a barrel would probably play nice in a cocktail with beer.

Gin: The botanical, herbal, and sometimes spicy flavors in gin are a dead match for the fruity, spicy, and floral esters in Belgian ales, specifically the pale ones. Personally, I think Saisons and Belgian wits work best with gin. If you don't believe me, add of few drops of really good artisanal gin to your next glass of Saison and you will see what I mean. Gin also works well with sour beers, as a lot of gin cocktails have a strong citrus component.

Rum (light): We need to break rum into two categories, as there is a clear difference between light and dark rum. Light rum is clean, sweet, and light, making it a good pairing for a lot of lighter styles of beers both in color and flavor. I like to use light rum with a Belgian blonde or pale lager in a beer version of the mojito. Light rum, by nature, is also a good match for fruit lambics and fruit beers.

Rum (dark or spiced): I almost always prefer dark rum to light rum, as it is more flavorful and complex. Because it is aged in oak, dark rum tends to have a lot of caramel, molasses, and toffee sweetness. It is a fine match for spiced beers, darker Belgians, and stouts. I am a huge fan of dark or spiced rum and Christmas beers. Sooooo warming, so good.

Tequila: Like rum, tequila can be clear or some tone of brown, depending on the length of oak aging. I almost never recommend mixing Anêjo in a cocktail, as it is mostly meant to be a sipping tequila. I always prefer Reposado in cocktails, though Blanco typically makes drinks look better. To me, tequila is an interesting blend of citrus, floral, and bitter flavors. Aged tequila has a little bit of oak, toast, and caramel to it, making it a perfect match for most IPAs. But be warned: Although these two beverages share a lot in common, they are horrible together, without anything else. Balance is key. Sugar and acid are needed to make the two sing.

Vodka: I really didn't want to talk about vodka, but I should probably mention it. Vodka is good for adding beer flavor to cocktails without adding beer. Case and point: hop vodka.

Whiskey: Whiskey is pretty tough to mix with because the spectrum of quality varies greatly. Some whiskeys are made for sipping while others are best shot down the throat as quickly as possible. To be honest, I think that bourbon works better with beer than whiskey, so I almost never use it in beer cocktails.

TO SHAKE (THE BEER) OR NOT TO SHAKE (THE BEER)— THAT IS THE QUESTION!

When I first started making beer cocktails, I made the horrible mistake of shaking the beer with the rest of the ingredients. This inevitably led to a bunch of shaker explosions and a huge mess.

However, beer is a great mixer because it's carbonated, and carbonation by nature helps mix drinks with little to no outside manipulation. Even for rocks drinks, I will usually shake all of the other ingredients—the spirits, bitters, sugar, and citrus—with ice first, then strain into a glass over ice or serve it straight up. Then I will add the beer.

The exception is the flip, a drink that requires an entire egg. In this case I like to shake all the ingredients together as vigorously as possible. The only issue is that if you are using a cheap shaker or your shaker glass isn't completely sealed in the shaker, the cocktail will explode all over you. Like *all* over you.

CONCEPTUALIZING BEER COCKTAILS

Understanding how to create a "regular" cocktail is really important for constructing beer cocktails. When it comes to cocktails, the less is more principle is key. The purest of cocktails are usually the booziest and require the least amount of ingredients. (It is important to note that the number of ingredients a cocktail contains has nothing to do with a drink's complexity.)

The reason why really great cocktails only need a few ingredients is because they start with one very, very important ingredient: a great spirit. When you have a well-made spirit, you don't need to do a lot with it to make a great cocktail. The spirit should be the star, and all the other ingredients should be supporting actors. When you taste a well-constructed cocktail you should be able to call out the main spirit by name, and it should never be overwhelmed or overshadowed by the other ingredients.

The difficult thing about making beer cocktails is deciding whether or not you want the beer or the spirit to be the star. Ideally, both are extremely well made and are delicious and intriguing by themselves, which makes picking the lead role extremely hard. In my opinion, the most successful beer cocktails are the ones that can transcend both the essence of the beer and the spirit, creating a flavor combination that would never have existed if both were not present. This is a very, very hard thing to achieve.

THE RATIOS

As we discussed on page 132, the tongue can taste five things: sweet, salty, bitter, sour, and umami. To this date, I'm only been able to create one cocktail that touches on every cell in the tongue (Smokin' Hops on page 246). The goal is not necessarily to activate all five tastes, however. Most people prefer cocktails that simply have a sweet and sour component. Some prefer really sweet, while others prefer really tart. Some do enjoy savory (umami). Few people love bitter or salty drinks. This is why the majority of cocktails, save for the booze-centric ones, have some sort of sugar and acid component to them. A common ratio is 2:1:1 for the booze : sugar : acid.

Sugar comes in many forms: granulated sugar, simple syrup (sugar diluted with water), agave nectar, honey, and sweet liqueurs are all used to add sweetness to cocktails. When it comes to acid, the majority of sourness from cocktails comes from citrus fruits, like lemons and limes, but can also come from other fruit sources.

For the most part, cocktails try to achieve balance. They should have a good, but not too strong, booze presence. They should have a balanced tartness and sweetness. And the best ones also have a *je ne sais quoi* element—something you can't quite place your finger on, but you know it's adding something special.

Since this is not a cocktail book, we can cut to the chase on the two exceptions. Booze-centric cocktails are those that feature little to no ingredients except booze. Examples are the Manhattan, martini, Negroni, and the Rob Roy. Artificial cocktails are exactly what you think they are: poor excuses for cocktails served up at the cheesiest of bars and restaurants. These are the drinks that taste unnatural and overly sweet, they are often blended, more often than not they have an unnatural color, and they and can be found in large glasses with ridiculous garnishes like umbrellas.

ADDING COMPLEXITY

As if balancing multiple brands for each spirits, multiple types of citrus, and various ways to incorporate sweetness into a cocktails wasn't enough, there is a whole dimension of other magical things that can be thrown into cocktails that will ultimately take the drink to the next level.

Bitters are the most common method of adding complexity to cocktails, but you can also add trace amounts of herbal liqueurs like amaro and chartreuse or rinse the glass with absinthe. Some bars also put herb-infused tinctures in drinks, which adds aroma without increasing the volume of a drink.

I liken these little cocktail mixing "extras" to dry hopping. They intensify the olfactory experience with the drink.

Try it at home: Make a really easy hop tincture by steeping whole leaf hops in grain neutral alcohol (like vodka or Everclear) for 24 hours. Strain the alcohol into a small dropper or spray bottle. Add a few drops or a mist of your hop tincture to classic cocktails, like martinis or a Sazerac, instead of or in addition to bitters.

To turn your tincture into bitters, add your own blend of herbs, spices, and roots to the hop infusion and sweeten the final product with a little bit of simple syrup, honey, or agave nectar. Try whole leaf cascade hops with dried orange peel, clove, milk thistle, dried rose petals, and honey.

BOURBON COCKTAILS

Liquid Pie

Recipe by the Beer Wench

I'm a huge fan of berries and bourbon. Vanilla, oak, and caramelized flavors from the bourbon paired with the juicy, tart, and fruity flavors of the berries form a flavor combination very reminiscent of pie.

My bourbon of choice is Breaking & Entering from my local distillery and beer mixology partner in crime, St. George Spirits. To lighten up the cocktail and give it a kick of effervescence, I opted to add a bit of pilsner to the mix. My personal favorite is Trumer Pils, brewed locally just blocks from my house in Berkeley, California. Extremely clean with hints of biscuit and a slight noble hop bitterness, Trumer Pils brought what I will call the "pie crust" character to the cocktail.

A signature quality of a pilsner is its nice thick head. The proper glassware for the pilsner, the tall thin glass, was designed to showcase this trait; however, this drink is best when presented in a champagne flute. The carbonation in the beer forces a big thick pink foam to come to the top of the glass, and it really is quite beautiful.

Ingredients

2 blackberries

6 blueberries

½ oz. agave nectar

½ oz. lemon juice

1 oz. St. George Spirits Breaking & Entering (bourbon)

3 oz. Bohemian pilsener

Instructions

Muddle the berries, agave nectar, and lemon juice until berries are completely macerated. Add bourbon and ice, shake vigorously, and strain into a champagne flute. Slowly add the pilsner, being careful not to let the foam get too out of control.

Oh My Darlin'

Recipe from Nat Harry, Bar Manager at Revival Bar + Kitchen (Berkeley, California) | Twitter: @alphacook

At first glance, you might be ultra skeptical about this recipe. You are probably thinking, "Citrus and bourbon? Really?" Aren't you supposed to drink bourbon neat, on the rocks, or even up? Is it really "kosher" to mix it with citrus and multiple citruses at that? Well, sit back, relax, and open your mind.

Bourbon and orange actually love each other, just like vanilla ice cream loves orange sherbet. See where I'm going with this? Blending bourbon with orange is akin to make an orange creamsicle. But before I get carried away with that analogy, it is important to note that this cocktail is not that sweet. Any perceived sweetness comes from the booze (bourbon and curacao in this case). The end product is actually quite refreshing.

West Coast–style IPAs are known for their intense grapefruit and citrus flavors. This is why they are a perfect match for this recipe. The IPA adds a much-desired balance to the cocktail by lightening the body of the drink with its carbonation while canceling some of the sweetness with the bitterness from the hops.

Ingredients

1 ¾ oz. bourbon

1 ½ oz. clementine puree syrup (see below)

½ oz. Pierre Ferrand Dry Curacao (or orange liqueur)

¼ oz. lemon juice

1 ½ oz. West Coast–style IPA

Orange or lemon twist for garnish

Instructions

Shake everything with ice except the beer, and pour the contents, including original ice, into a tall Collins glass. Top up with about 1 ½ oz. of IPA and stir well. Garnish with an orange or lemon twist.

CLEMENTINE PUREE SYRUP

For a medium-sized batch, use about 2 lb. of clementines, washing first as you will use the entire fruit. Trim the ends, bad spots, and overly tough or pithy parts of the rind. Quarter the fruit and place in a larger container. Cover the fruit with a rich simple syrup (1 part water : 1 ½ parts sugar) and puree in batches, blending on high power until smooth and there are no chunks or large pieces left. Add a bit of vodka for preserving if you wish. The syrup should keep up to two weeks if stored in the fridge.

GIN COCKTAILS

Witty Fizz

Recipe from the Beer Wench

Fruity, floral, and slightly spicy, the Belgian wit is a great match for the botanical profile of gin. Both are light in body and color yet complex in aroma and flavor.

This particular recipe was inspired by the classic "Silver Fizz," a gin-based cocktail with lemon juice, sugar, egg whites, and soda water. To add more flavor, I substituted raw agave nectar for the sugar and switched the soda water with a Belgian wit (like Allagash White). The result is a bright and refreshing, moderately tart, and slightly floral cocktail perfect for the hot spring and summer months.

Ingredients

1 ½ oz. gin

½ oz. fresh lemon juice

½ oz. raw agave nectar

1 egg white
(or ¼ oz. pasteurized
egg whites)

4 oz. Belgian witbier

Lemon peel for garnish

Instructions

Vigorously shake the gin, lemon juice, agave, and egg whites with ice. Strain the mixture into a Collins glass over ice, top with beer, and garnish with a lemon peel.

The Mad Botanist

Recipe from the Beer Wench

One thing that truly differentiates beer and spirits from wine, apart from the obvious, is that both allow for the addition of nontraditional ingredients. Although there are style guidelines and "rules" for both beer and spirits, innovators in both industries tend to bend them, if not completely break them.

The Mad Botanist was inspired by Bison Brewing's Saison de Wench, a Belgian-farmhouse style ale brewed with botanicals (rose, hibiscus, lemongrass, and pink peppercorn), and St. George Botanivore Gin, an artisan spirit distilled with nineteen botanicals.

To complement and enhance the floral and herbal characteristics in the beer, I chose to prepare the cocktail with a housemade hibiscus syrup and rose tincture. The result is a bright pink, slightly tart, and extremely aromatic cocktail.

It is important to note that this cocktail still works with other saison and gin brands than the ones mentioned. Use the most botanical versions you can find.

Ingredients

1 ½ oz. St. George Botanivore Gin

¼ oz. fresh lemon juice

¼ oz. hibiscus simple syrup

2 oz. Saison de Wench

3 drops rose tincture

Rose petal for garnish

Instructions

Add the gin, lemon, and hibiscus to the shaker. Shake with ice, and strain into champagne flute. Top with beer and 3 drops of rose tincture. Garnish with a rose petal.

HIBISCUS SIMPLE SYRUP

2 oz. dried hibiscus flowers (in a tea bag or cheesecloth)

2 c. water

2 c. sugar

Bring the water to a boil. Reduce the temperature and steep hibiscus for 7 minutes. Remove the tea bag, bring water back to a boil. Add the sugar slowly, stirring vigorously. Bring the temperature down. Simmer two minutes, remove from heat, and chill completely.

ROSE TINCTURE

1 oz. dried rose petals (red or pink)

¾ c. Everclear (or vodka)

Steep the rose petals in a tea bag in the Everclear for 3 to 4 weeks. Remove the tea bag squeezing out the liquid, and put the tinctue into a dropper bottle.

Red Light District

Recipe from Nicole Barker, owner of Red Creole Fusion Restaurant (Reno, Nevada) | @NicoleBarkerRed

From Nicole: I love these beer syrups; the honey is amazing with Lindemans Gueuze Cuvée René. The sour and sweet blends harmoniously and opens the floral components of the beer nicely. The cocktail is delicately sweet and surprisingly refreshing. Plus, blood orange makes for a stunning color.

Ingredients

St. George absinthe luge (or other absinthe) (see luge instructions)

1 ½ oz. Bols genever (or other genever or gin)

¾ oz. Bols sloe gin (or other gin)

¾ oz. blood orange juice

Lindemans Gueuze Cuvée René (or other gueuze)

¾ oz. beer honey syrup (recipe below)

Angostura bitters

Blood orange slice for garnish

Instructions

Absinthe luge: Fill a glass with ice and add about ¼ oz. of absinthe, swirl it around, and dump it out. Essentially, you are washing the glass with absinthe and ice.

Put the genever, sloe gin, blood orange juice, and beer syrup to a shaker with ice. Shake and double strain into the absinthe-luged glass. Add 1 oz. Lindemans Gueuze Cuvée René to the shaker, dry shake (shake without ice), and add to the glass, creating a nice foam on top. Add a few dashes of Angostura bitters and garnish with a blood orange slice.

BEER HONEY SYRUP

¼ c. Lindemans Gueuze Cuvée René

¼ c. local honey syrup

Warm honey in a small pan at a medium heat until liquid. Increase to high heat. Slowly pour in the beer and stir constantly for approximately 20 minutes, reducing the beer into the honey. Remove from heat and let cool.

RUM COCKTAILS

Strawberry Blonde Brewjito

Recipe from the Beer Wench

When it comes to refreshing cocktails, I'm a huge fan of the Mojito, a refreshingly effervescent mint-and-rum-based cocktail. Although the original mojito recipe is tasty on its own, it also makes a great base for variations. I love adding fruit, and berries work especially well with mint.

This particular recipe was inspired by Maui Brewing's Bikini Blonde Lager, a helles-style lager brewed with floral hops and pilsner and Munich malts. Refreshingly crisp, the Bikini Blonde Lager boasts light biscuit flavors, moderately low noble hop bitterness, and a clean, dry finish. Its rather neutral flavor profile makes it an excellent canvas for a light and fruity beer cocktail.

Strawberries, mint, agave nectar, rum, and beer come together to make this cocktail a perfect sipper for the beach, backyard barbecues, or even on those cold, rainy nights spent dreaming of the sunshine to come.

Ingredients

1 strawberry, quartered

5 mint leaves

¼ oz. agave nectar

½ oz. fresh lemon juice

1 oz. light rum

5 oz. Maui Brewing Bikini Blonde Lager, or other blonde or pilsner

Halved strawberry for garnish

Sprig of mint for garnish

Instructions

Muddle the strawberry, mint, and agave nectar until the strawberry is completely pulverized. Add lemon juice, rum, and ice, and shake vigorously for 5 to 10 counts. Add beer, shake lightly, and strain over ice into your glass of choice. Garnish with a halved strawberry and sprig of mint.

Trigger Warning

Recipe from Jacob Grier, writer and beverage consultant, author of
the beer cocktail book *Cocktails on Tap*, jacobgrier.com | Twitter: @jacobgrier

This cocktail may produce discomfort in those who have a low tolerance for capsaicin, perceive cilantro as a soapy flavor, suffer from a real or imagined gluten sensitivity, are in a state of shock over the price of limes, or believe that putting beer in a cocktail will lead only to discord. All others may find it refreshing and enjoyable.

Ingredients

1 ½ oz. Novo Fogo barrel-aged cachaça*

¾ oz. lime juice

¾ oz. habanero syrup

Small handful of cilantro leaves

2 oz. wheat beer

Instructions

Combine the cachaça, lime juice, habanero syrup, and cilantro in a shaker. Shake with ice and strain into a flute or cocktail glass. Top with the beer and stir gently to combine.

HABANERO SYRUP

2 c. sugar

2 c. water

5 habanero peppers, stemmed but not deseeded

Combine the sugar and water in a saucepan over medium heat and stir until dissolved. Bring it to a boil. Add the peppers and remove from heat, cover, and allow to steep for 20 minutes. Strain and keep refrigerated.

* Side note: Cachaça is the most popular distilled spirit in Brazil. It is kind of like a cousin to rum. Like rum, cachaça comes in two forms: unaged (white) and aged (gold). The major difference between cachaça and rum is that rum is usually made from molasses, while cachaça is made from fresh sugarcane juice. The caipirinha is the most popular cachaça cocktail.

Imperial Dark and Stormy

Recipe from Chris Elford, barman at Canon Seattle | Twitter: @ChrisElford

The Dark and Stormy is one of the most well-known high-ball cocktails, though I find it to be quite dull.

In this recipe, Chris adds a new level of intensity to what used to be a boring cocktail. The "dark" side is amplified with aged dark rum and 1 ounce of imperial stout, while the "stormy" side is deepened with a dose of fresh ginger syrup. The result is off the Richter.

Ingredients

1 ½ oz. Appleton VX Jamaican Rum (aged dark rum)

½ oz. fresh lime juice

¼ oz. fresh ginger syrup (Take strained fresh ginger juice and blend 1:1 with white sugar.)

2 oz. ginger beer (the spicier the better, in my opinion)

2 oz. imperial stout (I like Oskar Blues Ten FIDY or Brooklyn Black Chocolate Stout)

Lime wheel for garnish

Instructions

Shake the rum, lime juice, and ginger syrup to chill. Fine strain into an iced Collins glass. Add the ginger beer and stir briefly to combine. Float the imperial stout on top and garnish with a fresh lime wheel.

BEER FLIPS

Recipe from the Beer Wench

This recipe might creep you out a little because it calls for an entire egg—yolk and all. But let's not get ahead of ourselves here. The term *flip* refers to a class of cocktails made with a spirit, egg, sugar, and spice of sorts. A variation of the flip that most people are familiar with is eggnog, which calls for cream in addition to the other ingredients. Flips can be served hot or cold.

When the egg is emulsified with sugar, rum, and beer, the result is a super creamy, silky, and rich milkshake-like cocktail. It truly is dessert in a glass (and liquid dessert is always my favorite).

Beer flips can be made all year around, but I particularly love making them in the autumn and winter months with spiced ales and dark or spiced rum. Then again, I also like making them in the spring and summer with fruit syrups, light rum, and Belgian witbeers. The recipes are virtually all the same: 2 oz. rum, 1 oz. syrup, 3–4 oz. beer, and one whole egg. The technique is also the same.

The strongest recommendation I can make for this type of drink is to use organic eggs, if possible, or at least hormone and cage free. Not only will the drink taste better, but also the risk factor will be lower. These are raw eggs after all. Also, if using a whole egg freaks you out too much, you can substitute with an ounce of pasteurized egg whites from the carton.

What follows are a few of my favorite flip recipes. Feel free to adjust the amount of beer used in each. Adding less will make the rum come through stronger, and adding more will soften the alcohol burn.

Gingerbread Flip

Ingredients

2 oz. spiced rum

3–4 oz. holiday spiced dark ale

1 whole egg

1 oz. ginger syrup

Ground nutmeg for garnish

For ginger syrup: Bring 1 c. water, ½ c. sugar, and 8–10 slices of raw ginger to boil in a small saucepan. Simmer for 5 minutes, then allow to cool.

Pumpkin Pie Flip

Ingredients

2 oz. spiced rum

3–4 oz. pumpkin ale

1 whole egg

1 oz. ginger syrup

Ground nutmeg for garnish

Apple Pie Flip

Ingredients

2 oz. apple brandy

3–4 oz. Belgian tripel

1 whole egg

1 oz. ginger and cinnamon syrup

For ginger and cinnamon syrup: Follow the directions for Ginger Syrup but add a cinnamon stick with the raw ginger.

Lemon Meringue Pie Flip

Ingredients

2 oz. light rum

3-4 oz. Belgian wit

1 whole egg

1 oz. lemon syrup

For lemon syrup: Bring 1 c. water, 1 c. sugar, 4 oz. lemon juice, and 4–6 large lemon peels to a boil in a small saucepan. Simmer for 5 minutes, then allow to cool.

Blueberry Pie Flip

Ingredients

2 oz. light rum

3–4 oz. Belgian wit

1 whole egg

1 oz. blueberry syrup (pancake syrup works fine)

For blueberry syrup: Bring ½ c. fresh blueberries, ½ c. water, ½ c. sugar, and ¼ c. lemon juice to a boil in a small saucepan. Simmer for 5 minutes, then strain and allow to cool.

Instructions

Making a flip with beer can be dangerously messy. With any luck, you will end up with the cocktail in your mouth and not all over your clothes. First, crack the egg into your shaker pint and beat it with a whisk or fork until fully blended, almost as if you were making a scrambled egg. Add the syrup and the rum and dry shake (shake without ice). Make sure to form a really tight seal between the shaker pint and the tin before you shake. The egg will create pressure on the tin, so hold on tight.

After you vigorously dry shake for 10 seconds, add ice to the shaker and shake again, even more vigorously, for another 10 seconds. Strain into a large snifter or tulip glass and top with the beer. Please note that you can also shake the beer with all the ingredients; however, this is when things can get explosive. Also, the beer will still incorporate into the drink nicely when poured in after the shake. If the cocktail tastes too strong, feel free to top off with additional beer.

TEQUILA AND MEZCAL COCKTAILS

Barbecue Bloody Mary (with Beer!)

Recipe from the Beer Wench

The Bloody Mary has to be one of the most versatile cocktails out there, but few people have the audacity to alter it much from its vodka roots. I love switching out the vodka for other spirits, especially tequila. Of course, I also love adding beer.

One weekend I found myself craving just such a Bloody Mary, but I didn't have tequila in the house (insert sad face). I did have some mezcal, which got the brain ticking. Why not mix up a smoky, almost barbecue-like Bloody Mary with the mezcal?

In order to get that straight-off-the-grill, molasses barbecue flavor, I decided to use a stout in the recipe. The result? A badass Bloody Mary hybrid worthy of being garnished with a slice of bacon. In fact, you better garnish this baby with bacon.

Ingredients

1 ½ oz. mezcal

3 oz. tomato juice

½ oz. fresh lemon juice

½ tsp. Worcestershire sauce
(substitute with Bragg Liquid Aminos
for a vegetarian version)

½ tsp. celery salt

½ tsp. freshly ground pepper

½ tbsp. horseradish

Hot sauce (chipotle versions work best
in this recipe)

2 oz. dry stout

Instructions

In a pint glass, add the mezcal, tomato juice, lemon juice, Worcestershire, celery salt, pepper, horseradish, and hot sauce to taste. Stir to mix all ingredients together. Fill a pint glass with ice. Top with the stout and garnish how you like (but don't forget the bacon!)

Smokin' Hops

Recipe from the Beer Wench

Bitter, sour, spicy, sweet, and smoky, Smokin' Hops was designed for those of us who like to live life on the edge.

Mezcal fills the mouth and nose with hints of smoke, while fresh serrano chiles tingle the tongue. The mouth puckers slightly from the combination of fresh lemon and hop bitterness. Then all is calmed by the crisp and refreshing carbonation of the beer.

This cocktail can add a little kick to your routine in the summer. It's a perfect match for anything off the grill, especially smoked meats. It will warm you up in the winter as well. Just beware: this drink has bite.

Ingredients

1 oz. mezcal

1 oz. lemon juice

¼ oz. minced serrano chiles
(for less heat, substitute a few dashes of your favorite hot sauce)

½ oz. agave nectar

3 oz. West Coast IPA

Lemon peel for garnish

Instructions

In a shaker glass, muddle the serranos with the agave. Add the mezcal, lemon juice, and ice. Shake and strain into a Collins glass over ice. Top with IPA. Garnish with a lemon peel.

End of Days

Recipe from Chris Elford, Barman at Canon Seattle | Twitter: @ChrisElford

Although there are no official rules for beer mixology, some spirits pair extraordinarily well with certain styles of beer. For example, American India pale ale + tequila.

American IPAs are characterized by the use of American hops, which yield aromas of citrus, pine, and resin. They boast medium-high to very high hop bitterness, very light malt character, significant carbonation, and a dry finish.

This brings us to tequila. When it comes to buying tequila, products with 100 percent agave are by far the most preferred and highest quality on the market. Un-aged (Blanco) tequila is known for being floral, citrusy, and slightly bitter, making it directly complementary to the American IPA.

This cocktail also calls for Campari, a bright red, bitter, and woody Italian aperitif most known for being the primary ingredient in a Negroni. It adds a level of depth and complexity to the drink while complementing the bitter flavors in both the beer and the tequila.

For a richer, more rustic flavor, Chris Elford advises against using an overly filtered IPA for this cocktail.

Ingredients

¾ oz. blanco tequila

¾ oz. fresh lime juice

¾ oz. Campari

½ oz. Demerara syrup (1:1)

1 oz. chilled IPA

Grapefruit peel for garnish

Combine the tequila, lime juice, Camapri, and Demerara syrup in a shaker and fill with ice. Shake to chill, and strain into an ice-filled rocks glass. Add the IPA, stir to combine, and garnish with a grapefruit peel.

VODKA COCKTAILS

Hop Vodka Gimlet

Recipe from the Beer Wench

The gimlet is one of the most basic, classic cocktails out there. It traditionally consists of either vodka or gin and fresh lime juice. It can be served on the rocks or up. This hopped-up version calls for hop-infused vodka, which is ridiculously easy to make.

When it comes to making hop-flavored vodka, whole-leaf hops are preferred. Pellet hops are too concentrated and too difficult to filter, making them less than ideal for infusion. Whole leaf hops should be easy to find at homebrew shops but can be purchased online. You can probably even ask a local brewer for some, in a pinch.

HOP VODKA

Ingredients

750 ml bottle vodka (not too fancy, but not too cheap)

2–3 oz. whole-leaf hops (Centennial, Amarillo, and Simcoe work really well)

Instructions

Pour out about ¼ cup of vodka (or drink it, I'm not judging you). Add the hops to the bottle and steep for a week. Taste the vodka after a week. If it's not quite hoppy enough, let it steep up for another week.

HOP VODKA GIMLET

Ingredients

4 oz. hop vodka

1 oz. fresh lime juice

Instructions

Shake with ice and strain into a martini glass or shake and strain over ice in a rocks glass.

The Urbanite

Recipe from the Beer Wench

Let's face it, the Cosmo is sooooo last decade. Yet, weirdly enough, it still remains one of the most commonly ordered drinks at bars. I blame this partially on lack of bartender creativity combined with lack of knowledge on the consumer end. And so, I took it upon myself to sex up the extremely over-rated "Cosmo" with a beeralicious twist.

I'm not a fan of the sugary artificial cranberry juices that one finds in most stores, so removing the cranberry juice from the Cosmo was a no-brainer. Unfortunately, sour cranberry beers are rare and not readily accessible, so executing a perfect substitution was not an option. Instead, I opted to swap out cranberry juice for a Belgian kriek, a sour ale brewed with cherries.

Continuing to veer away from an overly sweet cocktail, I opted to use orange bitters in lieu of triple sec. I am quite proud of the result, even if it is a vodka cocktail. Now I could be wrong, but something tells me that if the ladies of *Sex and the City* had the chance, they would drink the Urbanite over the Cosmo any day.

Ingredients

1 ½ oz. vodka (citrus is typical)

1 oz. kriek

½ oz. fresh lime juice

2 dashes orange bitters

Lime twist for garnish

Instructions

Shake the vodka and lime juice, and strain into a martini glass. Add the kriek, finish with two dashes of orange bitters, and garnish with a lime twist.

The Muffin Top

Recipe from Nat Harry, bar manager at Revival Bar + Kitchen (Berkeley, California) | Twitter: @alphacook

Super light and refreshing and exploding with blueberry goodness, this cocktail really doesn't need much explaining. If a blueberry beer is hard to find, no worries. Muddle up some fresh blueberries with all the other ingredients, shake, and double strain over ice. Top off the drink with a Belgian wit.

Ingredients

1 ¾ oz. Stoli blueberry vodka

¾ oz. lemon juice

Scant ½ oz. simple syrup

2–3 oz. Sea Dog Wild Blueberry Ale or other blueberry beer

Lemon wheel for garnish

Instructions

Shake all ingredients except the beer with ice, strain into a Collins glass with fresh ice cubes. Top up with blueberry ale. Stir before serving and garnish with a lemon wheel.

Berlin Mule

Recipe from the Beer Wench

The Moscow Mule is one of the most popular vodka cocktails today, but the recipe is about as complicated as a vodka soda, gin and tonic, or rum and _____. I attribute the popularity of this cocktail, for the most part, to the copper cup that it's traditionally served in (people love to steal them).

As with the Cosmo, another overrated vodka cocktail, I took it upon myself to improve upon the Moscow Mule. I replaced the ginger beer with Berliner weisse, yet still maintaining the key ginger element with a housemade ginger simple syrup. The result is a super refreshing, tart, and slightly spicy beer cocktail that I think is actually worthy of that copper cup.

Ingredients

2 oz. vodka

1 oz. ginger syrup (page 242)

1 oz. fresh lime juice

4 oz. Berliner weisse

Lime wheel for garnish

Instructions

Shake the vodka, lime, and ginger syrup, and then strain over ice into a Moscow Mule copper cup. Top with the beer until the cup is full. Garnish with a lime wheel.

BEER RESOURCES

It is truly is an exciting time to be a beer lover! There are so many awesome resources for if you're interested in beer, it's almost impossible to narrow it down to a few sources. Still, here's a list of websites and books that inspire me the most:

WEBSITES

CraftBeer.com—From beer industry news to interviews with brewers and recipes for cooking—CraftBeer.com is the number one Internet resource for all things beer. Plus, the Brewers Association runs the site, so you know it's legit. (Disclaimer: I write for the site from time to time.)

BeerPulse.com—From new beer releases, brewery openings, and mergers to changes in beer legislation—BeerPulse is the number one news source for beer news in the world!

RateBeer.com—With the mission to be the most accurate, reliable, and comprehensive guide to the world's beer, RateBeer features trustworthy, expert reviews on over 30,00 beers. RateBeer gives its users access to a global guide to beer, breweries, bar and retail locations.

BeerAdvocate.com—Boasting a virtual archive of nearly ever beer brewed in the past few decades, BeerAdvocate (BA) is a global, grassroots network, powered by an independent community of beer enthusiasts and industry professionals who are dedicated to supporting and promoting beer.

TheBrewingNetwork.com—The Brewing Network (BN) is an Internet-based radio station focusing on homebrewing and general craft beer interest. The BN frequently features interviews with well-known (and well-respected) figures in both the homebrewing and craft brewing world.

BEER BOOKS

***Tasting Beer: An Insider's Guide to the World's Greatest Drink* by Randy Mosher**—The Holy Grail for all craft beer geeks and aspiring beer experts, *Tasting Beer* is the quintessential, all-encompassing guide to beer.

***The Complete Beer Course* by Joshua M. Bernstein**—For the last 15 years, Josh has been chronicling the craft beer revolution in some of the most esteemed publications, which include *Bon Appétit, Men's Journal,* the *New York Times, Time Out New York, Saveur, Draft Magazine, Wine Enthusiast, and more.* In *The Complete Beer Course,* Josh gives his readers the tools and knowledge to walk into any beer bar or bottle shop and understand every drop that's available to drink.

***The World Atlas of Beer* by Tim Webb and Stephen Beaumont**—Written by two of the world's leading experts on beer, *The World Atlas of Beer* is one of the most comprehensive, informative and up-to-the-minute books on beer. It also includes in-depth reviews of 500 of the worlds best beers—which kind of makes you want a scratch and lick version to be made.

Michael Jackson's Great Beers of Belgium—Revered as the best beer writer in the history of beer writing, every book written by the late Michael Jackson is absolutely brilliant. But if you had to chose just one, I would go with *Great Beers of Belgium*, an in-depth and extensive look into the brewing culture and history of Belgium.

***Let Me Tell You About Beer* by Melissa Cole**—Written in Melissa's trademark chatty style, *Let Me Tell You About Beer* covers everything from beer and food pairings to the history of beer styles to how to store your beer correctly. Great read for aficionados and beginners alike.

***The Complete Joy of Homebrewing* by Charlie Papazian**—Written by the founder of the American Homebrewers Association (whom many call the father of the modern-day American homebrewing movement), *The Complete Joy of Homebrewing* is by far the best-selling and most respected book on the subject of homebrewing.

***For The Love of Hops: The Practical Guide to Aroma, Bitterness and the Culture of Hops (Brewing Elements)* by Stan Hieronymus**—Whether you are a brewer or homebrewer looking to understand more about hops or self-claimed hophead seeking to geek out about the humulus luplus plant, *For the Love of Hops* is an absolute must-read.

BEER & FOOD BOOKS

***Dinner in the Beer Garden* by Lucy Saunders**—Written by one of first cookbook authors to explore craft beer, *Dinner in the Beer Garden* combines Lucy's passion for pairings with recipes featuring flavors of fresh and seasonal fruits and vegetables.

***The Craft Beer Cookbook* by Jacquelyn Dodd**—Known to her beloved fans as "The Beeroness," Jackie Dodd is a renowned food and beer blogger turned bonafide cookbook author. *The Craft Beer Cookbook* features 100 of Jackie's creative craft beer-infused recipes accompanied by dozens of mouthwatering photographs.

***The Brewmaster's Table* by Garrett Oliver**—Authored by one of the most renowned brewmasters and experts on beer pairings, *The Brewmaster's Table* illustrates the serendipitous chemistry that exists between beer and food, showcasing brilliant pairings that prove beer is, in fact, the perfect partner to any dining experience.

***What To Drink With What You Eat* by Karen Page and Andrew Dorenburg**—Although the primary focus of this book is mostly on food and wine pairings, beer and food lovers can still take away a lot of valuable information from *What To Drink With What You Eat*. Most of what I know about the symmetry between food and beverage, I've learned from reading the works of Karen and Andrew.

INDEX

Abbey beers, 68
Abita Amber, 35
adjuncts, 110
Affligem Blond, 69
Aktienbrauerei Zum Bierkeller, 24
Alaskan
    Baltic Porter, 81
    ESB, 53
    Smoked Porter, 61, 173
    Summer Ale, 29
    White, 72
    Alchemist Heady Topper, 44
    alcohol by volume (ABV), 13
    ale yeast, 120–121
ales, 14, 58–65
Allagash
    Dubbel Ale, 71, 172
    Tripel, 70
    White, 72
Almanac
    Brandy Barrel Pêche, 97
    Golden Gate Gose, 94
Alpine Captain Stout, 63
amber lagers, 30–37
American Barleywine, 79–80
American Black Ale/Black IPA, 44–45
American Brown Ale, 56–57
American India Pale Ale, 43, 111, 170
American Pale Ale, 53–55
American Stout, 63
American style, 50–51
Anchor
    Porter, 173
    Small Beer, 52
    Steam, 37
Anchor Brewing Co., 37, 53, 56, 80
    Bock Beer, 85
    Liberty Ale, 43
    Old Foghorn Ale, 80
Anchorage Galaxy White IPA, 95

Anderson Valley
    Barney Flats Oatmeal Stout, 63
    Belk's ESB, 53
    The Kimmie, The Yink & The Holy Gose, 94
appearance, 131
aroma, 132
Augustiner Dunkel, 35
Augustiner-Bräu, 37
Avery, 56
    Ellie's Brown Ale, 56
    Hog Heaven, 170
    Hog Heaven Barleywine, 80
    Maharaja, 44
    Out of Bounds Stout, 63
    White Rascal, 72
Ayinger
    Altbairisch Dunkel, 35
    Celebrator, 85
    Oktoberfest-Märzen, 37

Ballast Point
    Black Marlin, 61
    Fathom, 19
    Longfin Lager, 23
    Sculpin IPA, 43
Baltic porter, 80–81
Bar Harbor Lighthouse Ale, 60
Barleywines, 170–171
barrel-aged beers, 96–97
Base Camp In-Tents IPL, 28
base malt, 107
Bass & Co., 79
Baxter Tarnation California-style Lager, 37
Bear Republic Racer 5, 43
beer blends
    Beermosa, 231
    Black and Tan, 227
    Black Velvet, 230, 231
    Michelada, 230, 231
    Mulled Beer, 229
    Shandy, 228

beer cocktails
    beer flips, 242–243
    with bourbon, 235–236
    with gin, 237–239
    overview of, 232–234
    with rum, 240–241
    with tequila and mezcal, 244–246
    with vodka, 248–249
Beer Judge Certification Program (BJCP), 12, 79
Belgian beers, 12, 66–75
Belgian Blonde Ale, 69
Belgian dubbel, 70–71
Belgian Strong Ales, 71
Belgian tripel, 70, 172
Belgian-style IPA, 45
Bell's, 56
    Amber Ale, 55
    Best Brown, 56
    Expedition Stout, 173
    Hopslam, 44
    Oarsman, 94
    Porter, 173
    Third Coast Old Ale, 80, 170
    Two Hearted Ale, 43, 47, 117
Berliner Wine, 94
Bière de garde, 74
Bière de Mars (Mars), 74, 90
big beers, 76–85
Big Sky Moose Drool Brown, 56
Bison Brewing
    Chocolate Stout, 63
    Saison de Wench, 74
bitters, 51
Black IPA/American Black Ale, 44–45
Blanche de Bruxelles, 72
Blind Pig Brewery, 44
Bock Family, 83–85
Bohemian (Czech) Pilsener, 20
boiling, 103
Boon Geuze, 91
bottle-conditioned beers, 68

Boulevard
    Irish Ale, 65
    Tank 7 Farmhouse Ale, 74
bourbon barrels, 96–97
Bow Brewery, 40
Brasserie Castelain St. Amand, 74
breads and batters
    Beer Cornbread, 191
    Black Beer Bread, 194
    Classic Beer Batter Mahimahi Tacos with Zesty Coleslaw, 196
    Loose Leaf Ale Banana Bread, 192
    Pub Pretzel, 194–195
    Snow Wit Waffles, 193
Brettanomyces, 46, 123
BrewDog's The End of History, 78
Brewers Association, 12, 45
brewing process, 102–104
Bronder, Mark, 56
Brooklyn Brewery, 56
    Black Chocolate Stout, 173
    Black OPS, 83
Brouwerij Celis, 72
Bruery
    Black Tuesday, 97
    Hottenroth, 94
    Oude Tart, 92
    Rueuze, 91
    Trade Winds Tripel, 70
    White Oak, 80
Budweiser, 28
Burtonizing water, 127

Calicraft Cali Cöast, 29
California Common/Steam Beer, 37
Campaign for Real Ale (CAMRA), 50
Cantillon
    Gueuze, 91
    Kriek, 90
    Lou Pepe, 91

Captain Lawrence Golden
    Delicious, 97
cara malts, 108
caramel malts, 108
Cascadian Dark Ales (CDA), 44
cask beer, 50, 96
Catherine the Great, 83
Celis, Pierre, 72
cellaring beer, 141–142
Chimay
    Grande Reserve (Blue), 71
    Red, 71
    Tripel, 172
Chocolate Stout, 63
Cigar City Hornswoggled, 65
Cilurzo, Vinnie, 43–44
Cismontane The Citizen, 37
Classic (Premium) American
    Pilsner, 28
Coffee Stout, 63
color, 32, 112–113
The Commons Flemish Kiss, 95
condiments, sauces, and
    dressings
    Beer Mole, 202
    Beer Mole Baby Back Ribs, 202
Beer Mole Chili, 203
    Beer Mustard with Black Butte
    Porter, 197
    Beer Vinaigrette, 198–199
    Hoppyum IPA Barbecue Wing
    Sauce, 200–201
    Pale Ale Jalapeño Cheese
    Dip, 203
cooking with beer
basics of, 184–185
    breads and batters, 191–196
    condiments, sauces, and
    dressings, 197–203
    desserts, 216–223
    meat and seafood, 204–210
    soups and stews, 186–190
    vegetarian dishes, 211–215
cooling, 104
Coors Banquet, 28
corn, 110
Crooked Stave L'Brett d'Or, 95
crystal malts, 108, 109

dark ales, 58–65
dark lagers, 30–37
De Koninck, 55

De Struise Black Albert, 83
Deschutes
    Black Butte Porter, 61
    Hop in the Dark Cascadian
    Dark Ale, 45
    Mirror Mirror, 79
    Mirror Pond Pale Ale, 55
desserts
    Beeramisu Gelato, 221
    Blackout Stout Chocolate
    Cupcakes, 216–217
    Chocolate Beer Mousse with
    Bacon Spoon, 222–223
    Moody Tongue Cold-pressed
    Watermelon Cheesecake,
    218–219
    Strawberry Lemonade Beer
    Pound Cake, 220
Devils Backbone Vienna Lager, 35
Dinkel Acker Dark, 35
Dogfish Head, 56
    60 Minute IPA, 43
    Festina Peche, 94
    India Brown Ale, 56
    My Antonia, 28
    Olde School Barleywine, 80
    Piercing Pils, 19
    World Wide Stout, 78
Doppelbock (Double Bock), 84
Dortmunder
    Export, 25
    Union Export, 25
Dos Equis Amber Lager, 35
Dreher, Anton, 35
Drie Fonteinen
    Oude Geuze, 91
    Oude Kriek, 90
Dry (Irish) Stout, 63, 171–172
Duchesse de Bourgogne, 92
Duck-Rabbit
    Porter, 61
    Schwarzbier, 34
Duvel, 71

East India Company, 40
Eckhardt, Fred, 25
Eisbock, 84
English Barleywine, 78–79
English IPA, 42
English Mild, 60
English style, 50–51
esters, 119, 124–125

Extra Special Bitter (ESB), 51,
    52–53

Fantôme Printemps, 74
Farmhouse (Saison), 72–74
Faro, 90
fermentation, 104, 122–123.
    See also yeast
Firestone Walker
    Double Jack, 44
    Pivo Pils, 19
    Sucaba, 79
Flanders
    Oud Bruin (Brown Ale), 92–93
    Red Ale, 91–92
flavor, 133
Flying Dog
    Dogtoberfest, 37
    Horn Dog Barley Wine Style
    Ale, 79
    Old Scratch Amber Lager, 37
    Pearl Necklace, 171
    UnderDog Atlantic Lager, 28
Flying Fish Exit 4, 70
Foothills
    Brewing Baltic Porter, 81
    Sexual Chocolate, 83
Foreign Export Stout, 63
Founders
    Imperial Stout, 118
    Kentucky Breakfast Stout, 97
    Sweet Repute, 80
freshness, 140
fruit lambics, 90
Full Sail Amber, 55
Fuller's Brewery, 52
    ESB, 53

German Pilsner, 24, 110
German Purity Law, 18
glassware, 145–151
gluten-free grains, 110
Golden Road Berliner Weisse, 94
Goose Island
    Bourbon County Stout, 78, 97
    Honkers Ale, 52
    IPA, 42
    Mild Winter, 60
    Pere Jacques, 172
Gordon Bierch Czech Style
    Pilsner, 20
Gouden Carolus Tripel, 70

grains, 110
Grand Teton Bitch Creek ESB, 53
Great Divide Yeti Imperial
    Stout, 83
Great Lakes Brewing Co.
    Commodore Perry IPA, 42
    Conway's Irish Ale, 65
    Dortmunder Gold, 25
    Edmund Fitzgerald, 61, 173
    Eliot Ness, 35
    Oktoberfest, 37
Groll, Joseph, 20
Grossman, Ken, 55
Gueuze, 90–91

Hacker-Pschorr-Bräu, 37
Half Acre Gin Barrel Aged Pony
    Pilsner, 97
Hanssens Oude Gueuze, 91
Harpoon
    Bohemian Pilsner, 24
    Dark Gordon Biersch dunkels,
    35
    Hibernian Ale, 65
Heavy Seas Below Decks, 79
Hefeweizen/Weissbier, 26–27
Heineken, 21
Helles Bock (Maibock), 83
Herbed/Spiced IPA, 46
Herz, Julia, 124
High Water Campfire Stout, 63
high-gravity beers, 76–85
Hill Farmstead Biere de Norma, 74
Hitachino Nest White Ale, 72
Hodgson, George, 40
Hoegaarden Wit, 72
Hofbräu
    Maibock (Urbock), 85
    Oktoberfest, 37
hoppy beers, 48–57
hops, 111, 114–118

Ichtegem Old Brown, 93
Imperial (Double) India Pale
    Ale, 43–44
imperial, as term, 78
India Session Ale/Session Ale, 46
ingredients, 106–111, 114–127
Innis and Gunn Original, 64
International Bittering Units
    (IBU), 12–13
IPAs, 38–47

Irish Dry Stout, 111
Irish Red Ale, 65
Ithaca Cascazilla, 55

J. W. Lees Vintage Harvest Ale, 79
Jack's Abby Hoponius Union, 28
Jever Pilsener, 24
John Smith's Extra Smooth, 52
Jolly Pumpkin, 90
Jolly Pumpkin, Calabaza
    Blanca, 72

Kasteel Blond, 69
keg beer, 50
Kern River Citra Double IPA, 118
kilning, 18
Kölsch, 29
König Pilsener, 24
Köstritzer Schwarzbier, 34
Kulmbacher Mönchshof
    Premium Schwarzbier, 34

La Trappe Blond, 69
lacing, 69
Lactobacillus, 123
lager yeast, 122
lagers, 14
Lagunitas
    NightTime, 45
    Pils, 20
lambics, 88, 90
lautering process, 103
Leffe Blond, 69
Leipziger Gose, 94
Leipzig-style Gose, 93–94
Liefmans Goudenband, 93
Lindemans
    Cassis, 90
    Cuvée René, 91
    Faro lambic, 90
    Framboise, 90
Long Trail Hibernator, 64
Lost Abbey, 71
    Avant Garde, 74
    Judgment Day, 71
    Lost and Found, 172
    Red Poppy, 92
Lost and Found Abbey Ale, 71
Lost Coast, 56
    Downtown Brown, 56
Löwenbräu, 37
    Dunkel, 35

Ludwig II, 36–37

Magnolia Kalifornia Kölsch, 29
Maibock (Helles Bock), 83
Maillard reaction, 112–113
Maine Beer Co. Mean Old Tom, 63
malt, 106–109, 112–113
Maredsous 8, 71
Marin Duck Goose Gose, 94
Mars (Bière de Mars), 90
mash/mashing in, 103
Maui Brewing Co.
    Bikini Blonde Lager, 23
    CoCoNut PorTer, 61
Maytag, Fritz, 53
McAuliffe, Jack, 53
Meantime Brewing IPA, 42
meat and seafood
    Abbey Ale Braised Pork
        Shanks, 204
    Beer Mole Baby Back Ribs, 202
    Cerveza Carnitas, 206–207
    Classic Beer Batter Mahi-Mahi
        Tacos with Zesty Coleslaw, 196
    Moules à la Bière, 209
    Samuel Adams Boston Lager
        Marinated Sirloin, 205
    Summer Ale-Infused Lobster
        Roll with Summer Ale "Slaw,"
        208
    Thai-infused Beer-steamed
        Mussels, 210
Metropolitan Krankshaft
    Kölsch, 29
Milk/Sweet Stout, 63
milling, 103
mixology
    beer blends, 227–231
    beer cocktails, 232–249
    overview of, 226
Modern Times Black House, 63
Monk's Cafe Flemish Sour Ale, 92
Moonglow Weizenbock, 85
Moonlight Brewing Death and
    Taxes, 34
Moorhouse's Black Cat, 60
mouthfeel, 134
Munich
    Dunkel, 34–35
    Helles, 22–23

Napoleon, 94
Negra Modelo, 35
New Albion Brewing Company,
    53
New Belgium, 90
    Fat Tire amber ale, 55
    La Folie, 92
    Spring Blonde, 69
    Tripel, 172
New Glarus
    Back 40 Bock, 85
    Black Top, 45
    Thumbprint Enigma, 93
New Holland, 56
    Full Circle, 29
Night Shift Ever Weisse, 94
Ninkasi Oktoberfest
    Dortmund-Style Lager, 25
noble hops, 114
Nøgne Ø Porter, 81
Noonan, Greg, 44
North American hops, 114–115
North Coast, 56
North Coast, Old Rasputin,
    83, 173

Oakshire Overcast Espresso
    Stout, 63
Oatmeal Stout, 63
oats, 110
Odell Brewing
    90 Shilling Ale, 64
    Double Pilsner, 28
    Fernet Aged Porter, 97
    Mountain Standard Double
        Black IPA, 45
    St. Lupulin, 55
off-flavors, 134–137
O'Hara's Irish Red Ale, 65
Oktoberfest (Märzen), 36–37
Olde Saratoga Lager, 35
Ommegang, 90
    Abbey Ale, 172
    Hennepin, 74
    Rare Vos, 55
    Tripel Perfection, 172
    Witte, 72
Ordinary Bitter (Session Ale),
    51–52
Original Gravity (OG), 13
Orkney Brewery Dark Island, 64
Orval, 75

Oskar Blues
    Dale's Pale Ale, 55
    Mama's Little Yella Pils, 20
    Ten FIDY, 173
O'Sullivan, Shaun, 26–27
Oud Beersel Oude Kriek Vieille,
    90
Oyster Stout, 63, 171–172

Pabst Blue Ribbon, 28
packaging, 104
pairing
    approaches to, 158–163
    caviar, 170
    with cheese, 174–178
    designing perfect, 165–166
    duck, 172–173
    foie gras, 170–171
    getting started, 157–158
    lamb, 173
    lobster, 172
    overview of, 156–157
    oysters, 171–172
    with pizza, 180–181
    putting it together, 163–164
    steak, 173
    with tacos, 179–180
palate fatigue, 168–169
pale lagers, 16–29
Paulaner, 37, 83, 85
    Alt Münchner Dunkel, 35
    Hefeweizen, 27
    Oktoberfest, 37
    Premium Lager, 23
Pediococcus, 123
Perennial Artisan Ales Heart of
    Gold, 80
Peter the Great, 83
Pete's Wicked Ale, 56
Petrus
    Aged Pale, 93
    Oud Bruin, 93
pH, 126
Pilsner Urquell, 20
Pinkus Organic Ur Pils, 24
Piraat, 71
Porter, 61, 173
Portsmouth Gose, 94
pouring, 142–144
Pretty Things Jack D'or, 74
Prohibition, 19, 27

Radeberger Brewery, 24
    Pilsner, 24
Radler, 28
Real Ale (Cask Ale), 50
Red IPA, 46
Redhook ESB, 53
refrigeration, invention of, 18
Reinheitsgebot, 18, 26, 27, 35
Reissdorf Kölsch, 29
resources, 250–251
rice, 110
roasted malts, 108
Rochefort 10, 71
Rodenbach Grand Cru, 92
Rogue, 56
    Old Crustacean, 80, 170
runnings, 89
Russian Imperial Stout, 63,
    81–83, 173
Russian River Brewing Company,
    43–44
    Blind Pig IPA, 43
    Consecration, 97
    Damnation, 71
    Perdition, 55
    Pliny Bites, 44
    Pliny the Elder, 44
    Sanctification, 95
    Temptation, 97
rye, 110
Rye IPA, 46

Saison (Farmhouse), 72–74
Saison Dupont, 74
Salvator Doppel Bock, 85
Samuel Adams
    Black Lager, 34
    Noble Pils, 20
Samuel Smith
    IPA, 42
    Tadcaster Bitter, 52
Saranac Kölsch, 29
Schneider Weisse Weizenhell, 27
Schwarzbier (Black Lager),
    32–34
Scottish Ales, 64
Session Ale/India Session Ale, 46
Shipyard Old Thumper, 53
Sierra Nevada Brewing
    Company, 55, 56
    Bigfoot, 80, 170
    Celebration Ale, 43

Kellerweis, 27
    Ovila Abbey
    Dubbel, 172
    Pale Ale, 55, 117
    Sixpoint
    3Beans, 81
    Brownstone, 56
    Diesel, 63
skunked beer, 21
Slosberg, Pete, 56
Smithwick's Irish Ale, 65
Smuttynose Old Brown Dog
    Ale, 56
soups and stews
    Beer Mole Chili, 203
    Onion Soup, 186
    Stout Beef Stew, 190
    Texas-style Beer Chili,
    188–189
    Wisconsin Beer Cheese Soup,
    187
sour beers, 86–95, 88
Southampton
    Biere de Mars, 74
    Steem Beer, 37
Southern Tier
    2x Steam, 37
    Iniquity, 45
sparge, 103
Spaten Brewery, 18, 23
    Oktoberfest, 37
    Optimator, 85
    Pils, 24
    Premium Lager, 23
Spatenbräu, 37
Speciale Palm, 55
Spiced/Herbed IPA, 46
spontaneous fermentation,
    122–123
Sprecher
    Black Bavarian, 34
    Mai Bock, 85
St. Bernardus
    Abt 12, 71
    Pater 6, 71
Staatliches Hofbräu-München,
    37
Standard Reference Method
    (SRM), 12, 112–113
Steam Beer/California Common,
    37

Stone
    Imperial Russian Stout, 83
    Old Guardian Barleywine, 170
    Pale Ale, 55
    Ruination, 44
    Russian Imperial Stout, 173
    Smoked Porter, 173
    Sublimely Self-Righteous
    Ale, 45
storage, 140
Stoudt's Gold Lager, 23
Stouts, 62–63
straight lambic, 90
Sun King Wee Mac, 64
Surly
    Bender, 56
    Bitter Brewer, 52
    Darkness, 83
    Mild, 60
Sweet/Milk Stout, 63

tasting beer, 130–137
temperature, 142, 145
Therese of Hildburghausen, 37
Thirsty Dog
    Labrador Lager, 25
    Twisted Kilt Scotch Ale, 64
3 Floyds
    Brian Boru Old Irish Red
    Ale, 65
    Dreadnaught IPA, 44
    Jinx Proof, 25
    Zombie Dust, 55
3 Monts Flanders Golden Ale, 74
transferring, 104
Trappist beers, 68
Trappist Rochefort 6, 71
Trinity Brewing TPS Report, 95
Tröegs Troegenator Double
    Bock, 85
Trumer Pils, 24
21st Amendment
    Back in Black, 45
    Marooned on Hog Island, 171
    Sneak Attack Saison, 74
Two Brothers
    Domaine DuPage French Style
    Country Ale, 74
    Ebel's Weiss Beer, 27
Two-row malt, 107

ultraviolet light, 21
Unibroue
    Blanche de Chambly, 72
    La Fin du Monde, 70
Upland Raspberry Lambic, 90
Upright Brewing Oyster Stout,
    171

Val-Dieu Blond, 69
vegetarian recipes
    Beer Risotto, 212–213
    Chocolate Stout Baked Mac
    and Cheese, 211
    Double IPA Braised Beans with
    Salsa Verde, 214–215
Vermont Pub and Brewery, 44
Victory Brewing
    Baltic Thunder, 81
    Festbier, 37
    Golden Monkey, 70, 172
    Old Horizontal, 80
Vienna Lager, 35

water, 126, 127
Weihenstephaner Hefeweissbier,
    27
Weissbier/Hefeweizen, 26–27
Weizenbock, 84–85
Westbrook Gose, 94
Westmalle
    Dubbel, 71
    Trappist Tripel, 70
    Tripel, 172
Westvleteren 12, 71
Weyerbacher
    Blithering Idiot, 79
    Double Simcoe IPA, 44
wheat, 110
White IPA, 45
Widmer Hefeweizen, 27
wild beers, 95
Wild IPA, 46
wine, beer vs., 166–167
Witbier, 71–72
Wychwood Brewery Hobgoblin,
    53

Yards Brewing IPA, 42
Yazoo Sue, 173
yeast, 118–123
    discovery of, 18

About the Author

Known as The Beer Wench, Ashley V. Routson is a craft beer evangelist and social media maven on a mission to advance the craft beer industry through education, inspiration, and advocacy. By day, Ashley works in the craft beer industry and has spent years training others in beer tasting and craft beer marketing and sales support, as well as promoting craft beer brands. In her off hours, Ashley is a beer writer who has written for or been featured on NPR, *DRAFT* magazine, BeerAdvocate, and Time.com, among others. She's a regular contributor to both CraftBeer.com (run by the Brewer's Association) and the founder of IPA Day. Ashley has been a featured speaker at the Craft Brewers Conference, The Great American Beer Festival, and the Beer Bloggers Conference.

Find her on Instagram and Twitter: @TheBeerWench.

Acknowledgments

Thanks to my editor, Thom O'Hearn, and the team at Quarto Publishing Group for taking a chance on me, putting up with my hectic schedule, and allowing me to push my deadlines—patience truly is a virtue and all of you have it in spades!

Thanks to all the people that helped me pull this book together. Special thanks to my fantastic photographer, Bob McClenahan, who made this book (and me) look good and to all the breweries, bartenders, and fellow beer writers who were willing to share their recipes in this book. You all inspire me.

Thanks to the bars and breweries that provided the backdrop for most of the photography in this book: The Rare Barrel, Sierra Nevada Torpedo Room, Lagunitas Brewing Company, Forge Pizza, T-Rex BBQ Restaurant & Bar, Brotzeit Lokal, Revival Bar & Kitchen, and Perdition Smokehouse. Your businesses are what gave this book its great ambiance.

Thanks to all of the brewers and beer writers that have mentored and inspired me along the way. A special thank you to Daniel Del Grande from Bison Brewing for giving me my first "real" job in the craft beer industry—you have been such a great friend and mentor. Another special thank you goes to Julia Herz and Lucy Saunders—two very strong and inspirational women in the craft beer industry—for not only paving the way, but for being two of my greatest mentors.

Thanks to all my friends and followers on social media for your unyielding support, both on and offline. I truly believe that if it weren't for all of you, The Beer Wench would cease to exist. Thank you for believing in me and, more importantly, for helping me spread the message.

Thanks to Jonathan Otto for his relentless positivity and support during the writing of this book. Thank you for being my cheerleader, my punching bag, my sounding board—and most all, for being my best friend. I love you.

Last but definitely not least, thanks to my extraordinary parents and my sister, Rebecca, for their unconditional love and support over all the years. Thank you for being my biggest fans and for constantly pushing me to be the strongest, smartest, and best version of myself. You are the best family in the world and I love you more than anything and anyone in the world—even beer.